Henry Tattam

A compendious grammar of the Egyptian language as contained in the Coptic, Sahidic, and Bashmuric dialects;

Together with alphabets and numerals in the hieroglyphic and enchorial characters

Henry Tattam

A compendious grammar of the Egyptian language as contained in the Coptic, Sahidic, and Bashmuric dialects;
Together with alphabets and numerals in the hieroglyphic and enchorial characters

ISBN/EAN: 9783337730222

Printed in Europe, USA, Canada, Australia, Japan

Cover: Foto ©ninafisch / pixelio.de

More available books at **www.hansebooks.com**

A COMPENDIOUS GRAMMAR

OF THE

EGYPTIAN LANGUAGE

AS CONTAINED IN THE

COPTIC, SAHIDIC, AND BASHMURIC DIALECTS;

TOGETHER WITH

ALPHABETS AND NUMERALS IN THE HIEROGLYPHIC AND ENCHORIAL CHARACTERS.

BY THE

REV. HENRY TATTAM. LL. D., D. D., F. R. S.

Rector of Stanford Rivers.

SECOND EDITION

REVISED AND IMPROVED

WILLIAMS & NORGATE:

14, HENRIETTA STREET, COVENT GARDEN, LONDON,

AND

20, SOUTH FREDERICK STREET, EDINBURGH.

1863.

TO

JOHN LEE ESQ^{R.}

LL. D., F. R. S., P. A. S., &. &.

IN GRATEFUL REMEMBRANCE OF

THE MANY FACILITIES AFFORDED

IN THE PROSECUTION OF

HIS EGYPTIAN STUDIES

THIS VOLUME IS RESPECTFULLY DEDICATED

BY THE AUTHOR.

PREFACE.

Egyptian Literature has of late years attracted particular attention. All that has come down to us of the Language and Literature of ancient Egypt is contained in the Coptic, Sahidic, and Bashmuric Dialects; and in the Enchorial, Hieratic, and Hieroglyphic Inscriptions, and Manuscripts.

Without attempting to trace the origin of the Egyptian Language, we may just remark that the learned Rossius in his "Etymologiæ Ægyptiacæ," has shown the affinity of a number of Coptic and Sahidic words to the Oriental Languages; which affinity to a certain extent, it must be admitted, does exist.*)

---

*) In Rawlinson's Herodotus are the following observations. "The Egyptian Language might, from its grammar, appear to claim a Semitic origin, but it is not really one of that family, like the Arabic, Hebrew,

Nor need we be surprised at this, when we consider the intercourse of the Jews, Syrians, Persians,
Chaldeans, and Arabians with the Egyptians: but whether these words were originally Egyptian, or whether
they were adopted from other languages, it is impossible
for *us* to determine. M. Klaproth, a Gentleman well
acquainted with Asiatic Languages, has also pointed out
the resemblance of a considerable number of Egyptian

---

and others; nor is it one of the Sanscrit family, though it shows a
primitive affinity to the Sanscrit in certain points; and this has been
accounted for by the Egyptians being an offset from the early "undi-
vided Asiatic stock;" — a conclusion consistent with the fact of their
language being "much less developed than the Semitic and Sanscrit,
and yet admitting the principle of those inflictions and radical forma-
tions which we find developed, sometimes in one, sometimes in the other,
of those great families." Besides certain affinities with the Sanscrit,
it has others with the Celtic, and the languages of Africa; and Dr.
Ch. Meyer thinks that Celtic "in all its non-Semitic features most
strikingly corresponds with the old Egyptian." It is also the opinion
of M. Müller that the Egyptian bears an affinity both to the Arian and
Semitic dialects, from its having been an offset of the original Asiatic
tongue, which was their common parent before this was broken up into
the Turanian, Arian and Semitic.

.In its grammatical construction, Egyptian has the greatest resemblance to the Semitic; and if it has less of this character than the
Hebrew, and other purely Semitic dialects, this is explained by the
latter having been developed after the separation of the original tongue
into the Arian and Semitic, and by the Egyptian having retained a
portion of both elements. There is, however, a possibility that the
Egyptian may have been a compound language, formed from two or
more *after* the first migration of the race, and foreign elements may
have been then added to it, as in the case of some other languages.
Rawlinson's Herodotus vol. II. p. 279.

words to some of the dialects of the north of Asia, and the north of Europe: this discovery appears to have raised a doubt in his mind of the African origin of the Egyptians. The fact is, the remains we possess of the Egyptian Language, when separated from the Greek, with which it is in some measure mixed up, have no near resemblance to any one of the ancient or modern languages.*

The importance of the Ancient Egyptian Language to the Antiquary, will at once appear, when we consider that the knowledge of it is necessary before the inscriptions on the Monuments of Egypt can be properly understood, and the Enchorial and Hieratic Manuscripts can be fully deciphered.

Nor is it of less importance to the Biblical Student. The Egyptian Versions are supposed to have been made about the second century;** and if they were not

---

* Dr. Murray says, "The Coptic is an original tongue, for it derives all its indeclinable words and particles from radicals pertaining to itself. Its verbs are derived from its own resources. There is no mixture of any foreign language in its composition, except Greek." *Bruce's Travels,* vol. II. p. 473.

** Zosimus, as quoted by Fabricius, says, that the old Testament was translated into Egyptian, when the Septuagint Translation was made. "Biblia tunc non in Graecam tantum, sed etiam Aegyptiis in vernaculam linguam fuisse translata." p. 196.

The Talmudists say, "It is lawful for the Copts to read the Law in Coptic." *Tychsensius.* See also *Buxtorf's Talmudic Lex.* p. 1571. Also. "It is permitted to write the Law in Egyptian." *Babyl. Talmud,*

**

the first, they certainly were among the most early
Translations of the Scriptures into the Languages of the
East: and perhaps the Egyptian New Testament is of
equal or even of greater authority than any of the ancient Versions. The Coptic or Memphitic, and the Sahidic or Thebaic, are distinct versions. The Translations
of the old Testament, as will be readily supposed, were
made from the Septuagint, and not from the Hebrew
Scriptures. These versions will be found of great use
in assisting to determine the reading of many passages
of the Septuagint, and in fixing the meaning of many
expressions. We may also observe that the quotation
from Jeremy the Prophet, Matthew XXVII, 9. is found
in fragments of Jeremiah in these versions: it is different from the parallel passage in Zachariah XI, 12, 13.
and agrees with the quotation in St. Matthew. The Sahidic
New Testament contains many important readings, and
merits the closest attention of the Scholar and Divine.

The terms Coptic and Sahidic were adopted in
the first edition of the grammar, instead of Memphitic
and Thebaic, lest confusion should be created; as the

Seder Med. Schal. f. 115. These expressions seem to imply the existence of the Law in Coptic.

For the arguments in support of the Translation of the New Testament into Egyptian in the second century, see *Wilkinson's Introduction
to the Coptic New Testament*, and *The Introduction to the Sahidic Fragments*.

former terms are used in those Egyptian Publications which have issued from the Oxford University Press.

The defects and mistakes of the former edition the Author trusts have been corrected in this, and he has endeavoured to render this edition worthy of the confidence and patronage of the Students of Egyptian Literature.

Stanford Rivers Rectory.

May, 1862.

Observations

on the

Hieroglyphic and Enchorial Alphabets,

with a few remarks relative to their use.

The glory of Egypt has long since passed away, but enough of its learning remains in the Sculptured Monuments of Ancient Egypt, and in existing Papyri to excite the most intense interest. These stores had long engaged the attention of the Learned who had in vain endeavoured to decipher them till our indefatigable and learned countryman Dr. Young, and a little later in point of time M. Champollion, turned their energies to the subject with considerable success. And since their day the subject has not been permitted to slumber, for other learned men have entered the field, and put before the world all that these monuments have preserved, which had been hid from the researches of the wise for so many ages.

In the year 1814 Dr. Young commenced a laborious examination of the triple Inscription on the Rosetta Stone. This stone, which is much mutilated, was discovered by the French at Rosetta, and was shortly afterwards brought to this country. The Inscription is written in Greek, in Hieroglyphic, and in the Enchorial (εγχωρια)* or native character. Dr. Young entered upon the investigation after the Baron De Sacy and Mr. Akerblad had given up the attempt. By writing the Greek above the Enchorial, which reads from right to left, and comparing one part with another, Dr. Young succeeded in deciphering it, being aided by the words *King, Country, and,* &c. which had been discovered. Dr. Young next turned his attention to the Hieroglyphic Inscription, which was much mutilated: this he also deciphered by the aid of the two other Inscriptions. Having satisfactorily ascertained the name of *Ptolemy*, which was enclosed in a ring or oval, he justly conceived that the characters composing the name might be used otherwise than symbolically; he therefore proceeded to apply these characters *Phonetically,* or *Alphabetically,* as well as those contained in the name of *Berenice*, which he had ascertained, which was found with that of Ptolemy at Karnak: and by the aid of these characters he succeeded in de-

---

* This word is used in the Rosetta inscription and elsewhere.

ciphering other groups. Mr. Banks, who had received a communication from Dr. Young while he was in Egypt, discovered the names of *Ptolemy* and *Cleopatra* on a Temple and Obelisk at Philæ, which corresponded with the Greek dedicatory Inscriptions found upon the buildings, thus confirming Dr. Young's discoveries.

The letters in these names being thus ascertained and established, the system was taken up and extended by M. Champollion, and afterwards by Mr. Salt, our then consul general in Egypt. Since then, many eminent individuals, too numerous to name, have successfully pursued this branch of the Literature of Ancient Egypt, and the world is in possession of their labours.

From the researches of Dr. Young, M. Champollion, and others, the accompanying Alphabets are constructed.

The names of Kings, and of other distinguished individuals, are generally enclosed in ovals.

The characters are sometimes read from right to left, and at others from left to right, or from the top downwards; nor is the order in placing the characters always strictly observed, for in many instances it could not conveniently be done. We however state as a rule that the characters are always read from the side towards which the animals look.

The gender of nouns is expressed by Articles as in Coptic; the Hieroglyph ⊟ or ▢, corresponding with

π or φ, masculine singular, and ▄, with τ, θ or † sing.
fem. in Coptic, as in the names of Cleopatra, Arsinoe,
and Berenice. The character ⟋ has the power of
q in the Rosetta Inscription. If we may be allowed to
reason from analogy I should be induced to say that the
plural is formed by ⌇⌇⌇⌇ — or ♥ agreeing with ⲚⲒ
Coptic, or by these characters doubled; as ⌇⌇⌇, ═ or
♥, ⲚⲈⲚ, or ⲚⲒ. Coptic. The plural is also formed by
ⲓⲓⲓ, and the dual by ⲓⲓ, in the Rosetta Inscription. I am
also inclined to think that the genitive is formed by ⌇⌇⌇,
and the Prefixes, Pronouns, &c. by the grouping of se-
veral of the Phonetic characters: as ⟣, ⲚⲔ, or ⲚⲀⲔ,
⟣, ⲚϤ, or ⲚⲀϤ; ═ ⲚⲤ, or ⲚⲀⲤ &c.

The Alphabetic or Phonetic,* was one of the

---

* Clemens Alexandrinus, who flourished about the second century
is supposed to mention with correctness the kinds of writing used by
the Egyptians. His words are these:

Αυτικα οι παρ Αιγυπτιοις παιδευομενοι, πρωτον μεν παν-
των των Αιγυπτιων γραμματων μεθοδον εκμανθανουσι, την επι-
στολογραφικην καλουμενην δευτεραν δε, την ιερατικην, ἡ χρων-
ται οι ιερογραμματεις· ὑστατην δε και τελευταιαν την ιερο-
γλυφικην, ἡς ἡ μεν εστι δια των πρωτων στοιχειων κυριολο-
γικη ἡ δε συμβολικη· της δε συμβολικης ἡ μεν κυριολογειται
κατα μιμησιν ἡ δ᾽ ὡσπερ τροπικως γραφεται, ἡ δε αντικρυς
αλληγορειται κατα τινας αινιγμους ἡλιον γουν γραψαι βουλο-
μενοι κυκλον ποιουσι σεληνην δε σχημα μηνοειδες, κατα το
κυριολογουμενον ειδος τροπικως δε κατ οικειοτητα μεταγοντες
και μετατιθεντες, τα δ᾽ εξαλλαττοντες, τα δε πολλαχως μετασχη-
ματιζοντες χαραττουσιν. Strom. l. 4. c. 4.

„Jam vero qui docentur ab Aegyptiis, primum quidem discunt Aegy-

modes of Hieroglyphic writing; but besides this the
Egyptians had another called Symbolic, which is sub-
divided into various kinds. One kind of Symbolic writing was by direct imitation, or pictorial representations
of the things intended to be expressed; as a bullock or
a ram was represented by a figure of the animal; and a
bow and arrow by a graphic imitation of them. Another
kind of Symbolic writing was the Tropical or Figurative;
that is by metaphors and similitudes. The third kind of
Symbolic writing was called Enigmatical. For instance,

---

ptiarum litterarum viam ac rationem quae vocatur Epistolographica: secundo autem hieraticam, qua utuntur Hierogrammates: ultimam autem
Hieroglyphicam: cujus una quidem species est per prima elementa,
Cyriologica dicta: altera vero Symbolica. Symbolicae autem una quidem proprie loquitur per imitationem: alia vero scribitur velut Tropice:
alia vero fere significat per quaedam Aenigmata. Qui solem itaque
volunt scribere, faciunt circulum: lunam autem figuram lunae, cor-
nuum formam prae se ferentem, convenienter ei formae quae proprie
loquitur. Tropice autem per convenientiam traducentes et transferentes,
et alia quidem immutantes, alia vero multis figuris imprimunt.“

Porphyry has communicated much the same information on the
subject.

*Εν Αιγυπτω μεν τοις ιερευσι συνην ο Πυθαγορας, και την
σοφιαν εξεμαθε, και την Αιγυπτιων φωνην γραμματων δε τρισσας
διαφορας, επιστολογραφικων τε και ιερογλυφικων και συμβολικων·
των μεν κοινολογουμενων κατα μιμησιν, των δε αλληγορουμενων
κατα τινας αινιγμους.*

De Vit. Pythag. CII, 12.

„In Aegypto cum sacerdotibus vixit Pythagoras, et sapientiam
didicit, ac linguam Aegyptiorum: literarum autem tria genera, Episto-
lographicas, Hieroglyphicas, et Symbolicas, quarum illae (Hierogly-
phicae) quidem res exponunt imitatione. Hae (Symbolicae) vero sub
Aenigmatis quibusdam latenter ostendunt.“

***

to express the sun they formed a circle, and for the moon they traced the figure of a crescent.

At what period Hieroglyphic writing was first used in Egypt it is impossible to say; but the inscriptions on the monuments carry us back to a very ancient date. The name of Tirhakah king of Ethiopia, (2. Kings XIX, 9.) who flourished about 700 years before Christ, was discovered by Mr. Salt at Medinet Haboo, and at Birkel in Ethiopia in Phonetic Characters. M. Champollion also found at Karnak the name of Shishak king of Egypt, (1. Kings XIV, 25, 26.) Phonetically written, who lived about 970 years before Christ. "He is represented as dragging the chiefs of thirty conquered Nations to the feet of the Theban Trinity." Among these he found written in letters at full length, Joudaha Melek, "The king of the Jews." This may be considered as a commentary on the above named chapter. We may probably conclude in the words of the Poet:

„Nondum flumineas Memphis contexere biblos
Noverat: et saxis tantum volucresque feraeque
Sculptaque servabant magicas animalia linguas."
Lucan. Phars. lib. III. 221.

The Hieratic or Sacerdotal characters are immediately derived from the Hieroglyphic, which will at once appear evident on comparing them. "These characters appear to have been intended for simple imita-

tions of the Hieroglyphics: and from these the Enchorial or Popular characters seem to have been derived."

"The manuscripts, which belong to the time of
Psammetichus, appear to be decidedly Hieratic, and to
follow closely the traces of the distinct characters, while
those of Darius approach in some degree to the Enchorial form, which probably came into common use as the
"epistolographic" character, while the Hieratic was so called
as being more employed by the Priests for the purposes
of their religion."

I am indebted to the kindness of C. W. Goodwin
Esqr. for the Hieroglyphic and Enchorial Alphabets, and
for the following observations on those Alphabets.

"The Hieroglyphic writing comprises between 60
and 70 signs which are alphabetic, that is, which represent simple vowel and consonantial sounds. There
are also nearly 200 more which are syllabic, that is they
represent combinations of simple sounds. Some of these
latter signs are appropriated to particular words, others
are in common use, and occur in the spelling of words
of all kinds.

As an example of the Alphabetic signs we may take
the owl, which represents the letter *m*. It often however stands alone, like м in Coptic, in which case we
must suppose that a vowel sound *a* or *e* was either prefixed or postfixed in pronunciation. An example of the

syllabic signs is ✚ which represents the combination *am*. Signs of this kind are often com ined with one or more of the alphabetic signs. Thus for the simple ✚ we have sometimes ✚ 🦅, sometimes ❘🔒🦅 both of which combinations are sounded simply *am*. Many characters which are really syllabic were inserted in the earlier lists which were formed, as alphabetic. It is probable that all the Hieroglyphic characters were originally syllabic, and that those which subsequently became pure consonants, had at first a complementary vowel.

The Hieroglyphic list includes only those characters which are purely alphabetic. Those which are found in late inscriptions are marked with an asterisk. * A few of which the sound may be considered still open to doubt are marked with a query ?" —

"The Hieratic writing was formed from the Hieroglyphic, by a gradual modification of the original forms, many of which became so altered as to be capable of identification only by comparison of identical texts written in both kinds of characters, of which the Rituals furnish abundant examples. Many varieties of Hieratic exist, just as there are many kinds of handwriting amongst ourselves, all reducible to the old square Roman character.

About 600 B. C. the Demotic or Enchorial was ormed, being only an abbreviated or degenerated form of the Hieratic, trough which its letters may be traced

up to the original Hieroglyphics. — The Demotic or Enchorial writing comprises, like the Hieroglyphic and Hieratic, a limited number of purely alphabetical characters,
and also a good many syllabic ones. The list here given
is taken from the Demotic Grammar of Dr. Brugsch, and
comprises only those characters which may be considered
as purely alphabetic. The reading is from right to left."

Index to the Subjects.

Chap. VII.

Chap. VIII.

Enchorial or Demotic Alphabet.

A
I
OU
B
F, V
K
R
L
M
N
P
S
SH
T
ϫ, ϭ
KH, ϧ
H

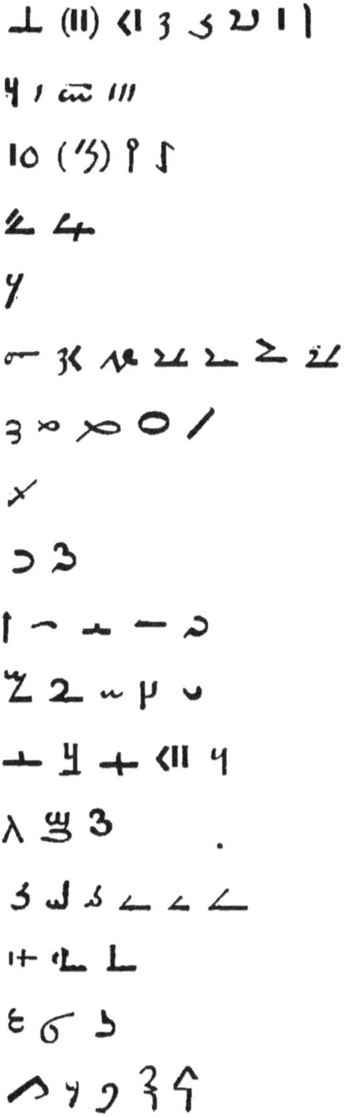

Hieroglyphic Alphabet.

A ·

I, E

U, OU,

B

F, V

K

R, L

M

N

P

S

Sh

T

T (x)

KH

H

All these figures admit of being turned the other way and read from left to right.

Enchorial or Demotic Numbers.

1	60
2	70
3	80
4	90
5	100
6	200
7	300
8	400
9	500
10	600
20	700
30	800
40	900
50	1000

Hieroglyphic Numbers.

1.	I.	21.	∩∩I.
2.	II.	22.	∩∩II.
3.	III.	30.	∩∩∩.
4.	IIII.	40.	∩∩∩∩.
5.	IIIII. |||	50.	∩∩∩∩∩.
6.	III III.	60.	∩∩∩ (∩)
7.	IIII III. ||||.	70.	∩∩∩∩
8.	IIII IIII. IIII / IIII.	80.	∩∩∩∩∩
9.	IIIII IIII. |||||.	90.	∩∩∩∩∩
10.	∩. ⊓.	100.	𝓎.
11.	∩I.	200.	𝓎𝓎.
12.	∩II.	300.	𝓎𝓎𝓎.
13.	∩III.	400.	𝓎𝓎𝓎𝓎.
16.	∩IIIIII.	500.	𝓎𝓎𝓎𝓎𝓎.
20.	∩∩.	1000.	⚘. ⚓.

CHAP. I.

The Coptic, or Egyptian Alphabet.

Egypt. Alphabet.		Names of Letters.		English sound.		Numb.
Ⲁ	ⲁ	ⲁⲗⲫⲁ	alpha	*a*		1
Ⲃ	ⲃ	ⲃⲏⲧⲁ	beta	*b*		2
Ⲅ	ⲅ	ⲅⲁⲙⲙⲁ	gamma	*g*		3
Ⲇ	ⲇ	ⲇⲉⲗⲧⲁ	delta	*d*		4
Ⲉ	ⲉ	ⲉⲓ	ei	*e* short		5
Ⲍ	ⲍ	ⲍⲏⲧⲁ	zeta	*z*		7
Ⲏ	ⲏ	ⲍⲏⲧⲁ	heta	*e* long		8
Ⲑ	ⲑ	ⲑⲏⲧⲁ	theta	*th*		9
Ⲓ	ⲓ	ⲓⲱⲧⲁ	iota	*i*		10
Ⲕ	ⲕ	ⲕⲁⲡⲡⲁ	kappa	*k*		20
Ⲗ	ⲗ	ⲗⲁⲩⲇⲁ	lauda	*l*		30
Ⲙ	ⲙ	ⲙⲓ	mi	*m*		40
Ⲛ	ⲛ	ⲛⲓ	ni	*n*		50
Ⲝ	ⲝ	ⲝⲓ	xi	*x*		60
Ⲟ	ⲟ	ⲟⲩ	ou	*o* short		70
Ⲡ	ⲡ	ⲡⲓ	pi	*p*		80

1

Egypt. Alphabet.		Names of Letters.	English sounds.	Numb.
Ｐ	p	po	ro	*r*	100
Ⲥ	c	ⲤⲓⲘⲀ	sima	*s*	200
Ⲧ	ⲧ	ⲦⲀⲨ	tau	*t*	300
Ⲩ	ⲩ	ⲉⲨ	hu	*u*	400
ⲫ	ⲫ	ⲫⲓ	phi	*ph*	500
Ⲭ	ⲭ	ⲭⲓ	chi	*ch*	600
Ⲯ	ⲯ	ⲯⲓ	psi	*ps*	700
Ⲱ	ⲱ	ⲱⲨ	ou	*o* long	800
Ⲱ	ⲱ	ⲱⲫⲓ	shei	*sh*	900
Ϥ	ϥ	ϥⲫⲓ	fei	*f*	90
ⲃ	ⲃ	ⲃⲫⲓ	khei	*kh*	
Ⲍ	ⲍ	ⲍⲟⲡⲓ	hori	*h*	
Ⲭ	ⲭ	ⲭⲀⲚⲭⲓⲀ	gangia	*gi*	
Ϭ	ϭ	ϭⲓⲘⲀ	shima	*sh*	
ϯ	ϯ	Ⲧⲫⲓ	dei	*ti*	

It will be seen from the foregoing Alphabet that
the Egyptians adopted the Greek Letters with the addition
of seven other characters. Anciently the Hieroglyphic,
Hieratic, and Demotic characters were only used in Egypt:
but when Christianity prevailed in that country those
characters were discontinued, and the Alphabet here given
was generally, if not altogether adopted in their stead.
It may be here observed that the five following letters,
viz. ⲅ, ⲇ, ⲍ, ⲝ and ⲯ were not used by the Egyptians
in their own language, but only in words adopted from
the Greek.

CHAP. II.

The pronunciation of the Letters.

The following is the pronunciation of the letters which now prevails among the Copts of Egypt.

ⲁ. is pronounced as *a* in *man* with us, and is often used in Bash. instead of ⲉ, ⲟ and ⲱ: as ⲁⲛⲅ for ⲟⲛⲃ, ⲛⲁⲃⲉ for ⲛⲟⲃⲉ, ⲁⲛⲉⲅ for ⲉⲛⲉⲅ, and ⲣⲉϥⲃⲁⲧⲉⲃ for ⲣⲉϥⲃⲱⲧⲉⲃ.

ⲃ. is sounded as *b* in ⲃⲁⲃⲩⲗⲱⲛ, and as *v* in ⲃⲕⲧⲱⲣ, ⲓⲱⲃⲁⲛ. It is also used instead of ϥ and ⲫ, as ⲃⲓ for ϥⲓ, and ϣⲃⲏⲣ for ϣⲫⲏⲣ, and it sometimes interchanges with ⲡ, as ⲁⲡⲁ for ⲁⲃⲃⲁ.

ⲅ. never occurs in Egyptian words, except when it is used instead of other Letters, or is found in Greek words. It is used instead of ⲕ and ⲭ, as ⲁⲛⲅ for ⲁⲛⲕ̄, ⲛⲅ̄ for ⲛⲕ̄, ⲧⲱⲛⲅ for ⲧⲱⲛⲕ, ⲙⲁⲁⲅⲉ for ⲙⲁⲁⲭⲉ; and in Greek words as ⲁⲛⲁⲅⲕⲏ.

ⲇ. was never used by the ancient Egyptians, and occurs only in foreign words, in which it is sometimes substituted for ⲧ, as ⲇⲁⲍⲓⲥ for ⲧⲁⲍⲓⲥ, ⲑⲉⲁⲇⲣⲟⲛ for ⲑⲉⲁⲧⲣⲟⲛ.

ⲉ. is pronounced as *ε* in Greek. It is used in Sahidic at the end of words instead of ⲓ in Coptic. It is also used instead of ⲁ in Bashmuric, as ⲅⲉⲡ for ⲅⲁⲡ. It is sometimes written instead of ⲏ.

ⲍ. is only used in words of foreign origin. It is sometimes written for ⲥ, as ⲍⲱⲛⲧ for ⲥⲱⲛⲧ. It is also written for ⲧ, as ⲧⲱⲡⲁⲍⲓⲟⲛ for ⲧⲱⲡⲁⲧⲓⲟⲛ.

н. is sounded like the Greek letter η̄, as мнпоте: it
was formerly pronounced with a sharp breathing, as
гнгемшн, ηγεμών. It is sometimes used for е and
ι, as гнвс for гевс, тнмι for тιмι.

ⲑ. This letter is pronounced as *th* in ѳаддеос. It is
also pronounced as д. ѳ is used instead of те for
expedition in writing. In Sahidic and Bashmuric т
is used instead of ѳ, as етве for еѳве. ѳ is sometimes used in Sahidic for б, as ѳеаүш for еббоуш.

ι. answers to ι in Greek, or *ee* in English. It often
changes with еι, as ιре, ειре: пιне, пеιне.

к. is sounded as χ in Greek. It is used in Sahidic instead of х, as каме for хаме; кроүр for хроүр.
In Sahidic it is often exchanged for г, as тшнг for
тшнк.

λ. in Bashmuric answers to p in Coptic, as λампι for
ромпι; λιмι for рιмι.

м. is pronounced as *m* in English.

n. also answers to *n* in English.

Ξ. this letter is seldom found in Egyptian words, but
principally occurs in words derived from other languages. It is sometimes used instead of кс, as ѳоүξ
for ѳоүкс; ξоүр for ксоүр.

о. is pronounced as *o* in Ровоам. It is often exchanged for ш long, as фшрх for форх.

п. is sounded as *b* by the modern Egyptians. п is used
in Sahidic for ф in Coptic, as паш Sah. for фаш
Coptic. It is sometimes used for в, as апа for
авва.

ρ. is pronounced as *r* in Ⲁⲣⲁⲙ. It is changed in Bashmuric for ⲗ, as ⲗⲉⲛ for ⲣⲁⲛ Coptic.

ⲥ. is enunciated as s in Ⲉⲥⲣⲱⲙ.

ⲧ. is pronounced as ⲇ; and it is occasionally used for
ⲇ, as Ⲧⲁⲛⲓⲉⲗ for Ⲇⲁⲛⲓⲉⲗ.

ⲩ. is sounded like *u*. It occurs in words of Greek origin instead of ι, η and ει; as ⲕⲩⲃⲱⲧⲟⲥ, for κιβωτός;
ⲥⲩⲙⲉⲛⲓⲛ, for σημαίνων; and ⲇⲩⲛⲁ for δεῖνα.

ⲫ. is pronounced as *f*; and in the beginning of words
as *b*; as ⲫⲁⲓ *bai*. In Sahidic and Bashmuric ⲡ is
always used instead of ⲫ.

ⲭ. has the sound of χ, or χ of the Greeks. It is exchanged with ϣ, and ϩ, as Ⲛ̄ϣⲓⲣ for ⲙⲉⲭⲓⲣ; and
ⲭⲱⲡ ϩⲱⲡ. In Sahidic ⲕ is used instead of ⲭ.

ⲯ. is pronounced as *ps* in Greek. It is rarely used in
Coptic, but sometimes it is found for ⲡⲥ in the expedition of writing, as ⲯⲓⲧ for ⲡⲥⲓⲧ; ⲯⲟⲗⲥⲉⲗ for
ⲡⲥⲟⲗⲥⲉⲗ.

ⲱ. is sounded like ω of the Greeks. It is frequently
exchanged with ο; and in Sahidic οο is often used
for ⲱ; and ⲁ in Bashmuric instead of ⲱ, as ⲁⲓⲕ for
ⲱⲓⲕ.

ϣ. possesses the same power as *ש* in Hebrew. It is
changed with ⲥ, ⲭ, ⲝ, ϭ, and sometimes with ϩ.

ϥ. is pronounced as *f*; and it is changed with ⲃ, and
sometimes with ⲫ, as ⲧⲏⲣⲫ for ⲧⲏⲣϥ.

ϧ. This letter answers to the ח of the Hebrews. Wilkinson says it has the sound of *kh*. It changes with
ⲭ and ⲕϩ, as ⲭⲉⲣ, ϧⲉⲣ; and ϧⲱⲕϩ, ϧⲱϧ. It never

occurs in Sahidic, ⳃ being always used in its stead.

ⳃ. is pronounced as *h* or ҇, and is used for the sharp breathing of the Greeks, as ϩⲟⲡⲗⲟⲛ ὅπλον, ϩⲩⲥⲱⲡⲟⲥ ὕσσωπος.

ⲝ. Sir Gardner Wilkinson says: "This letter is pronounced hard as *g* in go, and not as *dj*." It appears to answer to the Arabic ج. It changes with ⲅ, ⲭ, ⲱ, and ϭ; as ⲙⲁⲣⲭⲁⲣⲓⲧⲏⲥ, μαργαριτης, ⲅⲉⲛⲉⲫⲱⲣ for ⲝⲉⲛⲉⲫⲱⲣ, ⲝⲣⲱⲙ for ⲭⲣⲱⲙ, ⲱⲟⲩⲱⲧ for ⲝⲟⲩⲱⲧ, and ϭⲟϩ, ⲝⲟϩ.

ϭ. This letter is pronounced as *s* or *sh* by the present Copts; as ⲡⲥⲟϭⲛⲓ. *epsoshni;* ⲡⲉⲛϭⲟⲓⲥ, *pensuais.* It is exchanged with ⲥ and ⲱ, as ϭⲱⲛϩ for ⲥⲱⲛϩ, and ⲱⲱⲗ for ϭⲱⲗ. But it is chiefly exchanged with ⲝ in Sahidic and Bashmuric, as ϭⲓⲛ for ⲝⲓⲛ. It occurs in some words of Greek origin instead of ⲕ.

ϯ. The Copts of the present day pronounce this double letter as *di*; but there are some words in which we should evidently pronounce it as ti, as ⲃⲁⲡϯⲥⲙⲁ, ⲡⲗⲁϯⲁ etc. In Sahidic it is exchanged for ⲧⲉ. as ⲱⲟⲙϯ, Sah. ⲱⲟⲙⲧⲉ.

The following are examples of pronunciation as given by Sir G. Wilkinson while in Egypt. ⲉⲑⲃⲉ, pronounced as *átwa;* ⲥⲱⲧⲉⲙ, *sodam;* ϭⲟⲙ, *shôm;* ⲝⲟⲙ. *gôm;* ⲛⲓⲱϯ, *nshdee;* ⲡⲁⲛⲟⲩϯ, *banóode;* ⲡⲓⲟⲩⲱⲓⲛⲓ. *becouáynee;* ⲉ̀ⲃⲟⲗⳉⲉⲛ. *áwelkhán;* ⲉⲑⲃⲏⲧϥ, *atwátf;* ⲧⲡⲉ. *édbe;* ⲙⲉⲑⲙⲏⲓ, *metmái.*

CHAP. III.

Of Points and Abbreviations.

1. When the line in Coptic (`) or the horizontal line in Sah. (-) occurs over consonants, it generally expresses the vowel ε, as м̀ or м̄, εм: ǹ or n̄, εn. The vowel is sometimes written, and at other times it is expressed by the line above the consonant, as εmκλ2 or м̀κλ2, *af-fliction:* Sah. мn̄ for мεn, nм̄ for nεm, ϣм̄мо for ϣεммо.

It appears from some words derived from the Greek, that the line (`) has been used in Coptic to express the vowels λ, ε and о: as ǹλθωθ, *Ἀγαθώθ:* ǹоүϥι. *ὄνουφι;* and ξ̀εcтιn for ἐξέστην.

It is equally evident from the Sahidic, that the line (−) is used for λ, ε and о: as λn̄κ for λnoκ. *I;* n̄тk̄ for n̄тoκ, *thou:* оүn̄тϥ for оүonтλϥ. *he hath;* ϣm̄тε for ϣомтε. *three f.;* nм̄ for nεm *and;* 2n̄ for 2εn.

3. When the line (`) occurs above a vowel in words derived from the Greek, we find it expresses the soft or hard breathing of the Greeks; as ǹcλү. *Ἡσαῦ:* ὠcλnnλ. *ὡσαννά;* λ̀вιλ, *Ἀβιά:* or it denotes that the letter should be pronounced separately, and agrees with the diæresis of the Greeks, as cтоïχoc, *Στωϊκός.*

4. The line (`) is put over a letter in some words to distinguish them from others; as π̀εnε2, *ever,* from πεnε2, *thy oil* f.

5. A line above м̀ м̄. or ǹ n̄, distinguishes it from м or n radical, and from n, the definite article plural

before the infix; (see def. art. plur.) as ⲚⲰⲞⲨ is *glory:* but ⲚⲰⲟⲨ, without the point above the ⲛ. is *to them.*

6. Two points in Sahidic (̈) are sometimes put over the letter ï. as a contraction of ⲉⲓ. as ⲟⲩⲟⲓ̈ⲛ for ⲞⲨⲞⲈⲒⲚ, *light;* ⲡⲭⲟⲓ̈ⲥ for ⲡⲭⲞⲈⲒⲤ, *Lord.*

7. Two points are also put over the ï. when joined with another vowel in Sahidic, in the prefixes and suffixes to verbs, and in nouns and pronouns, thus: ⲦⲀⲬⲢⲞⲓ̈, ⲈⲢⲞⲓ̈, ⲚⲀⲓ̈, ⲈⲦⲎⲓ̈, ⲈⲌⲢⲀⲓ̈, ⲡⲀⲓ̈, ⲦⲀⲓ̈, ⲚⲀⲓ̈, ⲘⲈⲓ̈, ⲚⲞⲓ̈, Ⲏⲓ̈ &c.

8. The further use of the line (ˋ) and of the points (̈) will be pointed out as we proceed; but it may be here observed, that hardly two Manuscripts of the same work, agree in the lines above the letters; and we are still ignorant of a portion of them.

The Circumflex.

9. The circumflex (̂) is found in Sahidic Manuscripts over the vowels ⲁ̂, ⲉ̂, ⲏ̂, ⲓ̂, ⲟ̂ and ⲱ̂; and also over the ⲉⲓ and ⲟⲩ; as ⲟⲩⲁ̂, *one;* ⲚⲀ̂, *mercy;* ⲡⲎⲞⲨⲈ, *the heavens;* ⲚⲎ̂, *they;* ⳝⲦⲈⲔⲞ̂, *a prison;* ϬⲰ̂, *to remain;* ⲟⲩⲉⲓ, *one;* ⲟⲩ, *what?* In some cases the circumflex appears to be used instead of doubling the vowels, as ⲁ̂, ⲱ̂, for ⲀⲀ and ⲰⲰ. The circumflex is not always found in Sahidic Manuscripts.

The Apostrophe.

10. The apostrophe (') is generally found over the last letter of a word in Sahidic, but not always. Its use does not appear to be very apparent. I will not therefore add to the conjectures which have been put forth

concerning it. It is found thus: ⲡⲟⲣⲛⲓⲁˊ, ⲙⲁˊ, ⲛⲟⲩⲃˊ, Ⲗⲁⲅⲉⲓⲁˊ, ⲱⲁⲭⲉˊ, ⲥⲅⲓⲙⲉˊ, ⲫⲓⲉ̈ⲝⲓˊ, ⲃⲱⲕˊ, ⲭⲱⲕˊ, ⲫⲍⲉⲕⲓⲏⲗˊ, ⲱⲏⲣⲉⲱⲏⲙˊ, ⲛ̄ⲙ̄ⲙⲁⲛˊ, ⲣ̄ⲙ̄ⲙⲁⲟˊ, ⲅⲁⲧˊ, ⲱⲃⲏⲣˊ, ⲥⲱⲧⲏⲣˊ, ⲡⲟⲛⲏⲣⲟⲥˊ, ⲅⲁⲡˊ, ⲙ̄ⲡϥⲟⲩⲱⲱˊ, ⲛ̄ⲙⲟϥˊ.

·11. It sometimes occurs in the middle of a word, as ⲥⲟⲗˋⲥⲗ, ⲣ̄ˋⲅⲱⲃ, ⲱⲧ̄ⲣˋⲧⲱⲣ, ⲡⲉⲕˋⲕⲁⲅ.

The Abbreviations.

12. Some words in Coptic and Sahidic are abbreviated in the following manner, with a line or lines above the words.

Δ̄Λ̄Δ̄,	ⲁⲁⲅⲓⲁ,
Ⲉ̄ⲑ̄, Ⲉ̄ⲑ̄ⲩ̄,	ⲉⲑⲟⲩⲁⲃ,
ⲉⲣⲥ̄ᵒ,	ⲉⲣⲟⲥ,
ⲑ̄ⲥ̄, ⲑ̄ⲩ̄,	ⲑⲉⲟⲥ, ⲑⲉⲟⲩ,
ⲑⲓⲗⲏ̄ⲙ̄,	ⲧⲅⲓⲉⲣⲟⲩⲥⲁⲗⲏⲙ,
ⲓ̄ⲏ̄ⲗ̄,	ⲓⲥⲣⲁⲏⲗ,
ⲓ̄ⲏ̄ⲥ̄,	ⲓⲏⲥⲟⲩⲥ,
ⲓ̄ⲗ̄ⲏ̄ⲙ̄,	ⲓⲉⲣⲟⲩⲥⲁⲗⲏⲙ,
ⲓ̄ⲛ̄ⲥ̄,	ⲓⲏⲥⲟⲩⲥ ⲛⲁⲍⲁⲣⲉⲟⲥ ⲥⲱⲧⲏⲣ,
ⲓ̄ⲥ̄ⲗ̄,	ⲓⲥⲣⲁⲏⲗ,
ⲓ ⲱ ⲁ, ⲓ̄ⲱ̄ⲛ̄,	ⲓⲱⲁⲛⲛⲏⲥ,
ⲕ̄ⲉ̄, ⲕ̄ⲥ̄, ⲕ̄ⲛ̄,	ⲕⲩⲣⲓⲉ, ⲕⲩⲣⲓⲟⲥ, ⲕⲩⲣⲓⲟⲛ,
ⲕ̄ⲗ̄,	ⲕⲉⲫⲁⲗⲉⲟⲛ,
ⲙ̄ⲙ̄,	ⲙ̇ⲙⲁⲣⲧⲩⲣⲓⲁ.
ⲙⲥ̊ᵒⲩ,	ⲙⲥⲟⲩ,
ⲙⲉⲧⲭ̄ⲣ̄ⲥ̄,	ⲙⲉⲧⲭⲣⲏⲥⲧⲟⲥ,
ⲟ̄, ·	ⲟⲛ, as ⲙⲩⲥⲧⲏⲣⲓⲟ̄,
ⲟ̆,	ⲟⲩ, as ⲟ̆ⲟⲅ,

οΥ͞Ο,   ΟΥΟϢ,

π̅θ̅ρ,   ΠΑΡΘΕΝΟϹ,

π̅ν̅α,   ΠΝΕΥΜΑ.

π̅ν̅ε̅,   ΠΝΟΥΤΕ,

c̅ρ̅, c̅ω̅ρ̅, ϹΩΤΗΡ.   ☨, ΦΝΟΥϯ,

ⲋ Τ,

γ̅γ̅· ϢΗΡΕ,   ⳇ, ϹΤΑΥΡΟϹ,

Φϯ, ΦΝΟΥϯ.   ⳃ, ΜΑΡΤΥΡΟϹ,

Χ̅ρ̅, ΧΡΟΝΟϹ.   ⳃ, ΠΡΟϹ,

Χ̅c̅, Χ̅ρ̅c̅, ΧΡΙϹΤΟϹ, ⲋⲋ, ϬΟΕΙϹ. ϬΟΙϹ.

13. Coptic Manuscripts generally begin with ⲥⲩ̅ⲛθ ⲁⳑⳑⲓ, in the name of God: or with ⲥⲩ̅ⲛθ ΙϹΧⲩ̅ΡΟϹ, in the name of the powerful God.

14. The stops used in Manuscripts, are one or two points, as ⲝⲉ ⲁΝⲀⳉ ⲀϥⲘⲟⲨ. ⲞⲨⲞϢ &c.   Mark XV, 44. or as Ⲉⳑⲱⲓ: Ⲉⳑⲱⲓ: ⲈⳑⲈⳘⲀ ϹⲀⲂⲀⲬⲐⲀⲚⲓ: Mark XV, 24.

Part II.   Etymology.

The Articles.

1. The Egyptian Language has the definite and in-definite articles, and also the possessive.

The Definite Article.

Coptic.

Masc. Sing.	Fem. Sing.	Plur. Com.
ΠΙ. Π. Φ.	Τ. Θ. ϯ.	ΝΙ. ΝΕΝ.

Sahidic.

ⲡⲉ. ⲡ.   ⲧⲉ. ⲧ.   ⲛⲉ. ⲛ̄. ⲛⲛ̄.

Bashmuric.

ⲡⲓ. ⲡⲉ. ⲡ.   ϯ. ⲧⲉ. ⲧ.   ⲛⲓ. ⲛⲉ. ⲛ̄.

2. The Coptic uses the article ⲡⲓ and ⲡ promiscuously, either before double consonants or vowels, as ⲡⲓ-ⲕⲁϩⲓ and ⲡ-ⲕⲁϩⲓ; ⲡⲓ-ⲏⲓ and ⲡ-ⲏⲓ: ⲡⲓ-ⲟⲩⲣⲟ and ⲡ-ⲟⲩⲣⲟ: ϯ-ⲥⲙⲏ and ⲧ-ⲥⲙⲏ. The Coptic has ⲡⲓ and ϯ also before vowels, even before ⲓ. as ⲡⲓⲓⲁϩ, ϯⲓⲟⲩⲇⲉⲁ. But in the plural ⲛⲓ is generally used, but sometimes ⲛⲉⲛ, except before ⲉⲧ *who,* and the prefix, as we shall hereafter show. The articles ⲫ and ⲑ, are used instead of ⲡ and ⲧ. before the letters ⲃ, ⲓ, ⲙ, ⲛ, ⲟⲩ, ⲣ, as ⲫⲃⲁⲗ. ⲫⲙⲱⲓⲧ, ⲫⲟⲩⲁⲓ, ⲑⲃⲁⲕⲓ, ⲑⲙⲏⲥⲓ, ⲑⲛⲟⲩⲛⲓ: but we sometimes find these words written ⲡⲓⲃⲁⲗ. ⲡⲓⲙⲱⲓⲧ, ⲡⲓⲟⲩⲁⲓ, ϯⲃⲁⲕⲓ, ϯⲙⲏⲥⲓ, ϯⲛⲟⲩⲛⲓ.

3. The Sahidic has ⲡⲉ and ⲧⲉ singular, and ⲛⲉ plural before nouns, beginning with two consonants, as ⲧⲙⲁⲉⲓⲟ, ⲭⲣⲟ, ⲭⲡⲓⲟ, ⲟ̅ⲗⲟⲟⲧⲉ, ⲡⲣⲱ &c. The Articles ⲡ and ⲧ singular, and ⲛ plural, are used not only before vowels, or before one consonant, as before ⲟⲩⲱϣ, ⲥⲛⲟ̅, ⲛⲟⲩⲧⲉ, and ⲙⲁ; but even before consonants, when marked with the line or vowel above, as ⲡ̄ⲡⲉ, ⲧ̄ⲃⲃⲟ, ⲛ̄ⲧⲣⲉ etc. But either ⲡⲉ, ⲧⲉ. ⲛⲉ are used before ϩ, as ⲧⲉϩⲓⲏ, ⲛⲉϩⲓⲟⲟⲩⲉ; or ⲡϩ is contracted into ⲫ, and ⲧϩ into ⲑ, as ⲫⲏⲩ, from ⲡϩⲏⲩ. ⲫⲁⲡ, from ⲡϩⲁⲡ: ⲫⲏⲕⲉ from ⲡϩⲏⲕⲉ: ⲫⲟⲟⲩ from ⲡϩⲟⲟⲩ: and ⲑⲉ from ⲧϩⲉ. ⲑⲏ from ⲧϩⲏ, ⲑⲓⲙⲉ from ⲧϩⲓⲙⲉ, ⲑⲁⲓⲃⲉⲥ from ⲧϩⲁⲓⲃⲉⲥ, ⲑ̅ⲃⲥⲱ from

2 *

ⲧⲉ̄ⲃⲥⲱ, ⲟ̄ⲗⲗⲱ from ⲧⲉ̄ⲗⲗⲱ. Sometimes ⲡⲅ is found without the contraction, as ⲡⲅⲏⲧ, ⲡⲅⲓⲣ. The vowel ⲉ is
admitted before ⲟⲩ, and ⲉⲟⲩ is contracted into ⲉⲩ, as
ⲡⲉⲩⲟⲉⲓⲱ for ⲡⲉⲟⲩⲟⲉⲓⲱ, ⲧⲉⲩⲱ̣ⲏ for ⲧⲉⲟⲩⲱ̣ⲏ, and ⲧⲉⲩ-
ⲛⲟⲩ for ⲧⲉⲟⲩⲛⲟⲩ. Often ⲛ̄ is prefixed to vowels, as
ⲛ̄ⲁⲥⲉⲃⲏⲥ. ⲛ̄ is changed into ⲙ̄, before the letters ⲙ
and ⲡ, as ⲙ̄ⲙⲁⲉⲓⲛ. *the signs;* ⲙ̄ⲡⲏⲩⲉ, *the heavens;* ⲛ̄ⲛ̄
sometimes occurs, as ⲛ̄ⲛⲟ̄ⲗⲟ̄ⲃ, *the beds.* The ⲛ̄ plur. is
very rarely changed into ⲃ, ⲗ, ⲣ, before the same letters,
as ⲃ̄ⲃ̄ⲣ̄ⲣⲉ, for ⲛ̄ⲃ̄ⲣ̄ⲣⲉ, plur. *new;* ⲗ̄ⲗⲁⲟⲥ for ⲛ̄ⲗⲁⲟ̄ⲥ, *the
peoples;* ⲣ̄ⲣⲱⲙⲉ for ⲛ̄ⲣⲱⲙⲉ, *the men.* The Sahidic very
rarely has the Coptic articles ⲡⲓ. ϯ and ⲛⲓ. but they are
sometimes met with; and occasionally ⲧⲉⲓ and ⲛⲉⲓ arc
used instead of the articles.

The Indefinite Articles.

4. The indefinite article has no distinction of gender.

C o p t i c.

Sing.	Plur.
ⲟⲩ.	ⲅⲁⲛ.

S a h i d i c.

ⲟⲩ.	ⲅⲉⲛ. ⲅ̄ⲛ̄.

B a s h m u r i c.

ⲟⲩ.	ⲅⲁⲛ. ⲅⲉⲛ. ⲅ̄ⲛ̄.

5. Thus the indefinite article is used, as ⲟⲩⲥⲁϫⲓ.
a word; ⲅⲁⲛⲥⲁϫⲓ, *words;* ⲟⲩⲃⲁⲕⲓ. *a city;* ⲅⲁⲛⲃⲁⲕⲓ.
cities. When ⲟⲩ the indefinite article precedes the preposition ⲉ̀, as ⲉ̀ⲟⲩ, it is contracted into ⲉ̀ⲩ, as ⲉ̀ⲩⲱ̣ⲁϥⲉ

to a desert for ⲉⲟⲩⲱϣⲁϥⲉ. The Sahidic uses ⳨ⲉⲛ and ⳨ⲛ̄ in the plural, and the Bashmuric the Coptic and Sahidic plurals.

The Possessive Articles.

Coptic.

Sing. m	Sing. f.	Plur. com.
ⲫⲁ.	ⲑⲁ.	ⲛⲁ.

Sahidic.

ⲡⲁ.	ⲧⲁ.	ⲛⲁ.

6. These articles point out persons or things which belong to any one, as ⲡⲓⲁⲙⲁ⳨ⲓ ⲫⲁ ⲫϯ ⲡⲉ, *the power is of God.* Ps. LXI, 11. ⲑⲁ ⲛⲓⲙ ⲧⲉ ⲧⲁⲓ ⳨ⲓⲕⲱⲛ, *of whom is this image.* Mark XII, 16. ⲛⲁ ⲧⲕⲟⲩⲓ ⲡⲓⲥⲧⲓⲥ, *of little faith.* Luke XII, 28. ⲡⲁ ⲡⲉϥⲓⲱⲧ, *of his father.* Luke IX, 26. When used with the name of a person, ⲫⲁ signifies *the son of,* as ⲫⲁ ⲏ̅ⲗⲓ, *the son of Eli.* Luke III, 23.

CHAP. IV.

Of Nouns.

1. An Egyptian noun generally takes an article before it, or other particle, as ⲟⲩⲣⲱⲙⲓ, *a man;* ⳨ⲁⲛⲙⲟⲩⲙⲓ, *lions;* ⲡⲓⲣⲁⲛ, *the name;* ⲛⲓϭⲏⲡⲓ, *the clouds;* but when the article is prefixed to the adjective or the substantive, the other takes the prefix ⲛ̄, as ⲟⲩⲛⲓϣϯ ⲛ̄⳨ⲟϯ, Copt. ⲟⲩⲛⲟϭ

ⲚϨⲞⲦⲈ, Sah. *a great fear*. Act. V, 2. ⲞⲨⲔⲀϨⲒ ⲚϢⲈⲘⲘⲞ, *a strange land*, Copt. ⲦϢⲞⲢⲠ ⲚⲚⲦⲞⲖⲎ. *the first command- ment*. Sah. ⲞⲨⲚⲒϢ† ⲚⲚⲈϨⲠⲒ ⲠⲈⲫⲀⲒ, *this is a great lamen- tation*. Copt. The Ⲛ is also prefixed to the noun substan- tive or adjective after the verbs ⲞⲒ, and ϢⲰⲠⲈ. as ⲈϤⲞⲒ ⲚⲞⲨⲰⲒⲚⲒ, *it is light;* ⲀⲔϢⲰⲠⲈ ⲚⲂⲞⲎⲐⲞⲤ, *thou hast been a helper.*

2. Adjectives sometimes take the articles, as ⲠⲒⲚⲒϢ†, *great,* m.; †ⲚⲒϢ†, *great,* f.; but when they are united with the particles ⲈⲦ, ⲈϤ, ⲈⲤ and ⲈⲨ, they do not take the article. Adjectives are also distinguished by their prefixes and suffixes.

Of the Gender of Nouns.

3. Every noun of the three Dialects is either of the masculine or feminine gender, and is known by the mas- culine or feminine article being prefixed, or by the prefix or suffix, or it is known by its agreeing with the verb, or some other word in the sentence which has the sign of the gender; as †ⲂⲀⲔⲒ, *the city*, f.; ⲠⲒⲈ̀ⲭⲰⲢϨ, *the night,* m.; ⲈϤⲞϢ, *much,* m.; ⲈⲤⲞϢ, *much,* f.; ⲈⲐⲚⲀⲚⲈϤ. Copt. ⲚⲀⲚⲞⲨϤ, *good,* m.; Sah. ⲈⲐⲚⲀⲚⲈⲤ Copt. ⲚⲀⲘⲞⲨⲤ, Sah. *good,* f. The Plural has no distinction of gender, nor is there any neuter in the language, but instead of it the feminine is used. Nouns composed with the par- ticle ⲘⲈⲦ Copt. or ⲘⲚⲦ Sah. are all feminine. Those composed with ϬⲒⲚ, Sah. are also feminine, but those compounded with ⲭⲒⲚ, Coptic, are for the most part masculine.

4. There are some masculine nouns which become feminine by adding ı to them in the Coptic and Bashmuric, and ε in the Sahidic; as ⲃⲱⲕ, *a servant*, m.; ⲃⲱⲕⲓ, *a servant*, f. Copt. ⲥⲟⲛ, *a brother;* ⲥⲱⲛⲓ, *a sister*, Copt. ϣⲟⲙ, *a father in law.* ϣⲱⲙⲓ, Copt. ϣⲱⲙⲉ, Sah. *a mother in law.* ϣⲫⲏⲣ, *a friend*, m. ϣⲫⲏⲣⲓ, *a friend*, f. Copt. ϣⲃⲉⲉⲣ, *a friend*, m. ϣⲃⲉⲉⲣⲉ, *a friend*, f. Sah. ϭⲁⲙⲁⲩⲗ, *a camel*, m. ϭⲁⲙⲁⲩⲗⲉ, *a camel*, f. Sah. ϩⲓⲏⲃ, *a lamb*, m. ϩⲓⲏⲃⲓ, *a lamb*, f. Copt. ϩⲓⲉⲓⲃ, *a lamb,* m. ϩⲓⲉⲓⲃⲉ, *a lamb*, f. Sahidic.

5. Others form the feminine by changing the last short vowel of the masculine into a long one, as ⲃⲉⲗⲗⲉ, *blind*, m. ⲃⲉⲗⲗⲏ, Copt. ⲃⲗ̄ⲗⲏ, Sah. *blind*, f. ⲙⲟⲩⲓ, *a lion*, m. ⲙⲟⲩⲏ, *a lioness*, Copt. ⲟⲩⲣⲟ, *a king*, ⲟⲩⲣⲱ, *a queen*, Copt. ⲣ̄ⲣⲟ, *a king.* ⲣ̄ⲣⲱ, *a queen*, Sah. ⲃⲉⲗⲗⲟ. *an old man.* ⲃⲉⲗⲗⲱ. *an old woman*, Copt. ϩⲗ̄ⲗⲟ, *an old man.* ϩⲗ̄ⲗⲱ, *an old woman*, Sah. ϣⲙ̄ⲙⲟ, *a stranger*, m. ϣⲙ̄ⲙⲱ, *a stranger*, f. Sah. ⲥⲁⲃⲉ. *wise.* m. ⲥⲁⲃⲏ, *wise*, f. Copt. ϧⲁⲉ̀, *the end*, m. ϧⲁⲏ, *the end*, f. Copt.

6. Likewise by changing the vowel of the penultimate syllable of the masculine, as ϣⲏⲣⲓ, *a son.* ϣⲉⲣⲓ, *a daughter*, Copt. ϣⲏⲣⲉ, *a son.* ϣⲉⲉⲣⲉ, *a daughter*, Sah.

Of the Number of Nouns.

7. The number of nouns is two, the singular and the plural. These can only be distinguished from each other in general, by the singular or plural article being prefixed, as:

ⲞⲨ⳪ⲰⲘ, *a book;* Ⲡⲓ⳪ⲰⲘ, *the book;* ⳪ⲀⲚ⳪ⲰⲘ, *books;*
Ⲛⲓ⳪ⲰⲘ, *the books;* ⲞⲨⲚⲞⲂⲈ, *a sin;* ⲠⲚⲞⲨⲂⲈ, *the sin;*
⳪ⲈⲚⲚⲞⲂⲈ, *sins;* ⲚⲈⲚⲞⲂⲈ, *the sins,* Sah.

When nouns occur, without the article being prefixed, the singular or plural can only be known by its
connection with other words of the sentence.

8. Some adjectives take the prefixes ⲈϤ, masc. ⲈⲤ,
fem. and ⲈⲨ plur, as ⲈϤⲈⲘⲠⳡⲀ, *worthy,* m. ⲈⲤⲈⲘⲠⳡⲀ,
worthy, fem. ⲈϤⲞⲔⲘ̅. *sad,* m. Sah. ⲈⲨⲞⲔⲘ̅, *sad,* plur. Sah.
The adjectives which have the suffixes ϥ and ⲥ singular,
have the plural in ⲞⲨ, which variously is contracted with
the preceding vowel, as ⲠⲈⲐⲚⲀⲚⲈϤ, *good.* ⲠⲈⲐⲚⲀⲚⲈⲨ,
good, plur. ⲠⲈⲐⲚⲀⲀϤ, *great.* ⲠⲈⲐⲚⲀⲀⲨ, *great,* plur. ⲚⲀⳡⲰϤ,
much. ⲚⲀⳡⲰⲞⲨ, *much,* plur.

9. There are a considerable number of Nouns in
each dialect, which form their plural differently, which
we shall here endeavour to class according to their ter-
mination.

10. Coptic Plurals which end in ⲓ. ⲀⲂⲰⲔ, *a crow.*
ⲀⲂⲰⲔⲓ, *crows.* Ⲁϕⲱϕ, *a giant.* Ⲁϕⲱϕⲓ, *giants.* ⲘⲀ, *a place.*
ⲘⲀⲓ, *places.* Ⲙ̅ⲚⲞⲦ *a breast.* Ⲙ̅ⲚⲞ†, *breasts.* ⲢⲀⲘⲀⲟ̀,
rich. ⲢⲀⲘⲀⲟ̀ⲓ, *rich,* plur. ⳡϥⲈⲢ, *a companion.* ⳡϥⲈⲢⲓ, *com-
panions.* ⲃⲈⲗⲗⲟ, *old.* ⲃⲈⲗⲗⲟⲓ, *old,* plur.

11. Coptic Plurals which end in Ⲩ and their sing.
in ⲉ. ⳓⲀⲗⲈ, *lame.* ⳓⲀⲗⲈⲨ, *lame,* plur. ⲂⲈⲗⲗⲈ, *blind.* ⲂⲈⲗⲗⲈⲨ,
blind, plur. ⲐⲈⳡⲈ, *neighbour.* ⲐⲈⳡⲈⲨ, *a neighbours.* ⲘⲈⲐⲢⲈ,
a witness. ⲘⲈⲐⲢⲈⲨ, *witnesses.* ⲢⲈⲘⳇⲈ, *free.* ⲢⲈⲘⳇⲈⲨ, *free,*
plur. ⲤⲀⲂⲈ, *prudent.* ⲤⲀⲂⲈⲨ, *prudent,* plur. ⲃⲀⲉ̀, *last,*
ⲃⲀⲉⲨ, *last,* plur. ⳈⲀⲚⲈ, *humble.* ⳈⲀⲚⲈⲨ, *humble,* plur.

12. Coptic Plurals which end in ⲟⲩ, and their sing. in ⲉ and ⲟ; but which change them into ⲛⲟⲩ and ⲱⲟⲩ in the plural. ⲉ̀ⲃⲟ, *mule.* ⲉ̀ⲃⲱⲟⲩ, *mule,* plur. ⲉ̀ⲍⲉ, *an ox.* ⲉ̀ⲍⲏⲟⲩ and ⲉ̀ⲍⲱⲟⲩ, *oxen.* ⲓⲁⲣⲟ, *a river.* ⲓⲁⲣⲱⲟⲩ, *rivers.* ⲟⲩⲣⲟ, *a king.* ⲟⲩⲣⲱⲟⲩ, *kings.* ⲣⲁⲙⲁⲟ̀, *rich.* ⲣⲁⲙⲁⲱⲟⲩ, *rich,* plur. ⲣⲟ, *a door.* ⲣⲱⲟⲩ, *doors.* ⲥⲁⲓⲉ, *fair.* ⲥⲁⲓⲱⲟⲩ, *fair,* pl. ϣⲉⲙⲙⲟ, *a stranger.* ϣⲉⲙⲙⲱ́ⲟⲩ, *strangers.* ϣⲛⲉ, *a net.* ϣⲛⲏⲟⲩ. *nets.* ϣⲧⲉⲕⲟ, *a prison.* ϣⲧⲉⲕⲱⲟⲩ, *prisons.* ϣⲝⲉ, *a locust.* ϣⲝⲏⲟⲩ, *locusts.* To these may be added ⲁⲡⲏ, *head,* Bash. ⲁⲡⲛⲟⲩ, *heads.*

13. Coptic Plurals which end in ⲟⲩⲓ, and their singulars ending with a consonant, or with ⲱ.

ⲁϥ, *flesh.* ⲁϥⲟⲩⲓ, *flesh,* plur. ⲁⲭⲱ, *magician.* ⲁⲭⲱⲟⲩⲓ, *magicians.* ⲉⲧⲫⲱ, *a burden.* ⲉⲧⲫⲱⲟⲩⲓ, *burdens.* ⲣⲉϥⲭⲱ, *a singer.* ⲣⲉϥⲭⲱⲟⲩⲓ, *singers.* ⲥⲃⲱ, *a doctrine.* ⲥⲃⲱⲟⲩⲓ, *doctrines.* ⲥϕⲓⲣ, *a side.* ⲥϕⲓⲣⲱⲟⲩⲓ, *sides.*

14. Of Coptic Plurals which end in ⲟⲩⲓ, and their singulars in ⲉ, ⲉⲓ, ⲏ or ⲟⲩ, which are changed into ⲛⲟⲩⲓ or ⲱⲟⲩⲓ in the plural: as

ⲁϥⲉ, *a head.* ⲁϥⲛⲟⲩⲓ, *heads.* ⲁⲗⲟⲩ. *a boy.* ⲁⲗⲱⲟⲩⲓ, *boys.* ⲃⲉⲭⲉ, *wages.* ⲃⲉⲭⲛⲟⲩⲓ, *wages,* plur. ⲉⲣⲙⲏ, *a tear.* ⲉⲣⲙⲱⲟⲩⲓ, *tears.* ⲉⲣϕⲉⲓ, *a temple.* ⲉⲣϕⲛⲟⲩⲓ. *temples.* ⲟⲩⲛⲟⲩ, *an hour.* ⲟⲩⲛⲱⲟⲩⲓ, *hours.* ⲧⲉⲃⲛⲏ, *a labouring beast.* ⲧⲉⲃⲛⲱⲟⲩⲓ, *beasts.* ϕⲉ, *heaven.* ϕⲛⲟⲩⲓ, *heavens.* ϧⲣⲉ, *food.* ϧⲣⲛⲟⲩⲓ, *food,* plur.

15. Sahidic Plurals which end in ⲉ.

ⲁⲃⲱⲕ, *a crow.* ⲁ̀ⲃⲱⲕⲉ, *crows.* ⲗⲟⲟⲩ, *an ornament.* ⲗⲟⲟⲩⲉ, *ornaments.*

16. Sahidic Plurals which end in ⲉⲩ, and ⲏⲩ, and their singulars in ⲉ, as

ⲃⲗ̄ⲗⲉ, *blind.* ⲃⲗ̄ⲗⲉⲩ, *blind,* pl. ⲥⲁⲃⲉ, *prudent.* ⲥⲁⲃⲉⲉⲩ, *prudent,* plur. ⳣⲁϥⲉ, *a desert.* ⳣⲁϥⲉⲉⲩ, *deserts.* ϫⲓϫⲉ, *an enemy.* ϫⲓϫⲉⲉⲩ, *enemies.* ϯⲙⲉ, *a village.* ϯⲙⲉⲉⲩ, *villages.* ϩⲁⲉ, *last.* ϩⲁⲉⲉⲩ and ϩⲁⲉⲩⲉ, *last,* plur.

17. Sahidic Plur. which change the ⲉ sing. into ⲏⲩ pl. ⲁⲙⲣⲉ, *a baker.* ⲁⲙⲣⲏⲩ, *bakers.* ⲉϩⲉ, *an ox.* ⲉϩⲏⲩ, *oxen.* ⳣⲛⲉ, *a net.* ⳣⲛⲏⲩ, *nets.*

18. Sahidic Plurals which end in ⲉⲩⲉ, ⲏⲩⲉ, and ⲏⲟⲩⲉ, and their singulars in ⲉ, as

ⲁⲡⲉ, *a head.* ⲁⲡⲏⲩⲉ, *heads.* ⲡⲉ, *heaven.* ⲡⲏⲩⲉ, *heavens.* ϩⲁⲉ, *last.* ϩⲁⲉⲉⲩⲉ, *last,* plur. 'ⲉⲣⲉ, *food.* ϩⲣⲏⲩⲉ, and ϩⲣⲏⲟⲩⲉ, *food,* plur. ϭⲁⲗⲉ, *lame.* ϭⲁⲗⲉⲉⲩⲉ, *lame,* plur. The short ⲉ is changed into ⲏ when the plurals ends in ⲏⲩⲉ.

19. Sahidic Plurals which end in ⲟⲩ, and their singulars in ⲟ, which are changed into ⲱⲟⲩ, as

ⲓⲉⲣⲟ, *a river.* ⲓⲉⲣⲱⲟⲩ, *rivers.* ⲕⲣⲟ, *the shore.* ⲕⲣⲱⲟⲩ, *shores.* ⲙ̄ⲛⲧⲣ̄ⲣⲟ, *a kingdom.* ⲙ̄ⲛⲧⲣ̄ⲣⲱⲟⲩ, *kingdoms.* ⲣⲟ, *a door.* ⲣⲱⲟⲩ, *doors.* ⲣ̄ⲣⲟ, *a king.* ⲣ̄ⲣⲱⲟⲩ, *kings.* The following is formed not quite regularly: ⲉϩⲉ, *an ox.* ⲉϩⲟⲟⲩ, *oxen.*

20. Sahidic Plurals which end in ⲟⲩⲉ.

ⲉⲓⲱ, *an ass.* ⲉⲓⲱⲟⲩⲉ, *asses.* ⲉⲙⲣⲱ, *a harbour.* ⲉⲙⲣⲟⲟⲩⲉ, *harbours.* ⲉⲱ, *an ass.* ⲉⲟⲟⲩⲉ, *asses.* ⲕⲉ, *another.* ⲕⲟⲟⲩⲉ, *others.* ⲟⲩⲛⲟⲩ, *an hour.* ⲟⲩⲛⲟⲟⲩⲉ, *hours.* ⲟⲩⳣⲏ, *night.* ⲟⲩⳣⲟⲟⲩⲉ, *nights.* ⲣⲓⲙⲉ, *weeping.* ⲣⲙ̄ⲉⲓⲟⲟⲩⲉ, ⲣⲙ̄ⲉⲓⲟⲩⲉ, *tears.* ⲣⲟⲙⲡⲉ, *a year.* ⲣⲙ̄ⲡⲟⲟⲩⲉ, *years.* ⲥⲃⲱ, *a doctrine.* ⲥⲃⲟⲟⲩⲉ, *doctrines.* ⲥⲡⲓⲣ, *a side.* ⲥⲡⲓⲣⲟⲟⲩⲉ,

sides. **ⲧⲃⲛ̄ⲏ,** *a beast.* **ⲧⲃ̄ⲛⲟⲟⲩⲉ,** *beasts,* plur. **ⲋⲓⲏ,** *a way.*
ⲋⲓⲟⲟⲩⲉ, *ways.* **ⲋⲣⲉ,** *food.* **ⲋⲣⲉⲟⲩⲉ,** *food,* plur.

21. Coptic and Sahidic Plurals of a more irregular character.

Coptic.

Sing.	Plur.
ⲁⲋⲟ, *a treasure.*	**ⲁⲋⲱⲣ,** *treasures.*
ⲁⲃⲟⲧ, *a month.*	**ⲁⲃⲏⲧ,** *months.*
ⲁⲛⲁϣ, *an oath.*	**ⲁⲛⲁⲩϣ,** *oaths.*
ⲃⲏⲧ, *a palmwood.*	**ⲃⲁ†,** *palmwoods.*
ⲃⲱⲕ, *a servant.*	**ⲉ̀ⲃⲓⲁⲕ,** *servants.*
ⲉⲑⲟϣ, *an Ethiopian.*	**ⲉⲑⲁⲩϣ,** *Ethiopians.*
ⲉⲙⲕⲁⲋ, *grief.*	**ⲉⲙⲕⲁⲩⲋ,** *griefs.*
ⲉⲱ, *an ass.*	**ⲉⲉⲩ,** *asses.*
ϥⲩⲱ, *a pig.*	**ⲉϣⲁⲩ,** *pigs.*
ⲉϣⲱⲧ, *a merchant.*	**ⲉϣⲟ†,** *merchants.*
ⲏⲓ, *a house.*	**ⲏⲟⲩ,** *houses.*
ⲓⲟⲙ, *the sea.*	**ⲁⲙⲁⲓⲟⲩ,** *seas.*
ⲓⲱⲧ, *a father.*	**ⲓⲟ†,** *fathers.*
ⲙⲉⲛⲡⲓⲧ, *beloved.*	**ⲙⲉⲛⲡⲁ†,** *beloved.*
ⲙⲉϣⲱⲧ, *a plain.*	**ⲙⲉϣⲟ†,** *plains.*
ⲙⲱⲓⲧ, *a way.*	**ⲙⲓⲧⲱⲟⲩⲓ,** *ways.*
ⲟⲩⲣⲓⲧ, *a keeper.*	**ⲟⲩⲣⲁ†,** *keepers.*
ⲣⲉⲙⲏⲧ, *a tenth.*	**ⲣⲉⲙⲁ†,** *tenths.*
ⲥⲁⲃ, *a scribe.*	**ⲥⲃⲟⲩⲓ,** *scribes.*
ⲥⲟⲃⲧ, *a wall.*	**ⲥⲉⲃⲑⲁⲓⲟⲩ,** *walls.*
ⲥⲟⲛⲓ, *a robber.*	**ⲥⲓⲛⲱⲟⲩⲓ,** *robbers.*
ⲥⲟⲛ, *a brother.*	**ⲥⲛⲏⲟⲩ,** *brothers.*
ⲥϋⲓⲙⲓ, *a woman.*	**ⲋⲓⲟⲙⲓ,** *women.*

3*

Sing.	Plur.
ϣⲟⲙ, *a father in law.*	ϣⲙⲱⲟⲩ, *fathers in law.*
ϣⲃⲱⲧ, *a rod.*	ϣⲃⲟ†, *rods.*
ϩⲃⲱ, *a viper.*	ϩⲃⲟⲩⲓ, *vipers.*
ϩⲑⲟ, *a horse.*	ϩⲑⲱⲣ, *horses.*
ϩⲁⲗⲏⲧ, *a bird.*	ϩⲁⲗⲁ†, *birds.*
ϩⲟⲩⲓⲧ, *the first.*	ϩⲟⲩⲁ†, *first,* plur.
ϩⲱⲃ, *a work.*	ϩⲃⲏⲟⲩⲓ, *works.*
ⲭⲁⲙⲟⲩⲗ, *a camel.*	ⲭⲁⲙⲁⲩⲗⲓ, *camels.*
ⲭⲟⲓ, *a ship.*	ⲉⲭⲏⲟⲩ, *ships.*
ϭⲁⲗⲟⲭ, *a foot.*	ϭⲁⲗⲁⲩⲭ, *feet.*
ⲟ̅ⲥ̅, *a Lord.*	ϭⲓⲥⲉⲩ, *Lords.*

Sahidic.

Sing.	Plur.
ⲁϩⲟ, *a treasure.*	ⲁϩⲱⲱⲣ, *treasures.*
ⲃⲓⲣ, *a basket.*	ⲃⲣⲏⲟⲩⲉ, *baskets.*
ⲉⲃⲟⲧ, *a month.*	ⲉⲃⲁⲧⲉ, *months.*
ⲫⲓⲱⲧ, *a father.*	ⲉⲓⲟⲧⲉ, *fathers.*
ⲟⲩⲣⲓⲧ, *a keeper.*	ⲟⲩⲣⲁⲧⲉ, *keepers.*
ⲥⲟⲛ, *a brother.*	ⲥⲛⲏⲩ, *brothers.*
ⲥϩⲓⲙⲉ, *a woman.*	ϩⲓⲟⲙⲉ, *women.*
ⲟⲩϩⲟⲣ, *a dog.*	ⲟⲩϩⲟⲟⲣ, *dogs.*
ϩⲁⲗⲏⲧ, *a bird.*	ϩⲁⲗⲁⲁⲧⲉ, *birds.*
ϩⲃⲱ, *a viper.*	ϩⲃⲟⲩⲓ, *vipers.*
ϩⲧⲟ, *a horse.*	ϩⲧⲱⲣ, ϩⲧⲱⲱⲣ, *horses.*
ϩⲱⲃ, *a work.*	ϩⲃⲏⲩ, ϩⲃⲏⲩⲉ, *works.*
ⲭⲟⲓ, *a ship.*	ⲉⲭⲏⲩ́, *ships.*
ⲭⲟⲉⲓⲥ, *Lord.*	ⲭⲉⲓⲥⲟⲟⲩⲉ, *Lords.*

Of Cases of Nouns.

22. Strictly speaking the three Dialects of Egypt have no cases of nouns. But these are indicated by certain particles which precede, or are prefixed to the nouns, or by prepositions, as,

	Coptic.	Sahidic and Bashmuric.
Nom.	Ⲛ̀ⲬⲈ.	Ⲛ̄Ⳓ̄ⲓ.
Gen.	Ⲛ̀ⲦⲈ, Ⲙ̀, Ⲛ̀.	Ⲛ̄ⲦⲈ, Ⲙ̄, Ⲛ̄.
Dat.	Ⲉ̀, Ⲙ̀, Ⲛ̀.	Ⲉ̄, Ⲙ̄, Ⲛ̄.
Acc.	Ⲉ̀, Ⲙ̀, Ⲛ̀.	Ⲉ, Ⲙ̄, Ⲛ̄.
Voc.	ⲱ̀, ⲠⲒ.	ⲱ, ⲠⲈ.
Abl.	Ⲉ̀, Ⲙ̀, Ⲛ̀, or a preposition.	Ⲉ, Ⲙ̄, Ⲛ̄, or a preposition.

23. It will be seen that what are called cases in Greek and Latin are here denoted by particles which precede the noun, as in the nominative and genitive, or by particles prefixed.

The Nominative Case.

24. The sign of the nominative case is Ⲛ̀ⲬⲈ in Coptic, and Ⲛ̄Ⳓ̄ⲓ in Sahidic and Bashmuric, as ⲀⳘⲈⲢⲞⲨⲱ̀ Ⲛ̀ⲬⲈ ⲒⲎ̄Ⲥ̄, ⲠⲈⲬⲀ ⲚⲱⲟⲨ, *Jesus answered (and) said to them*, Luke VI, 3. ⲀⳆⲒ̀ ⲀⲈ Ⲛ̀ⲬⲈ ⲘⲀⲢⲒⲀ̀ ⳁⲘⲀⲄⲆⲀⲖⲒⲚⲎ, *But Mary Magdalen came.* John XX, 18. ⲀⳆⲈⲒ̂ Ⲛ̄Ⳓ̄ⲓ ⲒⲰⲀⲚⲚⲎⲤ, *John came.* Mat. III, 1. Sah. ⲦⲞⲦⲈ ⲀⳆⲈⲒ̂ Ⲛ̄Ⳓ̄ⲓ ⲒⳞ̄ ⲈⲂⲞⲖⲍⲚ̀, ⲦⲄⲀⲖⲒⲖⲀⲒⲀ, *than Jesus came out of Galilee.* Mat. III, 13. Sah.

The Genitive Case.

25. The genitive case is indicated by ⲚⲦⲈ preceding the noun, as ⲞⲨⲂⲀⲔⲒ ⲚⲦⲈ ⲦⲤⲀⲘⲀⲢⲒⲀ, *a city of Samaria.* John IV, 4. ⲪⲞⲨⲰⲒⲚⲒ ⲚⲦⲈ ⲠⲈⲔⲈⲞ, *the light of thy face.* Ps. XLIV, 3. ⲞⲨϢⲀϪⲈ ⲚⲦⲈ ⲦⲘⲈ, *the word of truth*, Sah. 2. Cor. VI, 7. Sah. But the prefix Ⲙ or Ⲛ, is frequently used as the sign of the genitive case, especially in the Sahidic, as ⲪⲢⲀⲚ ⲘⲠⲀⲒⲰⲦ, *the name of my father.* John V, 44. ⲞⲨⳠⲀϪⲒ ⲚⲈⲘⲒ, *the word of knowledge.* 1. Cor. XII, 8. ⲦϢⲈⲈⲢⲈ ⲚⲤⲒⲰⲚ, *the daughter of Sion.* Mat. XXI, 5. Sah. ⲠϢⲎⲢⲈ ⲚⲆⲀⲨⲈⲒⲆ, *the son of David.* Mat. XXI, 9. Sah. ⲠϢⲎⲢⲈ ⲘⲠⲢⲰⲘⲈ, *the son of man.* Luke XXII, 48. Sah. ⲦϬⲞⲘ ⲘⲠⲚⲞⲨⲦⲈ, *the power of God.* Luke XXII, 69. Sah. The prefix Ⲙ is used principally before Ⲃ, Ⲙ and ⲫ, and always before ⲡ, but seldom before ⲗ and ⲣ.

The Dative Case.

26. The dative case takes the prefix Ⲙ or Ⲛ, and sometimes ⲉ̀, as ⲀϤⲦⲦⲞⲦϤ ⲘⲠⲒⲤ⳪, *he hath given help* (his hand) *to Israel.* ⲠⲈϪⲀϤ ⲚⲤⲒⲘⲰⲚ, *he said to Simon.* ⲀϤⲒ ⲈⲠⲎⲒ ⲘⲘⲀⲢⲒⲀ, *he came to the house of Mary.* Ⲛ⳾ ϢⲰⲘ ⲘⲠⳅⲢⲞ, *to give tribute to the king*, Luke XXIII, 2. Sah. ⳾ ⲚⲚϨⲎⲔⲈ, *to give to the poor*, Luke XIX, 8. Sah. ⲚⲈⲔϪⲰ ⲘⲘⲞⲤ ⲈⲞⲨⲞⲚ ⲚⲒⲘ, *sayest thou it to all?* Luke XII, 41. Sah. When ⲉ is prefixed to the indefinite article ⲞⲨ, the ⲈⲞⲨ are frequently contracted into ⲈⲨ, as ⲈⲤⲦⲚⲦⲰⲚ ⲈⲨⲂⲀⲂⲒⲗⲈ ⲚϢⲀ⳦ⲦⲘ, *it is like to a grain of mustard seed.* Luke XIII, 19. Sah.

The Accusative Case.

27. The signs of the accusative case are Ṁ, Ṅ or
è, as ⲁⲛϫⲓⲙⲓ ⲙ̇ⲡⲓⲙⲁⲛⲥⲱⲛⲍ, *we found the prison*, Acts
V, 21. ⲁϥⲣⲱⲃⲧ ⲛ̇ⲍⲁⲛϫⲱⲣⲓ, *he hath cast down the strong*,
Luke I, 52. ⲁⲗⲗⲁ ⲉ̀ⲣⲉⲧⲉⲛⲉ̀ϭⲓ ⲛ̇ⲟⲩϫⲟⲙ, *but ye shall re-*
ceive power. Acts I, 8. ⲁⲛⲛⲁⲩ ⲉ̀ⲡ̅ⲟ̅ⲥ̅, *we have seen the*
Lord. John XX, 25. ⲁ ⲙⲱⲩⲥⲏⲥ ϫⲉⲥⲧ̅ ⲙ̇ⲡⲍⲟϥ, *Moses*
lifted up the serpent. John I, 14. Sah. ⲡⲁⲓ ⲉⲧⲉ ⲣ̅ⲟⲩⲟⲉⲓⲛ
ⲉⲣⲱⲙⲉ ⲛⲓⲙ, *which enlighteneth every man.* John I, 9. Sah.
But the ⲉ is most frequently used as the sign of the
accusative.

The Vocative Case.

28. The sign of the vocative case is ⲱ̀ preceding
the noun, as ⲱ̀ ⲑⲉⲟⲫⲓⲗⲉ, *o Theophilus.* Acts I, 1., but
it does not often occur. The definite article is used as
the sign of the vocative, as ⲫⲣⲉϥⲧ̇ⲥⲃⲱ ⲛ̇ⲁⲅⲁⲑⲟⲥ, Copt.
ⲡⲥⲁⲍ ⲛ̇ⲁⲅⲁⲑⲟⲥ, *o good Master!* Sah. Mat. XIX, 16.
ⲡⲁϣⲫⲏⲣ, *O my friend!* Copt. ⲡⲉϣⲃⲉⲉⲣ, *O friend!* Sah.
Mat. XX, 13. ⲉⲩϫⲱ ⲙ̇ⲙⲟⲥ ϫⲉ ⲡϫⲟⲉⲓⲥ ⲛⲁ ⲛⲁⲛ ⲡϣⲏⲣⲉ
ⲛ̇ⲇⲁⲩⲉⲓⲇ, *saying, O Lord thou son of David, have mercy*
on us, Sah. Mat. XX, 30. ⲧϣⲉⲣⲓ ⲛ̇ⲥⲓⲱⲛ, Copt. ⲧϣⲉⲉⲣⲉ
ⲛ̇ⲥⲓⲱⲛ, *O daughter of Sion!* John XII, 15. Sah.

The Ablative Case.

29. This case sometimes takes the prefix Ṁ, Ṅ or
 è, as ⲉⲛⲟⲃⲉ ⲛⲓⲙ, *from all sin.* Sah. ⲉⲡⲛⲟⲩⲧⲉ, *from God.*

Ⲛ ⲘⲘⲞⲔⲘⲈⲔ, *from the thoughts.* Sah. But the ablative is generally represented by some preposition.

The Bashmuric takes the same particles as the Sahidic to all the cases, except the Ablative.

CHAP. V.

Of Adjectives.

1. There are some adjectives, the number and gender of which are known by the suffixes, or the articles, as ⲠⲒⲚⲒϢϮ, *great,* m. ϮⲚⲒϢϮ, *great,* f. and ⲈⲐⲚⲀⲚⲈϤ, *good,* m. ⲈⲐⲚⲀⲚⲈⲤ, *good,* f. ⲚⲀⲀϤ or ⲈⲐⲚⲀⲀϤ, *great,* m. Sah. ⲚⲀⲀⲤ, *great,* f. Sah. ⲈⲐⲚⲀⲀⲨ, *great,* plur. Sah.

Ⲉ, ⲈⲦ, or ⲈⲐ united to verbs forms adjectives, as ⲞⲨⲀⲂ *to be clean, holy.* ⲈⲐⲞⲨⲀⲂ, *clean, holy.*

ⲚⲀϢⲈ or ⲈⲚⲀϢⲈ, Sah. *much.* ⲚⲀϢⲱϤ or ⲈⲚⲀϢⲱϤ, Sah. *much,* m. ⲚⲀϢⲱⲤ or ⲈⲚⲀϢⲱⲤ, Sah. *much,* f. ⲚⲀϢ-ⲱⲞⲨ or ⲈⲚⲀϢⲱⲞⲨ, Sah. *much,* plur.

ⲚⲀⲚⲈ and ⲚⲀⲚⲞⲨ, ⲈⲚⲀⲚⲞⲨ, Sah. *good.* ⲚⲀⲚⲈϤ, ⲚⲀⲚⲞⲨϤ, ⲈⲚⲀⲚⲞⲨϤ, Sah. *good,* m. ⲚⲀⲚⲈⲤ, and ⲚⲀⲚⲞⲨⲤ, ⲈⲚⲀⲚⲞⲨⲤ, Sah. *good,* f. ⲈⲐⲚⲀⲚⲈⲨ, ⲈⲦⲚⲀⲚⲞⲨⲞⲨ, Sah. *good,* plur.

ⲚⲀⲈⲒⲀⲦ or ⲚⲀⲒⲀⲦ, Sah. *blessed.* ⲚⲀⲒⲀⲦⲔ, *blessed thou,* m. ⲚⲀⲒⲀⲦϤ, *blessed he.* ⲚⲀⲒⲀⲦⲤ, *blessed she.* ⲚⲀⲒⲀⲐⲎⲨⲦⲚ̄, *blessed ye.* ⲚⲀⲒⲀⲦⲞⲨ, *blessed they.*

ⲚⲈⲤⲈ or ⲈⲚⲈⲤⲈ, *fair, beautiful.* ⲚⲈⲤⲱⲒ, *fair I.* ⲚⲈⲤⲱϤ, ⲈⲐⲚⲈⲤⲱϤ or ⲈⲚⲈⲤⲱϤ, *fair he.* ⲚⲈⲤⲱⲤ, ⲈⲐⲚⲈⲤⲱⲤ or ⲈⲚⲈⲤⲱⲤ, *fair she.* ⲈⲚⲈⲤⲱⲞⲨ or ⲈⲚⲈⲤⲞⲞⲨ, *fair they.*

ⲤⳘⲀⲢⲰⲞⲨⲦ, and ⲤⳘⲀⳘⲀⲀⲦ, Sah. *blessed*. ⲔⲤⳘⲀ-
ⲢⲰⲞⲨⲦ, *blessed thou*. ϥⲤⳘⲀⲢⲰⲞⲨⲦ, ϥⲤⳘⲀⳘⲀⲀⲦ, Sahidic.
blessed he. ⲚⲎⲈⲦⲤⳘⲀⲢⲰⲞⲨ, ⲚⲈⲦⲤⳘⲀⳘⲀⲀⲦ, Sah. *blessed
they*.

ⲞⲨⲀⲀ, Sah. *alone*. ⲞⲨⲀⲀⲔ, *alone thou*. ⲞⲨⲀⲀϥ, *alone
he*. ⲞⲨⲀⲀⲦⲞⲨ, *alone they*.

ⳘⳘⲀⲨⲀⲦ, and ⳘⲀⲨⲀⲀⲦ, Sah. *alone*. ⳘⳘⲀⲨⲀⲦⲔ,
ⳘⲀⲨⲀⲀⲔ, Sah. *alone thou.* m. ⳘⳘⲀⲨⲀϯ, *alone thou* f.
ⳘⳘⲀⲨⲀⲦϥ. ⳘⲀⲨⲀⲀϥ, Sah. *alone he*. ⳘⳘⲀⲨⲀⲦⲤ, ⳘⲀⲨ-
ⲀⲀⲤ, Sah. *alone she*. ⳘⲀⲨⲀⲀⲚ, Sah. ⳘⳘⲀⲨⲀⲦⲈⲚ, *alone
we*. ⳘⳘⲀⲨⲀⲦⲞⲨ, ⳘⲀⲨⲀⲀⲨ, Sah. *alone they*.

ⲦⲎⲢ, *all*. ⲦⲎⲢⲔ, *the whole thou*, m. ⲦⲎⲢϥ, ⲦⲎⲢⲈϥ,
Sah. *all he*. ⲦⲎⲢⲤ. ⲦⲎⲢⲈⲤ, Sah. *all she*. ⲦⲎⲢⲈⲚ, ⲦⲎⲢⲚ̄,
all we. ⲦⲎⲢⲦⲚ̄, Sah. *all ye*. ⲦⲎⲢⲞⲨ, *all they*.

Of the Comparison of Adjectives.

2. Comparatives are formed by ⲞⲨⲞ, Copt. ⲞⲨⲞ,
ⲞⲨⲈ, Sah. ⲞⲨⲀ, ⲞⲨⲈ, Bash. *more,* as ⲞⲨⲞ̀ ⲦⲀⲒⲞ̀
Ⲉ̀ⲞⲦⲈ ⳘⲰⲨⲤⲎⲤ, *more (greater) honour than Moses.*
ⲞⲨⲞⲨⲞ̀ ⲦⲀⲒⲞ̀ Ⲉ̀ⲞⲦⲈ ⲠⲒⲎⲒ, *more (greater) honour than
the house.* Heb. III, 3. ⳘⲚ̄ⲦⲀⲚ ⲞⲨⲞ ⲈϯⲞⲨ ⲚⲞⲈⲒ̈Ⲕ,
Sah. *we have not more than five breads loaves.* Luc. IX, 13.

Ⲉ̀ⲞⲦⲈ is also a sign of the comparative, as Ⲉ̀ⲞⲦⲈ-
ⲢⲞⲒ, *more than me,* Mat. X, 37. and with Ⲉ̀, as ϯⳘⲈⲦⲤⲞⲬ
Ⲛ̀ⲦⲈ ⲫϯ ⲈⲤⲞⲒ Ⲛ̀ⲤⲀⲂⲈ Ⲉ̀ⲞⲦⲈ Ⲉ̀ⲚⲒⲢⲰⳘⲒ, *the foolishness of
God is wise more (wiser) than men.* 1. Cor. I, 25.

3. The comparative is also expressed by adding
Ⲛ̀ⲞⲨⲞ to the positive; as ϯⳘⲈⲦⳘⲈⲐⲢⲈ Ⲛ̀ⲦⲈ ⲫϯ ⲞⲨ-
ⲚⲒϢϯ ⲦⲈ Ⲛ̀ⲞⲨⲞ, *the witness of God is greater.* 1. John

4

V, 9. It is also expressed by adding ⲉ, or ⲛ to the positive, as ⲙⲏ ⲛ̄ⲧⲟⲕ ⲉⲕⲛⲁⲁⲕ ⲉⲡⲛ̄ⲓⲱⲧ ⲓⲁⲕⲱⲃ, *art thou greater than our father Jacob?* John IV, 12. Sah. ⲟⲩⲛⲟϭ ⲛ̄ⲛⲟⲃⲉ, *greater sin.* John XIX, 11. Sah. ⲛ̄ⲛⲟϭ ⲉⲡⲉⲛϩⲏⲧ, *greater than our heart.* 1. John III, 20. Sah. ⲙⲏ ⲉⲛⲭⲟⲟⲣ ⲉⲣⲟϥ, *are we stronger than he?* 1. Cor. X, 22. Sah.

4. Sometimes there is no word to express the comparative, and it can only be collected from the sense of the passage; as ⲛⲓⲙ ⲅⲁⲣ ⲡⲉ ⲡⲓⲛⲓϣϯ, *for which is great (greater)* Luke XXII, 27. ⲧⲙⲛ̄ⲧⲙⲛ̄ⲧⲣⲉ ⲙ̄ⲡⲛⲟⲩⲧⲉ ⲛⲁⲁⲁⲥ, *the witness of God is great (greater)* 1. John V, 9. Sah.

5. The positive is sometimes used for the superlative as ⲛⲓⲙ ⲡⲉ ⲡⲓⲛⲓϣϯ ⲃⲉⲛ ϯⲙⲉⲧⲟⲩⲣⲟ ⲛ̄ⲧⲉ ⲛⲓⲫⲏⲟⲩⲓ, ⲛⲓⲙ ⲡⲉ ⲡⲛⲟϭ ϩⲛ̄ ⲧⲙⲛ̄ⲧⲉⲣⲟ ⲛ̄ⲙ̄ⲡⲏⲩⲉ, Sah. *who is the great (greatest) in the kingdom of heaven?* Mat. XVIII, 1. Sah.

6. The superlative is formed by adding ⲉ̀, ⲉ̀ⲃⲟⲗ, ⲉ̀ⲃⲟⲗⲟⲩⲧⲉ, or some such word to the positive, as ⲁ̀ⲛⲟⲕ ⲅⲁⲣ ⲡⲉ ⲡⲓⲕⲟⲩϫⲓ ⲉ̀ⲃⲟⲗⲟⲩⲧⲉ ⲛⲓⲁ̀ⲡⲟⲥⲧⲟⲗⲟⲥ ⲧⲏⲣⲟⲩ, and Bash. ⲁⲛⲟⲕ ⲅⲁⲣ ⲡⲉ ⲡⲕⲟⲩⲓ ⲟⲩⲧⲉ ⲛⲓⲁⲡⲟⲥⲧⲟⲗⲟⲥ ⲧⲏⲣⲟⲩ, *for I am the least of all the Apostles.* 1. Cor. XV, 9.

7. The superlative is more often formed by adding ⲉ̀ⲙⲁϣⲱ, Copt. ⲉⲙⲁⲧⲉ, Sah. ⲉⲙⲁϣⲁ, Bash. *greatly, very much,* to the positive, as ⲁ̀ⲧⲁⲯⲩⲭⲏ ϣⲑⲟⲣⲧⲉⲣ ⲉ̀ⲙⲁϣⲱ, *my soul is exceedingly troubled.* Ps. VI, 3. ⲉ̀ⲙⲁϣⲱ, ⲉⲙⲁⲧⲉ and ⲉⲙⲁϣⲁ are also repeated; as ⲁϥⲉⲣ ⲣⲁⲙⲁⲟ̀ ⲛ̄ϫⲉ ⲡⲓⲣⲱⲙⲓ ⲉ̀ⲙⲁϣⲱ ⲉ̀ⲙⲁϣⲱ, *the man was exceeding rich.* Gen. XXX, 43. ϫⲉⲕⲁⲥ ⲉⲣⲉ ⲧⲉⲧⲛ̄ⲁⲅⲁⲡⲏ ⲣ̄ϩⲟⲩⲟ ⲉⲙⲁⲧⲉ ⲉⲙⲁⲧⲉ, *that your love may abound exceedingly.* Sahidic.

Phil. I, 9. and in Bash. ⲝⲉⲕⲉⲥ ⲉⲣⲉ ⲧⲉⲧⲉⲛⲁⲅⲁⲡⲏ ⲉⲗ-ⲍⲟⲩⲁ ⲉⲙⲁϣⲁ. The superlative is also formed by ⲛ̀ⲍⲟⲩⲟ repeated, as ⲟⲩⲟⲍ ⲛ̀ⲍⲟⲩⲟ̀ ⲛ̀ⲍⲟⲩⲟ̀ ⲛⲁⲩⲉⲣϣϕⲏⲣⲓ, *and they were exceedingly astonished.* Mark VII, 37.

CHAP. VI.

Of Personal Pronouns.

Singular.

Coptic.	Sahidic.	Bash.	
ⲁ̀ⲛⲟⲕ	ⲁ̄ⲛⲟⲕ	ⲁ̀ⲛⲟⲕ	
	ⲁ̄ⲛⲅ̄	ⲁ̀ⲛⲁⲕ	*I.*
	ⲁ̄ⲛⲕ̄		
ⲛ̀ⲑⲟⲕ	ⲛ̄ⲧⲟⲕ	ⲛ̀ⲧⲁⲕ	*thou,* m.
	ⲛ̄ⲧⲕ̄		
ⲛ̀ⲑⲟ	ⲛ̄ⲧⲟ	ⲛ̀ⲧⲁ *thou,* f.	
ⲛ̀ⲑⲟϥ	ⲛ̄ⲧⲟϥ	ⲛ̀ⲧⲁϥ *he.*	
ⲛ̀ⲑⲟⲥ	ⲛ̄ⲧⲟⲥ	ⲛ̀ⲧⲁⲥ *she.*	

Plural.

Coptic.	Sahidic.	Bash.	
ⲁ̀ⲛⲟⲛ	ⲁ̄ⲛⲟⲛ	ⲁ̀ⲛⲁⲛ	*we.*
	ⲁ̄ⲛⲛ̄		
ⲛ̀ⲑⲱⲧⲉⲛ	ⲛ̄ⲧⲱⲧⲛ̄	ⲛ̀ⲧⲁⲧⲉⲛ	*ye.*
	ⲛ̄ⲧⲉⲧⲉⲛ	ⲛ̀ⲧⲁⲧⲛ̀	
	ⲛ̄ⲧⲉⲧⲛ̄		
ⲛ̀ⲑⲱⲟⲩ	ⲛ̄ⲧⲟⲟⲩ	ⲛ̀ⲧⲁⲩ *they.*	

4·

Personal Pronouns.

2. Of the Genitive Case.

Singular.

Coptic.	Sahidic.	Bash.
ⲚⲐⲒ	ⲚⲦⲀⲒ	ⲈⲚⲐⲒ *mei, of me.*
ⲚⲦⲀⲔ	ⲚⲦⲀⲔ	ⲚⲐⲔ *of thee,* m.
ⲚⲦⲈ	ⲚⲦⲈ	ⲚⲦⲈ *of thee,* f.
ⲚⲦⲀϥ	ⲚⲦⲀϥ / ⲚⲦϥ	ⲚⲐϥ / ⲚⲦⲈϥ } *of him.*
ⲚⲦⲀⲤ	ⲚⲦⲀⲤ / ⲚⲦⲤ̄	ⲚⲐⲤ } *of her.*

Plural.

Coptic.	Sahidic.	Bash.
ⲚⲦⲀⲚ	ⲚⲦⲀⲚ / ⲚⲦⲚ̄	ⲚⲐⲚ̄ } *of us.*
ⲚⲐⲰⲦⲈⲚ	ⲚⲦⲈⲦⲚ̄	ⲚⲐⲦⲈⲚ
ⲚⲦⲰⲦⲈⲚ	ⲚⲦⲈⲦⲎⲨⲦⲚ̄	ⲚⲦⲈⲦⲈⲚ } *of you*
ⲚⲦⲈⲐⲎⲚⲞⲨ		ⲚⲦⲈⲦⲎⲚⲞⲨ
ⲚⲦⲰⲞⲨ	ⲚⲦⲀⲨ	ⲚⲐⲞⲨ, *of them.*

Of the Dative Case.

Singular.

Coptic.	Sahidic.	Bash.
ⲚⲎⲒ	ⲚⲀⲒ	ⲚⲎⲒ *mihi, to me.*
ⲚⲀⲔ	ⲚⲀⲔ	ⲚⲎⲔ *to thee,* m.
ⲚⲈ	ⲚⲈ	*to thee,* f.
ⲚⲀϥ	ⲚⲀϥ	ⲚⲎϥ / ⲚⲈϥ } *to him*
ⲚⲀⲤ	ⲚⲀⲤ	ⲚⲎⲤ *to her.*

Plural.

ⲚⲀⲚ	ⲚⲀⲚ	ⲚⲎⲚ *to us.*
ⲚⲰⲦⲈⲚ	ⲚⲎⲦⲚ̄	ⲚⲎⲦⲈⲚ *to you.*
ⲐⲎⲚⲞⲨ	ⲦⲎⲚⲞⲨ	ⲦⲎⲚⲞⲨ *with an accus.*
ⲚⲰⲞⲨ	ⲚⲀⲨ	ⲚⲎⲞⲨ, ⲚⲎⲨ ⎱ *to them.*
		ⲚⲈⲨ ⎰

3. The dative is also formed by the word **ⲡⲟ** Copt. and **ⲗⲁ** Bash. by prefixing **ⲉ̀** to them: and by **ⲦⲞⲦ,** Copt. **ⲦⲞⲞⲦ,** Sah. **ⲦⲀⲀⲦ,** Bash. by prefixing **ⲉ̀** or **ⲛ̀** to them.

Singular.

˙Coptic.	Sahidic.	Bash.
ⲉ̀ⲡⲟⲓ	ⲉⲣⲟⲓ, ⲉⲣⲀⲓ	ⲉⲗⲀⲓ *to me.*
ⲉ̀ⲡⲟⲕ	ⲉⲣⲟⲕ, ⲉⲣⲀⲕ	ⲉⲗⲀⲕ *to thee,* m.
ⲉ̀ⲡⲟ	ⲉⲣⲟ, ⲉⲣⲀ	ⲉⲗⲀ *to thee,* f.
ⲉ̀ⲡⲟϥ	ⲉⲣⲟϥ, ⲉⲣⲀϥ	ⲉⲗⲀϥ *to him.*
ⲉ̀ⲡⲟⲥ	ⲉⲣⲟⲥ, ⲉⲣⲀⲥ	ⲉⲗⲀⲥ *to her.*

Plural.

ⲉ̀ⲡⲟⲚ	ⲉⲣⲟⲚ, ⲉⲣⲀⲚ	ⲉⲗⲀⲚ *to us.*
ⲉ̀ⲡⲱⲦⲉⲚ	ⲉⲣⲱⲦⲚ̄	ⲉⲗⲀⲦⲉⲚ ⎱ *to you.*
ⲉ̀ⲡⲱⲦⲉⲚ ⲐⲎⲚⲞⲨ	ⲉⲣⲀⲦ ⲦⲎⲨⲦⲚ̄	ⲉⲗⲀⲦⲦⲎⲚⲞⲨ ⎰
ⲉ̀ⲡⲱⲞⲨ	ⲉⲣⲟⲟⲨ	ⲉⲗⲀⲨ *to them.*

Singular.

Coptic.	Sahidic.	Bash.
ⲉ̀ or Ⲛ̀ⲦⲞⲦ	ⲉ̀ or Ⲛ̄ⲦⲞⲞⲦ	ⲉ̀ or Ⲛ̄ⲦⲀⲀⲦ *to me.*
Ⲛ̀ⲦⲞⲦⲕ	Ⲛ̄ⲦⲞⲞⲦⲕ	Ⲛ̄ⲦⲀⲀⲦⲕ *to thee,* m.
Ⲛ̀ⲦⲞ†	Ⲛ̄ⲦⲞⲞⲦⲉ	*to thee,* f.
Ⲛ̀ⲦⲞⲦϥ	Ⲛ̄ⲦⲞⲞⲦϥ	Ⲛ̄ⲦⲀⲀⲦϥ *to him.*
Ⲛ̀ⲦⲞⲦⲥ	Ⲛ̄ⲦⲞⲞⲦⲥ	Ⲛ̄ⲦⲀⲀⲦⲥ *to her.*

Plural.

Ė or ⲚⲦⲞⲦⲈⲚ   Ē or ⲚⲦⲞⲞⲦⲚ̄   ė or ⲚⲦⲀⲀⲦⲈⲚ *to us.*

ⲈⲦⲈⲚⲐⲎⲚⲞⲨ   ⲈⲦⲞⲞⲦ ⲐⲎⲨⲦⲚ̄   *to you.*

ⲈⲦⲞⲦⲞⲨ ⎱
            ⎰ ⲚⲦⲞⲞⲦⲞⲨ   ⲚⲦⲀⲀⲦⲞⲨ *to them.*
ⲚⲦⲀⲦⲞⲨ ⎰

4. The accusative Pronoun is formed by ⲘⲘⲞ Copt. and Sah., ⲘⲘⲀ and ⲘⲀ Bash.

Singular.

Coptic.	Sahidic.	Bash.	
ⲘⲘⲞⲒ	ⲘⲘⲞⲒ, ⲘⲘⲞⲈⲒ	ⲘⲘⲀⲒ	*me.*
ⲘⲘⲞⲔ	ⲘⲘⲞⲔ	ⲘⲘⲞⲔ	*thee,* m.
ⲘⲘⲞ	ⲘⲘⲞ		*thee,* f.
ⲘⲘⲞϥ	ⲘⲘⲟϥ	ⲘⲘⲀϥ	*him.*
ⲘⲘⲞⲤ	ⲘⲘⲞⲤ	ⲘⲘⲀⲤ	*her.*

Plural.

ⲘⲘⲞⲚ	ⲘⲘⲞⲚ	ⲘⲘⲀⲚ	*us.*
ⲘⲘⲰⲦⲈⲚ	ⲘⲘⲰⲦⲚ̄	ⲘⲘⲀⲦⲈⲚ	*you.*
ⲘⲘⲰⲞⲨ	ⲘⲘⲞⲞⲨ	ⲘⲘⲀⲨ	*them.*

ⲘⲘⲞ with other words sometimes expresses the various cases of the personal pronoun, as ⲚⲒⲘ ⲘⲘⲰⲞⲨ *some of them.* 1. Cor. X, 10. ⲈⲂⲞⲖ ⲘⲘⲟϥ, *from him.*

5. Another form of the accusative is ⲂⲎ, Copt. ⲈⲎ, Sah., which take Ⲧ with the suffixes.

Singular.

Coptic.	Sahidic.
ⲃⲏⲧ	ⲍⲏⲧ *my face, me.*
ⲃⲏⲧⲕ	ⲍⲏⲧⲕ *thee,* m.
ⲃⲏϯ	ⲍⲏⲧⲉ *thee,* f.
ⲃⲏⲧϥ	ⲍⲏⲧϥ *him.*
ⲃⲏⲧⲥ	ⲍⲏⲧⲥ *her.*

Plural.

ⲃⲏⲧⲉⲛ	ⲍⲏⲧⲛ̄ *us.*
ⲃⲏⲧⲟⲩ	ⲍⲏⲧⲟⲩ *them.*

6. The ablative case is formed by the following prepositions with the suffixes.

	Coptic.	Sahidic.	Bash.
ⲛ̀ⲧⲉ	ⲛ̀ⲧⲟⲧ	ⲛ̄ⲧⲟⲟⲧ	ⲛ̀ⲧⲁⲁⲧ
ⲉ̀ⲃⲟⲗ	ⲉ̀ⲃⲟⲗⲙ̀ⲙⲟ	ⲉ̄ⲃⲟⲗⲙ̄ⲙⲟ	ⲉ̀ⲃⲁⲗⲙ̀ⲙⲁ
	ⲉ̀ⲃⲟⲗⲛ̀ⲃⲏⲧ	ⲉ̄ⲃⲟⲗⲛ̄ϩⲏⲧ	ⲉ̀ⲃⲁⲗⲛ̀ϩⲏⲧ
ⲉ̀ⲃⲟⲗϩⲁ	ⲉ̀ⲃⲟⲗϩⲁⲣⲟ		
ⲉ̀ⲃⲟⲗϩⲓ	ⲉ̀ⲃⲟⲗϩⲓⲱⲧ	ⲉ̄ⲃⲟⲗϩⲓⲱⲱ	
ⲉ̀ⲃⲟⲗϩⲓⲧⲉⲛ	ⲉ̀ⲃⲟⲗϩⲓⲧⲟⲧ	ⲉ̄ⲃⲟⲗϩⲓⲧⲟⲟⲧ	ⲉ̀ⲃⲁⲗϩⲓⲧⲁⲁⲧ
ⲉ̀ⲃⲟⲗϩⲓⲭⲉⲛ	ⲉ̀ⲃⲟⲗϩⲓⲭⲱ		
ϩⲓⲧⲉⲛ	ϩⲓⲧⲟⲧ	ϩⲓⲧⲟⲟⲧ	ϩⲓⲧⲁⲁⲧ &c.

Possessive Pronouns.

7. The possessive pronouns are sometimes expressed by the genitive personal pronouns, as ⲛ̀ⲧⲏⲓ, Copt. ⲛ̄ⲧⲁⲓ, Copt. ⲛ̀ⲧⲁⲕ, Copt. and Sah. ⲛ̀ⲧⲁϥ Copt. and Sah. &c. yet they are formed of the definite article with ⲱ in the singular and ⲟⲩ in the plural, as

Sing. Masc. Sing. Fem.

Coptic.	Sahidic.		Coptic.	Sahidic.
ϕⲱⲓ	ⲡⲱⲓ	*mine.*	ⲑⲱⲓ	ⲧⲱⲓ
ϕⲱⲕ	ⲡⲱⲕ	*thine,* m.	ⲑⲱⲕ	ⲧⲱⲕ
ϕⲱ	ⲡⲱ	*thine,* f.	ⲑⲱ	ⲧⲱ
ϕⲱϥ	ⲡⲱϥ	*his.*	ⲑⲱϥ	ⲧⲱϥ
ϕⲱⲥ	ⲡⲱⲥ	*her.*	ⲑⲱⲥ	ⲧⲱⲥ
ϕⲱⲛ	ⲡⲱⲛ	*our.*	ⲑⲱⲛ	ⲧⲱⲛ
ϕⲱⲧⲉⲛ	ⲡⲱⲧⲛ̄	*your.*	ⲑⲱⲧⲉⲛ	ⲧⲱⲧⲛ̄
ϕⲱⲟⲩ	ⲡⲱⲟⲩ	*their.*	ⲑⲱⲟⲩ	ⲧⲱⲟⲩ

Plural Common.

ⲛⲟⲩⲓ *mine.*

ⲛⲟⲩⲕ *thine,* m.

ⲛⲟⲩ *thine,* f.

ⲛⲟⲩϥ
ⲛⲱϥ } *his.*

ⲛⲟⲩⲥ *her.*

ⲛⲟⲩⲛ *our.*

ⲛⲟⲩⲧⲉⲛ
ⲛⲱⲧⲉⲛ } *your.*

ⲛⲟⲩⲟⲩ
ⲛⲱⲟⲩ } *their.*

Demonstrative Pronouns.

Singular.

	Masc.			Fem.	
Coptic.	Sahidic.	Bash.	Coptic.	Sahidic.	Bash.
ϕⲁⲓ	ⲡⲁⲓ	ⲡⲉⲓ	ⲑⲁⲓ	ⲧⲁⲓ	ⲧⲉⲓ *this.*

Plural.

Coptic and Sahidic.	Bashmuric.
ⲚⲀⲒ	ⲚⲈⲒ *these.*

Another form of the demonstrative pronoun is as follows.

Masc.		Fem.	
Coptic.	Sahidic.	Coptic.	Sahidic.
ⲪⲎ	ⲠⲎ *he.*	ⲐⲎ	ⲦⲎ *she.*

Plural.

ⲚⲎ *they.*

8. The demonstrative pronoun is often joined with the relative pronoun ⲈⲦ, as

Singular.

Masc.		Fem.	
Coptic.	Sahidic.	Coptic.	Sahidic.
ⲪⲎⲈⲦ	ⲠⲎⲈⲦ *he, who.*	ⲐⲎⲈⲦ	ⲦⲎⲈⲦ *she, who.*

Plural.

ⲚⲎⲈⲦ *they, who.*

Ⲙ̄ⲘⲀⲨ is frequently united with the demonstrative and relative pronouns both singular and plural, as ⲪⲎⲈⲦⲈⲘ̄ⲘⲀⲨ, *he.* Luke XXII, 12. Copt. ⲚⲒⲒⲞⲨⲆⲀⲒ ⲈⲦϢⲞⲠ Ⲙ̄ⲠⲒⲘⲀ ⲈⲦⲈⲘ̄ⲘⲀⲨ, *the jews dwelling in that place,* Acts XVI, 3. Copt. ⲂⲈⲚ ⲦⲞⲨⲚⲞⲨ ⲈⲦⲈⲘ̄ⲘⲀⲨ, *in that hour.* Copt. ⲞⲨⲞⲪ Ⲁ̀ ⲦⲈⲤⲤⲘⲎ ϢⲈⲚⲀⲤ Ⲉ̀ⲂⲞⲖ ϢⲒⲬⲈⲚ ⲠⲒⲔⲀϪ̀Ⲓ ⲦⲎⲢϥ ⲈⲦⲈⲘ̄ⲘⲀⲨ, *and the fame of it went out through all that land.* Mat. IX, 26.

5

Relative Pronouns.

9. The relative pronoun is ε. ετ, ετε. or εθ before the letters м, ν and ο in Copt.; and εντ. *qui, quae, quod,* and likewise ε, ετ, ετε, ντ, in Sahidic and Bashmuric. ννηὲτ ᴀγτλογον, *to those who sent us.* John I, 22. ϕηὲτ cωτεм νcωτεν, *he who heareth you.* ϕηὲτ ϣωϣ ṁмωτεν, *he who despiseth you.* Luke X, 16.

10. The interrogative pronouns undergo no variation, which are these, νιм, *who?* ᴀϣ, εϣ, *who? what?* ογ, *who?* ογηρ, *how many?*

Of Prepositions.

11. There are some substantives which are used as prepositions, as рᴀτ Copt. λετ, Bash. *a foot.* ро, *a mouth.* τοτ, *a hand.* ϧнτ, *a neck.* ϩнτ, *a heart.* ϩрᴀ, *a face.* xω, *a head.* These, being united with some particles become prepositions, as ὲрᴀτ *to me.* Mat. VI, 18. ϧᴀрᴀτ, Copt. ϩᴀрᴀτ, Sah. *under me.* Mat. VIII, 9. ὲро, ϧᴀро, *under thee.* Ezech. XXVII, 30. ϧᴀроϥ, *against him.* Ex. XVI, 8. ντοτϥ *from him.* Deut. XV, 3. νϧнτογ, *in them.* Psalm V, 10. ⲛϩнτк, Sah. *in thee.* Ezech. XXVIII, 15. ὲϩрᴀι, *against me.* Ps. CI, 8. ὲϩрнι ὲxωι, *against me.* Ps. III, 1. &c.

Prepositions.

ὲ, acc., dat., *ad, in* &c.

ὲβολⲛϧнτ, Copt. *from, e.x.* ὲβολⲛϧнτϥ, ὲβολⲛϧнτογ &c.

εβολⲛϩнτ, Sah. *from, e.x.* εβολⲛϩнτϥ, εβολⲛϩнτⲛ &c.

ὲβολϩᴀ, *from, ab, e.x.*

ⲉⲃⲟⲗϩⲁⲣⲟ, *a, ab.* ⲉ̀ⲃⲟⲗϩⲁⲣⲟϥ, ⲉ̀ⲃⲟⲗϩⲁⲣⲟⲛ &c.

ⲉⲃⲟⲗϩⲓⲧⲛ̄, Sah. *a, ab.*

ⲉⲃⲟⲗϩⲓⲧⲙ̄, Sah. *a, ab.*

ⲉ̀ⲃⲟⲗϩⲓⲧⲟⲧ, *per, a, ab.* ⲉ̀ⲃⲟⲗϩⲓⲧⲟⲧⲕ, ⲉ̀ⲃⲟⲗϩⲓⲧⲟⲧϥ, &c.

ⲉⲃⲟⲗϩⲓⲧⲟⲟⲧ, S. *per, a, ab.* ⲉⲃⲟⲗϩⲓⲧⲟⲟⲧⲕ, ⲉ̀ⲃⲟⲗϩⲓⲧⲟⲟⲧϥ.

ⲉ̀ϩⲟⲧⲉⲣⲟ, *supra, plus quam.* ⲉ̀ϩⲟⲧⲉⲣⲟⲕ, ⲉ̀ϩⲟⲧⲉⲣⲟϥ, &c.

ⲛ̀, acc., dat., *ad, ab, from,* &c.

ⲛ̀ⲧⲉⲛ, ⲛ̄ⲧⲛ̄, Sah. *from.*

ϣⲁ, *ad, usque ad,* ϣⲁⲣⲟⲓ, ϣⲁⲣⲟⲕ, ϣⲁⲗⲁⲕ, Bash. &c.

ⳉⲁ, Copt. *sub, contra,* ⳉⲁⲧⲟⲧⲕ. *apud te,* ⳉⲁⲧⲟⲧϥ, *apud eum.*

ϩⲁ, Sah. *sub, ad, pro.* ϩⲁⲧⲟⲧⲕ, etc.

ϩⲁⲧⲙ̄, Sah. *apud, ad,* &c.

ϩⲁⲧⲛ̄, Sah. *apud,* &c.

ϩⲓ, *in, cum,* ϩⲓⲧⲟⲧ, ϩⲓⲧⲟⲟⲧ, Sah. ϩⲓⲧⲟⲟⲧⲥ, Sah. &c.

To these may be added ⲁⲧⲟ́ⲛⲉ, ⲉⲑⲃⲉ, ⲉⲧⲃⲉ, Sah. ⲟⲩⲃⲉ, ⲟⲩⲧⲉ and others.

The Pronoun Infixes and Suffixes.

12. The pronoun infixes and suffixes are added to words, instead of the possessive and personal pronouns.

13. The pronoun infixes are inserted between the article and the noun, and used instead of the possessive pronouns. They are the following: ⲁ, *my.* ⲉⲕ, *thy.* ⲉ or ⲟⲩ, *thy,* f. ⲉϥ, *his.* ⲉⲥ, *her.* ⲉⲛ or ⲛ̄, *our.* ⲉⲧⲉⲛ or ⲉⲧⲛ̄ *your.* ⲟⲩ or ⲉⲩ, *their.*

An example of the infixes with the articles is here given.

The Infixes.

	Singular.		Plural.
with artic. masc.	with artic. fem.		
ⲡ-ⲁ,	ⲧ-ⲁ,	ⲛ-ⲁ,	*my*.
ⲡ-ⲉⲕ,	ⲧ-ⲉⲕ,	ⲛ-ⲉⲕ,	*thy*, m.
ⲡ-ⲉ,	ⲧ-ⲉ,	ⲛ-ⲉ,	*thy*, f.
ⲡ-ⲟⲩ,	ⲧ-ⲟⲩ,	ⲛ-ⲟⲩ,	*thy*, f. Sah.
ⲡ-ⲉϥ,	ⲧ-ⲉϥ,	ⲛ-ⲉϥ,	*his*.
ⲡ-ⲉⲥ,	ⲧ-ⲉⲥ,	ⲛ-ⲉⲥ,	*her*.
ⲡ-ⲉⲛ,	ⲧ-ⲉⲛ,	ⲛ-ⲉⲛ,	*our*.
ⲡ-ⲛ̄,	ⲧ-ⲛ̄,	ⲛ-ⲛ̄,	*our*, Sah.
ⲡ-ⲉⲧⲉⲛ,	ⲧ-ⲉⲧⲉⲛ,	ⲛ-ⲉⲧⲉⲛ,	*your*.
ⲡ-ⲉⲧⲛ̄,	ⲧ-ⲉⲧⲛ̄,	ⲛ-ⲉⲧⲛ̄,	*your*.
ⲡ-ⲟⲩ,	ⲧ-ⲟⲩ,	ⲛ-ⲟⲩ,	*their*.
ⲡ-ⲉⲩ,	ⲧ-ⲉⲩ,	ⲛ-ⲉⲩ,	*their*, Sah.

ⲟⲩ is sometimes used for the infix of the second person feminine, instead of ⲉ in Coptic, but it seldom occurs.

14. The suffixes are used with words instead of the infixes, and are these which follow.

The Suffixes.

Singular.	Plural.
ⲓ or ⲧ, *me*, or *my*.	ⲛ or ⲉⲛ, *us*, or *our*.
ⲕ, *thee*, or *thy*, m.	ⲧⲉⲛ, *you*, or *your*.
ⲉ or ⲓ,*) *thee*, or *thy*, f.	ⲧⲛ̄, *you*, or *your*, Sah.

---

*) The ⲓ following ⲧ is changed into ⲑ.

Singular.	Plural.
є, *thee,* or *thy,* f.	ⲟⲩ. ⲁⲩ, *they,* or *their.*
ϥ, *him,* or *his.*	• ⲉⲟⲩ or ⲏⲩ, *they,* or *their,* Sah.
ⲥ, *her,* or *hers.*	

A small number of words vary from the general rule.

The Infixes.

15. The infixes to nouns will be understood by the following examples.

ϣⲏⲣⲓ, *a son,* with the m. article, and infixes.

Singular.	Plural.
Artic. and Infixes to a noun masc.	Artic. and Infixes to a noun masc.
ⲡⲁ-ϣⲏⲣⲓ, *my son.*	ⲛⲁ-ϣⲏⲣⲓ, *my sons.*
ⲡⲉⲕ-ϣⲏⲣⲓ, *thy son,* m.	ⲛⲉⲕ-ϣⲏⲣⲓ, *thy sons,* m.
ⲡⲉ-ϣⲏⲣⲓ, *thy son,* f.	ⲛⲉ-ϣⲏⲣⲓ, *thy sons,* f.
ⲡⲟⲩ-ϣⲏⲣⲉ, *thy son,* f. Sah.	ⲛⲟⲩ-ϣⲏⲣⲉ, *thy sons,* f. Sah.
ⲡⲉϥ-ϣⲏⲣⲓ, *his son.*	ⲛⲉϥ-ϣⲏⲣⲓ, *his sons*
ⲡⲉⲥ-ϣⲏⲣⲓ, *her son.*	ⲛⲉⲥ-ϣⲏⲣⲓ, *her sons.*
ⲡⲉⲛ-ϣⲏⲣⲓ, *our son.*	ⲛⲉⲛ-ϣⲏⲣⲓ, *our sons.*
ⲡⲛ̄-ϣⲏⲣⲉ, *our son,* Sah.	ⲛⲛ̄-ϣⲏⲣⲉ, *our sons,* Sah.
ⲡⲉⲧⲉⲛ-ϣⲏⲣⲓ, *your son.*	ⲛⲉⲧⲉⲛ-ϣⲏⲣⲓ, *your sons.*
ⲡⲉⲧⲛ̄-ϣⲏⲣⲉ, *your son,* Sah.	ⲛⲉⲧⲛ̄-ϣⲏⲣⲉ, *your sons,* Sah.
ⲡⲟⲩ-ϣⲏⲣⲓ, *their son.*	ⲛⲟⲩ-ϣⲏⲣⲓ, *their sons.*
ⲡⲉⲩ-ϣⲏⲣⲉ, *their son,* Sah.	ⲛⲉⲩ-ϣⲏⲣⲉ, *their sons,* Sah.

CⲱNI, *a sister*, with the fem. article and infixes.

Singular.	Plural.
Artic. and Infixes to a noun fem.	Artic. and Infixes to a noun fem.
TA-CⲱNI, *my sister*.	NA-CⲱNI, *my sisters*.
TEK-CⲱNI, *thy sister*, m.	NEK-CⲱNI, *thy sisters*, m.
TE-CⲱNI, *thy sister*, f.	NE-CⲱNI, *thy sisters*, f.
TOⲨ-CⲱNE, *thy sister*, f. Sah.	NOⲨ-CⲱNE, *thy sisters*, f. Sah.
TEϥ-CⲱNI, *his sister*.	NEϥ-CⲱNI, *his sisters*.
TEC-CⲱNI, *her sister*.	NEC-CⲱNI, *her sisters*.
TEN-CⲱNI, *our sister*.	NEN-CⲱNI, *our sisters*.
TN̄-CⲱNE, *our sister*, Sah.	NN̄-CⲱNE, *our sisters*, Sah.
TETEN-CⲱNI, *your sister*.	NETEN-CⲱNI, *your sisters*.
TETN̄-CⲱNE, *your sister*, Sah.	NETN̄-CⲱNE, *your sisters*, Sah.
TOⲨ-CⲱNI. *their sister*.	NOⲨ-CⲱNI, *their sisters*.
TEⲨ-CⲱNE, *their sister*, Sah.	NEⲨ-CⲱNE. *their sisters*, Sah.

16. It will be seen from the foregoing examples, that the *infixes* are the same to a masculine and feminine noun, singular and plural.

The Suffixes.

17. The following examples will show the position of the suffixes.

Adjectives with the Suffixes.

ENECE or NECE, *fair*.	THp, *all.*
ENECⲱI. *fair, I.*	THpK, *all, thou*, m.
ENECⲱK, *fair, thou*, m.	THpK̄, *all, thou*, m. Sah.
ENECⲱϥ, *fair, he.*	THpϥ, *all, he.*
ENECⲱC, *fair, she.*	THpC, *all, she.*
ENECⲱN, *fair, we.*	THpEN, *all, we.*

ⲉⲛⲉⲥⲱⲟⲩ, *fair, they.*

ⲉⲛⲉⲥⲟⲟⲩ, *fair, they,* Sah.

ⲧⲏⲣⲡ̄, *all, we,* Sah.

ⲧⲏⲣⲧⲉⲛ, *all, ye.*

ⲧⲏⲣⲧⲛ̄, *all, ye,* Sah.

ⲧⲏⲣⲟⲩ, *all, they.*

ⲛⲁⲁ or ⲉⲛⲁⲁ, *great.*

ⲛⲁⲁⲓ, *great, I.*

ⲛⲁⲁⲕ, *great, thou,* m.

ⲛⲁⲁϥ, *great, he.*

ⲛⲁⲁⲥ, *great, she.*

ⲛⲁⲁⲩ, *great, they.*

ⲛⲁⲛⲉ or ⲛⲁⲛⲟⲩ, *good.*

ⲛⲁⲛⲟⲩⲓ, *good, I.*

ⲛⲁⲛⲉϥ, *good, he.*

ⲛⲁⲛⲉⲥ, *good, she.*

ⲛⲁⲛⲉⲩ, *good, they.*

ⲙⲁⲩⲁⲧ, *alone.* ⲙⲁⲩⲁⲧⲕ, *alone, thou,* m. ⲙⲁⲩⲁ†, *alone, thou,* f. ⲙⲁⲩⲁⲧϥ, *alone, he.* ⲙⲁⲩⲁⲧⲥ, *alone, she.* ⲙⲁⲩⲁⲧⲉⲛ, *alone, we.* ⲙⲁⲩⲁⲧⲉⲛⲑⲏⲛⲟⲩ, *alone, ye.* ⲙⲁⲩⲁⲧⲟⲩ, *alone, they.*

Prepositions with the Suffixes.

Coptic and Sahidic.	Bash.	
ⲉⲣⲁⲧ,	ⲉⲗⲉⲧ,	*to me.*
ⲉⲣⲁⲧⲕ,	ⲉⲗⲁⲧⲕ,	*to thee,* m.
ⲉⲣⲁ†,	ⲉⲗⲉⲧⲓ,	*to thee,* f.
ⲉⲣⲁⲧⲉ,		*to thee,* f. Sah.
ⲉⲣⲁⲧϥ,	ⲉⲗⲉⲧϥ,	*to him.*
ⲉⲣⲁⲧⲥ,	ⲉⲗⲉⲧⲥ,	*to her.*
ⲉⲣⲁⲧⲉⲛ,	ⲉⲗⲉⲧⲉⲛ,	*to us.*
ⲉⲣⲁⲧⲛ̄,		*to us,* Sah.
ⲉⲣⲁⲧⲉⲛⲑⲏⲛⲟⲩ,	ⲉⲗⲉⲧⲧⲏⲛⲟⲩ,	*to you.*
ⲉⲣⲁⲧⲧⲏⲩⲧⲛ̄,		*to you,* Sah.
ⲉⲣⲁⲧⲟⲩ,	ⲉⲗⲉⲧⲟⲩ,	*to them.*

Coptic.	Sahidic.
ⲈⲐⲂⲈ,	ⲈⲦⲂⲈ, *de, ob.*
ⲪⲐⲂⲎⲦ,	ⲈⲦⲂⲎⲎⲦ, *of me.*
ⲈⲐⲂⲎⲦⲔ,	ⲈⲦⲂⲎⲎⲦⲔ, *of thee,* m.
ⲈⲐⲂⲎ†,	ⲈⲦⲂⲎⲎⲦⲈ, *of thee,* f.
ⲪⲐⲂⲎⲦϥ,	ⲈⲦⲂⲎⲎⲦϥ, *of him.*
ⲪⲐⲂⲎⲦⲤ,	ⲈⲦⲂⲎⲎⲦⲤ, *of her.*
ⲈⲐⲂⲎⲦⲈⲚ,	ⲈⲦⲂⲎⲎⲦⲚ̄, *of us.*
ⲈⲐⲂⲈⲐⲎⲚⲞⲨ,	ⲈⲦⲂⲈⲐⲎⲨⲦⲚ̄, *of you.*
ⲪⲐⲂⲎⲦⲞⲨ,	ⲈⲦⲂⲎⲎⲦⲞⲨ, *of them.*

Coptic.	Sahidic.
ⲚⲈⲘ,	ⲚⲘ̄, *with.*

Coptic.	Sahidic.	Bashmuric.
ⲚⲈⲘⲎⲒ,	ⲚⲘ̄ⲘⲀⲒ, ⲘⲞⲒ,	ⲚⲈⲘⲎⲒ. *with me.*
ⲚⲈⲘⲀⲔ,	ⲚⲘ̄ⲘⲀⲔ,	*with thee,* m.
ⲚⲈⲘⲈ,	ⲚⲘ̄ⲘⲈ,	*with thee,* f.
ⲚⲈⲘⲀϥ,	ⲚⲘ̄ⲘⲀϥ, Ⲟϥ,	ⲚⲈⲘⲎϥ, *with him.*
ⲚⲈⲘⲀⲤ,	ⲚⲘ̄ⲘⲀⲤ,	ⲚⲈⲘⲎⲤ, *with her.*
ⲚⲈⲘⲀⲚ,	ⲚⲘ̄ⲘⲀⲚ, ⲞⲚ,	*with us.*
ⲚⲈⲘⲰⲦⲈⲚ,	ⲚⲘ̄ⲘⲎⲦⲚ̄,	ⲚⲈⲘⲎⲦⲈⲚ. *with you.*
ⲚⲈⲘⲱⲞⲨ,	ⲚⲘ̄ⲘⲀⲨ,	ⲚⲈⲘⲎⲞⲨ, *with them.*

Ⲛ̄ⲤⲀ, *after.*

Ⲛ̄ⲤⲰⲒ, *after me.* ⲚⲤⲰⲔ, *after thee,* m. Ⲛ̄ⲤⲰ, *after thee,* f. Ⲛ̄ⲤⲰϥ, *after him.* ⲚⲤⲰⲤ, *after her.* ⲚⲤⲰⲚ, *after us.* ⲚⲤⲰⲦⲈⲚ, Ⲡ̄ⲤⲰⲦⲚ̄, *after you,* S. Ⲛ̄ⲤⲰⲞⲨ, *after them.*

Of Numbers.

18. The Coptic Numbers are generally expressed by the letters of the Alphabet with a line above them,

as ⲅ̄ ⲚⲈⲌⲞⲞⲨ. *three days.* Matt. XII, 40. Ⲇ̄ ⲚⲀⲂⲞⲦ. *four months.* John IV, 35; sometimes they are expressed by words, as ϤⲦⲞⲨ-ⲪⲞⲞⲨ, *four days.* Acts V, 30. But the Sahidic numbers are usually expressed by words.

19. Numbers admit the articles, and are also found without them, as ⲠⲒⲒ̄Ⲃ̄, *the twelve.* Matt. X, 2. 5. ⲠⲒⲤⲚⲀⲨ, *the two.* Deut. XVII, 6. ⲰⲐⲎⲚ ⲤⲚⲞⲨⲦ, *two tunics.* Luke III, 11.

The Cardinal Numbers.

	Coptic.		Sahidic.	
	Masc.	Fem.	Masc.	Fem.
Ⲁ̄	ⲞⲨⲀⲒ,	ⲞⲨⲈ.	ⲞⲨⲀ,	ⲞⲨⲈⲒ,
	ⲞⲨⲰⲦ		ⲞⲨⲰⲦ	
Ⲃ̄	ⲤⲚⲀⲨ,	ⲤⲚⲞⲨⲦ,	ⲤⲚⲀⲨ,	ⲤⲈⲚⲦⲈ, ⲤⲚ̄ⲦⲈ,
Ⲅ̄	ⲰⲞⲘⲦ,	ⲰⲞⲘⲦ,	ⲰⲞⲘⲚ̄Ⲧ, ⲰⲘ̄ⲚⲦ. ⲰⲞⲘⲦⲈ,
Ⲇ̄	ϤⲦⲰⲞⲨ,	ϤⲦⲞⲈ,	ϤⲦⲞⲞⲨ,	ϤⲦⲞⲈ, ϤⲦⲞ,
Ⲉ̄	ⲦⲞⲨ,	ⲦⲈ, Ⲧ,	ⲦⲞⲨ,	ⲦⲈ,
Ⲋ̄	ⲤⲞⲞⲨ,	ⲤⲞ,	ⲤⲞⲞⲨ,	ⲤⲞⲞ, ⲤⲞⲈ.
Ⲍ̄	ⲰⲀⲰϤ,	ⲰⲀⲰϤⲒ,	ⲤⲀⲰϤ. ⲤⲈⲰϤ, ⲤⲀⲰϤⲈ.
Ⲏ̄	ⲰⲘⲎⲚ,	ⲰⲘⲎⲚⲒ.	ⲰⲘⲞⲨⲚ,	ⲰⲘⲞⲨⲚⲈ,
Ⲑ̄	ⲮⲒⲦ,	ⲮⲒⲦ.	ⲮⲒⲦ,	ⲠⲤⲒⲦⲈ.
Ⲓ̄	ⲘⲈⲦ,	ⲘⲎⲦ,	ⲘⲎⲦ,	ⲘⲎⲦⲈ,
Ⲕ̄	ⲪⲰⲦ,	ⲪⲞⲨⲰⲦ,	ⲪⲞⲨⲰⲦ,	ⲪⲞⲨⲰⲦⲈ.
Ⲗ̄	ⲘⲀⲠ,		ⲘⲀⲀⲂ. ⲘⲀⲂ. ⲘⲀⲀⲂⲈ.
Ⲙ̄	ⲌⲘⲈ,		ⲌⲘⲈ,	ⲌⲘⲎ,
Ⲛ̄	ⲦⲀⲒⲞⲨ,		ⲦⲀⲒⲞ,
Ⲍ̄	ⲤⲈ,		ⲤⲈ.

6

	Coptic.		Sahidic.	
	Masc.	Fem.	Masc.	Fem.
ū	ϣⲂⲈ		ϣⲂⲈ, ϣϥⲈ.	
ⲡ̄	ⳉⲀⲘⲚⲈ,		ⳍⲘⲈⲚⲈ,	
ⳋ	ⲡⲓⲤⲦⲀⲨ,	ⲡⲓⲤⲦⲈⲞⲨⲓ.	ⲡⲤ̄ⲦⲀⲒⲞⲨ, ⲡⲈⲤⲦⲀⲒⲞⲨ,	
ⲣ̄	ϣⲈ,		ϣⲈ.	
ⲥ̄	ⲤⲚⲀⲨⲚ̀ϣⲈ.	ⲤⲚⲀⲨϣⲈ,	ϣⲎⲦ,	
ⲧ̄	ϣⲞⲘⲦⲚ̀ϣⲈ,		ϣⲘ̄ⲚⲦϣⲈ, ϣⲘ̄ⲦϣⲈ, ϣⲞⲘⲈⲦϣⲈ,	
ⲩ̄	ⳋⲦⲞⲞⲨⲚ̀ϣⲈ,		ⳋⲦⲞⲞⲨϣⲈ, ⳋⲦⲞⲨϣⲈ, ⳋⲦⲈⲨϣⲈ,	
ⲫ̄	ⳁⲞⲨⲚ̀ϣⲈ,	ⳁⲞⲨϣⲈ.	ⳁⲞⲨⲚ̄ϣⲈ.	
ⲭ̄	ⲤⲞⲞⲨⲚ̀ϣⲈ,	ⲤⲞⲞⲨϣⲈ.	ⲤⲞⲞⲨⲚ̄ϣⲈ, ⲤⲈⲨϣⲈ,	
ⲯ̄	ϣⲀϣϥⲚ̀ϣⲈ,		ⲤⲀϣϥⲚ̄ϣⲈ.	
ⲱ̄	ϣⲘⲎⲚⲚ̀ϣⲈ,		ϣⲘⲞⲨⲚϣⲈ.	
ⳛ̄			ⲯⲓⲤⲚ̄ϣⲈ.	
ⲁ̄	ϣⲞ,		ϣⲞ.	
ⲃ̄	ϣⲞⲤⲚⲀⲨ,		ⲤⲚⲀⲨⲚ̄ϣⲞ.	
ⲧ̄	ⲐⲂⲀ.		ⲦⲂⲀ.	

20. The following numbers are prefixes to nouns, viz. ϣⲘ̄ⲚⲦ, ϣⲘ̄Ⲧ, ϣⲞⲘⲦ, *three*, Sah. ϣⲘ̄ⲦϣⲞ, *three thousand.* ⳋⲦⲈ, Copt. ⳋⲦⲞⲨ, ⳋⲦⲈⲨ, Sah. *four.* ⲤⲈⲨ, Sah. *six.* ⲘⲎ̄Ⲧ, Sah. *ten.* ⲭⲞⲨⲦ, Sah. *twenty.*

The following are suffixes to numbers: ⲞⲨⲈ. Sah. *one.* ⲘⲚ̄ⲦⲞⲨⲈ, *eleven.* ⲤⲚⲞⲞⲨⲤ, ⲤⲚⲞⲨⲤ, m. ⲤⲚⲞⲞⲨⲤⲈ, ⲤⲚⲞⲨⲈ, f. Sah. *two.* ⲘⲚ̄ⲦⲤⲚⲞⲨⲤ, *twelve.* ϣⲞⲘⲦ, Sahidic. *three.* ⲦⲀⳋⲦⲈ, ⲀⳋⲦⲈ, Sah. *four.* ⲦⲎ, ⲦⲈ, Sah. *five.* ⲦⲀⲤⲈ, ⲀⲤⲈ. Sah. *six.* ϣⲘⲎⲚ, Copt. ϣⲘⲎⲚⲈ, f. Sah. *eight.* ⲘⲚ̄ⲦⲞⲨⲈ.

The Bashmuric has the following variations, ⲞⲨⲈⲒ, m. ⲞⲨⲈⲒ, f. *one.* ϣⲀⲘⲈⲚⲦ, *three.* ϣⲀ. *a thousand.*

The Ordinal Numbers.

21. The *first*, in ordinal numbers is expressed differently from the others; as

Copt.		Sahidic.		Bash.	
Masc.	Fem.	Masc.	Fem.	Masc.	Fem.
ϩⲟⲩⲓⲧ,	ϩⲟⲩⲓϯ,	ϣⲟⲣⲡ,	ϣⲟⲣⲡⲓ,	ϣⲁⲣⲉⲡ,	ϣⲁⲣⲡⲓ, *first.*
ϣⲟⲣⲡ,	ϣⲱⲣⲡ,				
ϣⲉⲣⲡ.					

22. The remaining cardinals are formed by putting ⲙⲁϩ Copt. and ⲙⲉϩ Sah. and Bash. before the cardinal numbers, as ⲡⲓⲙⲏⲓⲛⲓ ⲙ̄ⲙⲁϩⲃ̄, *the second miracle.* John IV, 54. Copt. ⲡⲙⲉϩ ϣⲟⲙⲛ̄ⲧ, *the third.* Matt. XXII, 26. Sah. ⲃⲉⲛ ϯⲙⲁϩ ⲥⲛⲟⲩϯ ⲛ̄ⲣⲟⲙⲡⲓ, *in anno secundo,* Dan. II, 1. Coptic. ⲧⲙⲉϩ ⲥⲛ̄ⲧⲉ, *the second,* f. Luke XII, 38. Sahidic.

ⲥⲟⲩ is used instead of ⲙⲁϩ and ⲙⲉϩ with the cardinal numbers when the days of the month are spoken of, as ⲥⲟⲩⲕ̄ⲉ ⲛ̄ⲁⲑⲱⲣ, *the twenty fifth day of Athor.* Exod. XII, 3. Copt. ⲛ̄ⲥⲟⲩⲕ̄ⲍ ⲙ̄ⲡⲓⲁⲃⲟⲧ, *the twenty seventh day of the month.* Gen. VIII, 4. ⲥⲟⲩϫⲟⲩⲧ ⲯⲓⲥ ⲛ̄ϩⲁⲑⲱⲣ, *the twenty ninth day of the month Athor.* Zoeg. Sah.

ⲁϫⲡ Copt. and ϫ̄ⲡ, Sah. occur with the cardinal numbers when hours are spoken of, as ⲛ̄ⲁϫⲡ ⲑ̄ ⲙ̄ⲡⲓⲉϩⲟⲟⲩ, *the ninth hour of the day.* Acts X, 3. ⲛ̄ⲡⲛⲁⲩ ⲛ̄ϫ̄ⲡ ⲥⲟⲉ, *about the sixth hour.* Sah. Matt. XX, 5.

ⲣⲉ, Copt. and Sah. *part,* is used with numbers, as ⲡⲓⲣⲉ ⲉ̄, *the fifth part.* Gen. XLI. 34. ⲟⲩⲟϩ ⲁϥⲣⲱⲕϩ ⲛ̄ⲥⲉ ⲫⲣⲉ ⲅ̄ ⲛ̄ⲛⲓϣϣⲏⲛ, *and the third part of the trees was burnt up.* Rev. VIII, 7. ⲡⲣⲉϣⲟⲙ̄ⲛⲧ, *the third part*, Numb. XXVIII, 5. Sah. The Copt. has also ⲧⲉⲣⲉ, or ⲧⲉⲣ, and the Sah. ⲧⲣⲉ. *part.*

ⲟⲩⲱⲛ, more often ⲟⲩⲛ̄, and sometimes ⲟⲩⲉⲛ, and ⲟⲩⲛⲉ́, Sah. *a part*, is put before numbers, as ⲟⲩⲱⲛ ⲁⲩⲁⲁϥ ⲛ̄ϥⲧⲟⲟⲩ ⲛ̄ⲟⲩⲱⲛ, ⲟⲩⲟⲩⲱⲛ ⲙ̄ⲡⲟⲩⲁ ⲡⲟⲩⲁ, *they made four parts, a part to each one*, John XIX, 23. Sah. ⲡⲟⲩⲛ̄ ⲛ̄ϥⲧⲟⲟⲩ, *fourth part*, Ezech. V, 2. Sah. ⲡⲟⲩⲉⲛ ⲛ̄ϯⲟⲩ, *the fifth part*, Zoeg. Sah. ⲡⲟⲩⲛⲉ ϣⲟⲙ̄ⲛ̄ⲧ, *the third part*, Tukius.

ⲡⲉϥ Copt. and Sah. is prefixed to numbers signifying days, as ⲡⲉϥϥⲧⲟⲟⲩ ⲅⲁⲣ ⲡⲉ. *for it is four days.* John XI, 39. ⲉⲡⲉϥϥⲧⲟⲟⲩ ⲡⲉ ⲉⲩ ⲍⲙ̄ ⲧⲓⲧⲁⲫⲟⲥ, *it is four days he is in the sepulchre.* v. 17. Sah.

ⲁ, et ⲛⲁ *about.* Copt. and Sah. as ⲁϥⲧⲟⲩ ϣⲉ ⲛ̄ⲣⲱⲙⲉ. *about four hundred men*, Acts V, 36. Sah. ⲛⲁ ϥⲧⲟⲩ ϣⲉ ⲧⲁⲓⲟⲩ ⲛ̄ⲣⲟⲙⲡⲉ, *about four hundred and fifty years.* Acts XIII, 20. Sah.

The plural of number is occasionally expressed by repeating the number, as, ⲕⲁⲧⲁ ⲣⲣ̄ ⲛⲉⲙ ⲕⲁⲧⲁ ⲛ̄ⲛ̄, *by hundreds, and by fifties.* Mark VI, 40.

CHAP. VII.

Of Verbs.

23. Egyptian verbs have no passive voice differing from the active, but the passive may be known thus, ⲗⲥ-ⲑⲁⲙⲓⲟ ⲛ̀ⲭⲉ ⲧ̀-ⲥⲟⲫⲓⲁ̀ ⲉ̀ⲃⲟⲗⲃⲉⲛ ⲛⲉⲥ-ⲅ̄ⲃⲏⲟⲩⲓ, *wisdom is justified of her works*, Matt. XI, 19. ⲟⲩⲟⲅ ⲁⲩⲟⲩⲱⲛ ⲛ̀ⲭⲉ ⲛⲉϥ-ⲥⲱⲧⲉⲙ, *and his ears were opened*, Mark VII, 35.

24. The passive is more commonly expressed by the verb in the third person plural of the verb active, as ⲡⲉⲛ-ⲣⲱⲙⲓ ⲛ̀ⲁⲡⲁⲥ ⲗⲩⲁⲱϥ ⲛⲉⲙⲁϥ, *our old man was crucified with him*. Rom. VI, 6. ⲉⲩⲛⲁⲡⲱⲛⲅ ⲉⲃⲟⲗ ⲙ̄ⲡⲉⲥ-ⲛⲟϥ ⲛ̄ⲧⲉ ⲥⲧⲉⲫⲁⲛⲟⲥ, *the blood of Stephen was shed.* Acts XXII, 20. Sah. ⲟⲩⲟⲅ ⲟⲩⲙⲏⲓⲛⲓ ⲛ̀ⲛⲟⲩⲧⲏⲓϥ, *and no sign shall be given.* Matt. XII, 39. ⲁⲩ-ⲕⲟⲥⲉⲛ ⲛⲉⲙⲁϥ, *we are buried with him.* Rom. VI, 4.

25. But sometimes the passive voice can only be discovered by the sense of the passage read. But see further on verbs passive.

The Prefixes and Suffixes to Verbs.

Person.	The Prefixes. Coptic.	Sahidic.	The Suffixes.
1.	ⲧ̄	ⲧ̄	ⲓ
2. m.	ⲕ, ⲭ	ⲕ	ⲕ
2. f.	ⲧⲉ	ⲧⲉ	ⲉ

Person.	The Prefixes.		The Affixes.
	Coptic.	Sahidic.	
3. m.	ϥ	ϥ	ϥ
3. f.	c	c	c
1. plur.	ⲧⲉⲛ	ⲧⲛ̄, ⲧⲉⲛ	ⲛ
2.	ⲧⲉⲧⲉⲛ	ⲧⲉⲧⲛ̄, ⲧⲉⲧⲉⲛ	ⲧⲉⲛ
3.	ⲥⲉ	ⲥⲉ	ⲩ

Indicative Mood.

The 1st Present Tense.

Singular.

Coptic.	Sahidic.
ϯ	ϯ, *I do,* or *am doing.*
ⲕ, ⲭ	ⲕ, *thou art,* m.
ⲧⲉ	ⲧⲉ, *thou art,* f
ϥ	ϥ, *he is.*
c	c, *she is.*

Plural.

ⲧⲉⲛ	ⲧⲛ̄, ⲧⲉⲛ, *we are.*
ⲧⲉⲧⲉⲛ	ⲧⲉⲧⲛ̄, ⲧⲉⲧⲉⲛ, *ye are.*
ⲥⲉ	ⲥⲉ, *they are.*

The 2nd Present Tense.

Singular.

Coptic.	Sahidic.	Bash.
ⲉⲓ	ⲉⲓ	ⲉⲓ, *I am,* or.
ⲉⲕ	ⲉⲕ	ⲉⲕ, *thou art,* m.

Coptic.	Sahidic.	Bash.
ЄΡЄ	ЄΡЄ	ЄΛЄ, *thou art,* f.
ЄϤ) ЄΡЄ	ЄϤ) ЄΡЄ	ЄϤ) ЄΛЄ. *he and she.*
ЄC)	ЄC)	ЄC) *is.*

he is.

Plural.

ЄN	N̄, ЄN	ЄN. *we are.*
ЄTЄT.ЄN	ЄTЄTN̄	ЄTЄTЄN, *ye are.*
ЄY. OY; ЄΡЄ	ЄY, OY. ЄΡЄ	ЄY, OY ЄΛЄ, *they are.*

The Imperfect Tense.

Singular.

Coptic.	Sahidic.	Bash.
NAI ΠЄ	NЄI ΠЄ	NAI ΠЄ, *I was.*
NAK ΠЄ	NЄK ΠЄ	NAK ΠЄ. *thou,* m.
NAΡЄ ΠЄ	NЄΡЄ ΠЄ	NAΡЄ ΠЄ. *thou,* f.
NAϤ ΠЄ) NAΡЄ	NЄϤ ΠЄ) NЄΡЄ	NAϤ ΠЄ) NAΡЄ *he and she.*
NAC ΠЄ) ΠЄ	NЄC ΠЄ) ΠЄ	NAC ΠЄ) ΠЄ. *is.*

he.

Plural.

NAN ΠЄ	NЄN ΠЄ	NAN ΠЄ, *we were.*
NAΡЄTЄN ΠЄ	NЄTЄTN̄ ΠЄ	NAΡЄTЄN ΠЄ, *ye.*
NAYΠЄ.NAΡЄΠЄ	NЄY ΠЄ. NЄΡЄ ΠЄ	NAYΠЄ, NAΡЄ ΠЄ, *they.*

The 1st Perfect Tense.

Singular.

Coptic.	Sahidic.	Bash.
AI	AI	AI. *I have.*
AK	AK	AK, *thou hast,* m.
AΡЄ	AΡЄ	AΡЄ, *thou hast.* f.
Aϥ) à	Aϥ) λ	Aϥ) à *he and she.*
AC)	AC)	AC) *hath.*

he hath.

Plural.

Coptic.	Sahidic.	Bash.
ⲁⲛ	ⲁⲛ	ⲁⲛ, *we have.*
ⲁⲣⲉⲧⲉⲛ	ⲁⲧⲉⲧⲛ̄	ⲁⲧⲉⲧⲛ̄, *ye have.*
ⲁⲩ, ⲁ	ⲁⲩ, ⲁ	ⲁⲩ, ⲁ, *they have.*

The 2nd Perfect Tense.

Singular.

Coptic.	Sahidic.	Bash.
ⲉ̀ⲧⲁⲓ,	ⲛ̄ⲧⲁⲓ,	ⲉⲧⲁⲓ, *I have.*
ⲉ̀ⲧⲁⲕ,	ⲛ̄ⲧⲁⲕ,	ⲉⲧⲁⲕ, *thou hast,* m.
ⲉ̀ⲧⲁⲣⲉ,	ⲛ̄ⲧⲁⲣ,	ⲉⲧⲁⲣⲉ, *thou hast,* f.
ⲉ̀ⲧⲁϥ, ⲉⲧⲁ̀,	ⲛ̄ⲧⲁϥ, ⲛ̄ⲧⲁ,	ⲉⲧⲁϥ, *he hath.* ⲉ̀ⲧⲁ, *he a. she.*
ⲉ̀ⲧⲁⲥ,	ⲛ̄ⲧⲁⲥ,	ⲉⲧⲁⲥ, *hath.*

Plural.

Coptic.	Sahidic.	Bash.
ⲉ̀ⲧⲁⲛ,	ⲛ̄ⲧⲁⲛ,	ⲉⲧⲁⲛ, *we have.*
ⲉ̀ⲧⲁⲣⲉⲧⲉⲛ,	ⲛ̄ⲧⲁⲧⲉⲧⲛ̄,	ⲉⲧⲁⲣⲉⲧⲉⲛ, *ye have.*
ⲉ̀ⲧⲁⲩ. ⲉⲧⲁ̀,	ⲛ̄ⲧⲁⲩ, ⲛ̄ⲧⲁ,	ⲉⲧⲁⲩ, ⲉⲧⲁ, *they have.*

The Pluperfect Tense.

Singular.

Coptic.	Sahidic and Bash.
ⲛⲉ ⲁⲓ ⲡⲉ,	ⲛⲉ ⲁⲓ ⲡⲉ, *I had.*
ⲛⲉ ⲁⲕ ⲡⲉ,	ⲛⲉ ⲁⲕ ⲡⲉ, *thou,* m.
ⲛⲉ ⲁⲣⲉ ⲡⲉ,	ⲛⲉ ⲁⲣⲉ ⲡⲉ, *thou,* f.
ⲛⲉ ⲁϥ ⲡⲉ, ⲛⲉ ⲁ ⲡⲉ,	ⲛⲉ ⲁϥ ⲡⲉ, ⲛⲉ ⲁ ⲡⲉ, *he.*
ⲛⲉ ⲁⲥ ⲡⲉ,	ⲛⲉ ⲁⲥ ⲡⲉ, *she.*
ⲛⲉ ⲁ ⲡⲉ, ⲛⲉ ⲁⲣⲉ ⲡⲉ,	ⲛⲉ ⲁ ⲡⲉ, ⲛⲉ ⲁⲣⲉ ⲡⲉ, *he and she.*

Plural.

Coptic.	Sahidic and Bash.
ⲚⲈ ⲀⲚ ⲠⲈ,	ⲚⲈ ⲀⲚ ⲠⲈ, *we.*
ⲚⲈ ⲀⲢⲈⲦⲈⲚ ⲠⲈ,	ⲚⲈ ⲀⲦⲈⲦⲚ̄ ⲠⲈ, *ye.*
ⲚⲈ ⲀⲨ ⲠⲈ,	ⲚⲈ ⲀⲨ ⲠⲈ, *they.*

The Present Tense Indefinite.

Singular.

Coptic.	Sahidic.	Bash.
ϢⲀⲒ,	ϢⲀⲒ,	ϢⲀⲒ, *I am.*
ϢⲀⲔ,	ϢⲀⲔ,	ϢⲀⲔ, *thou,* m.
ϢⲀⲢⲈ,	ϢⲀⲢⲈ,	ϢⲀⲖⲈ, *thou,* f.
ϢⲀϥ,} ϢⲀⲢⲈ,	ϢⲀϥ,} ϢⲀⲢⲈ,	ϢⲀϥ,} *he.* ϢⲀⲖⲈ, *he & she.*
ϢⲀⲤ,	ϢⲀⲤ,	ϢⲀⲤ, *she.*

Plural.

ϢⲀⲚ,	ϢⲀⲚ,	ϢⲀⲚ, *we.*
ϢⲀⲢⲈⲦⲈⲚ,	ϢⲀⲦⲈⲦⲚ̄,	ϢⲀⲦⲈⲦⲈⲚ, *ye.*
ϢⲀⲨ, ϢⲀⲢⲈ,	ϢⲀⲨ, ϢⲀⲢⲈ,	ϢⲀⲨ, ϢⲀⲖⲈ, *they.*

The Imperfect Tense Indefinite.

Singular.

Coptic.	Sahidic.
ⲚⲈ ϢⲀⲒ ⲠⲈ,	ⲚⲈ ϢⲀⲒ ⲠⲈ, *I was.*
ⲚⲈ ϢⲀⲔ ⲠⲈ,	ⲚⲈ ϢⲀⲔ ⲠⲈ, *thou,* m.
ⲚⲈ ϢⲀⲢⲈ ⲠⲈ,	Ⲛϥ ϢⲀⲢⲈ ⲠⲈ, *thou,* f.
ⲚⲈ ϢⲀϥ ⲠⲈ,} ⲚⲈ ϢⲀⲢⲈ ⲠⲈ,	ⲚⲈ ϢⲀϥ ⲠⲈ,}ⲚⲈ ϢⲀⲢⲈ *he.* ⲠⲈ, *he & she.*
ⲚⲈ ϢⲀⲤ ⲠⲈ,	ⲚⲈ ϢⲀⲤ ⲠⲈ,} *she.*

7

Plural.

Coptic.	Sahidic.
ⲛⲉ ϣⲁⲛ ⲡⲉ,	ⲛⲉ ϣⲁⲛ ⲡⲉ, *we.*
ⲛⲉ ϣⲁⲣⲉⲧⲉⲛ ⲡⲉ,	ⲛⲉ ϣⲁⲧⲉⲧⲛ̄ ⲡⲉ, *ye.*
ⲛⲉ ϣⲁⲩ ⲡⲉ, ⲛⲉ ϣⲁⲣⲉ ⲡⲉ,	ⲛⲉ ϣⲁⲩ ⲡⲉ, ⲛⲉϣⲁⲣⲉ ⲡⲉ, *they.*

Singular.

Bash.

ⲛⲉ ϣⲁⲓ ⲡⲉ, *I was.*

ⲛⲉ ϣⲁⲕ ⲡⲉ, *thou,* m.

ⲛⲉ ϣⲁⲗⲉ ⲡⲉ, *thou,* f.

ⲛⲉ ϣⲁϥ ⲡⲉ,   ⎫   *he.*

               ⎬ ⲛⲉ ϣⲁⲗⲉ ⲡⲉ, *he* and *she.*

ⲛⲉ ϣⲁⲥ ⲡⲉ,   ⎭   *she.*

Plural.

ⲛⲉ ϣⲁⲛ ⲡⲉ, *we.*

ⲛⲉ ϣⲁⲧⲉⲧⲉⲛ ⲡⲉ, *ye.*

ⲛⲉ ϣⲁⲩ ⲡⲉ, ⎫

           ⎬ *they.*

ⲛⲉ ϣⲁⲗⲉ ⲡⲉ, ⎭

The 1st Future Tense.

Coptic.	Sahidic.	Bash.
ϯⲛⲁ,	ϯⲛⲁ,	ϯⲛⲉ, vel ⲁ, *I shall.*
ⲭⲛⲁ,	ⲕⲛⲁ,	ⲕⲛⲉ, *thou,* m.
ⲧⲉⲛⲁ,	ⲧⲉⲛⲁ,	*thou,* f.
ϥⲛⲁ,	ϥⲛⲁ,	ϥⲛⲉ, *he.*
ⲥⲛⲁ,	ⲥⲛⲁ,	ⲥⲛⲉ, *she.*

Plural.

Coptic.	Sahidic.	Bash.	
ⲧⲉⲛⲛⲁ,	ⲧⲉⲛⲛⲁ, ⲧⲉⲛⲁ, ⲧⲉⲛⲛⲉ, vel ⲁ,		*we.*
ⲧⲉⲧⲉⲛⲛⲁ,	ⲧⲉⲧⲛ̄ⲛⲁ, ⲧⲉⲧⲛ̄ⲁ,		*ye.*
ⲥⲉⲛⲁ,	ⲥⲉⲛⲁ,	ⲥⲉⲛⲉ, *they.*	

The 2nd Future Tense.

Singular.

Coptic.	Sahidic.	Bash.
ⲈⲒⲚⲀ,	ⲈⲒⲚⲀ,	ⲀⲒⲚⲀ vel ⲚⲈ, *I shall.*
ⲈⲔⲚⲀ,	ⲈⲔⲚⲀ,	ⲀⲔⲚⲀ, *thou*, m.
ⲈⲠⲈⲚⲀ,	ⲈⲠⲈⲚⲀ,	ⲀⲠⲈⲚⲀ, *thou*, f.
ⲈϤⲚⲀ,⎱ ⲈⲠⲈ..ⲚⲀ,	ⲈϤⲚⲀ,⎱ ⲈⲠⲈ..ⲚⲀ,	ⲀϤⲚⲀ,⎱ ⲀⲠⲈ..ⲚⲀ,*he&she.*
ⲈⲤⲚⲀ,⎰	ⲈⲤⲚⲀ,⎰	ⲀⲤⲚⲀ,⎰

he.

she.

Plural.

ⲈⲚⲚⲀ,	ⲚⲚⲀ, ⲈⲚⲚⲀ,	ⲀⲚⲚⲀ, vel ⲚⲈ, *we.*
ⲈⲠⲈⲦⲈⲚⲚⲀ,	ⲈⲦⲈⲦⲚ̄ⲚⲀ,ⲈⲦⲈⲦⲚ̄Ⲁ,	ⲀⲠⲈⲦⲈⲚⲚⲀ, *ye.*
ⲈⲨⲚⲀ, ⲞⲨⲚⲀ,	ⲈⲨⲚⲀ, ⲞⲨⲚⲀ,	ⲀⲨⲚⲀ, *they.*

The Prefixes Copt. are sometimes written ⲀⲒⲚⲀ, ⲀⲔⲚⲀ, ⲀⲠⲈⲚⲀ, etc.

The 3rd Future Tense.

Singular.

Coptic.	Sahidic.	Bash.
ⲈⲒⲈ̀,	ⲈⲒⲈ,	ⲈⲒⲈ, *I shall.*
ⲈⲔⲈ̀,	ⲈⲔⲈ,	ⲈⲔⲈ, *thou*, m.
ⲈⲠⲈ̀,	ⲈⲠⲈ,	ⲈⲠⲈ, *thou* f.
ⲈϤⲈ̀,⎱ ⲈⲠⲈ̀,	ⲈϤⲈ,⎱ ⲈⲠⲈ,	ⲈϤⲈ,⎱ ⲈⲠⲈ, *he and she.*
ⲈⲤⲈ̀,⎰	ⲈⲤⲈ,⎰	ⲈⲤⲈ,⎰

he.

she.

Plural.

ⲈⲚⲈ̀,	ⲈⲚⲈ,	ⲈⲚⲈ, *we.*
ⲈⲠⲈⲦⲈⲚⲈ̀,	ⲈⲦⲈⲦⲚ̄Ⲉ,	ⲈⲦⲈⲦⲚ̄Ⲉ, *ye.*
ⲈⲨⲈ̀, ⲈⲠⲈ̀,	ⲈⲨⲈ, ⲈⲠⲈ,	ⲈⲨⲈ, ⲈⲠⲈ, *they.*

7 *

The 4th Future Tense.

Singular.

Coptic.	Sahidic.	Bash.
ⲧⲁ,	ⲧⲁ, ⲧⲁⲣⲓ,	ⲧⲁ, *I shall.*
	ⲧⲁⲣⲉⲕ,	*thou,* m.
ⲧⲉⲣⲁ,	ⲧⲉⲣⲁ,	ⲧⲉⲣⲁ, *thou,* f.
	ⲧⲁⲣⲉϥ,	*he.*
	ⲧⲁⲣⲉⲥ,	*she.*

Plural.

ⲧⲁⲣⲛ̄,		*we.*
ⲧⲁⲣⲉⲧⲛ̄,	ⲧⲁⲗⲉⲧⲉⲛ, *ye.*	
ⲧⲁⲣⲟⲩ,		*they.*

The Imperfect Tense.

Singular.

Coptic.	Sahidic.
ⲛⲁⲓⲛⲁ,	ⲛⲉⲓⲛⲁ, *I should.*
ⲛⲁⲕⲛⲁ,	ⲛⲉⲕⲛⲁ, *thou,* m.
ⲛⲁⲣⲉⲛⲁ,	ⲛⲉⲣⲉⲛⲁ, *thou,* f.
ⲛⲁϥⲛⲁ,} ⲛⲁⲣⲉ..ⲛⲁ,	ⲛⲉϥⲛⲁ,} ⲛⲉⲣⲉ..ⲛⲁ, *he & she.*
ⲛⲁⲥⲛⲁ,}	ⲛⲉⲥⲛⲁ,} *she.*

(center column: *he.* / *he & she.* / *she.* — ⲛⲁϥⲛⲁ, ⲛⲁⲥⲛⲁ grouped; ⲛⲉϥⲛⲁ *he.*, ⲛⲉⲥⲛⲁ *she.*)

Bash.

ⲛⲁⲓⲛⲉ vel ⲛⲁ, *I should.*

ⲛⲁⲕⲛⲉ, *thou,* m.

ⲛⲁⲣⲉⲛⲉ, *thou,* f.

ⲛⲁϥⲛⲉ,} ⲛⲁⲣⲉ *he.*
ⲛⲁⲥⲛⲉ,} ..ⲛⲉ, *he & she.*
　　　　　　she.

Plural.

Coptic.	Sahidic.
ⲚⲀⲚⲚⲀ ⲠⲈ,	ⲚⲈⲚⲚⲀ ⲠⲈ, *we.*
ⲚⲀⲢⲈⲦⲈⲚⲚⲀ ⲠⲈ,	ⲚⲈⲦⲈⲦⲚ̄Ⲁ ⲠⲈ, *ye.*
ⲚⲀⲨⲚⲀ, ⲚⲀⲢⲈ..ⲚⲀ ⲠⲈ,	ⲚⲈⲨⲚⲀ, ⲚⲈⲢⲈ..ⲚⲀ ⲠⲈ, *they.*

Bash.

ⲚⲀⲚⲚⲈ ⲠⲈ, *we.*

ⲚⲀⲢⲈⲦⲈⲚⲚⲈ ⲠⲈ, *ye.*

ⲚⲈⲨⲚⲈ, ⲚⲀⲢⲈⲚⲈ ⲠⲈ, *they.*

The Subjunctive Mood.

Singular.

Coptic.	Sahidic.	Bash.	
Ⲛ̀ⲦⲀ,	Ⲛ̄ⲦⲀ,	Ⲛ̀ⲦⲀ, *that I.*	
Ⲛ̀ⲦⲈⲔ,	Ⲛ̄Ⲅ,	Ⲛ̀Ⲅ, *thou,* m.	
Ⲛ̀ⲦⲈ,	Ⲛ̄ⲦⲈ,	Ⲛ̀ⲦⲈ, *thou,* f.	
Ⲛ̀ⲦⲈϥ,} Ⲛ̀ⲦⲈ,	ⲚⲈϥ, Ⲛ̄ϥ,} Ⲛ̄ⲦⲈ,	ⲚⲈϥ, Ⲛ̄ϥ,} Ⲛ̄ⲦⲈ, *he.* *he & she.*	
Ⲛ̀ⲦⲈⲤ,}	Ⲛ̄Ⲥ,}	ⲚⲈⲤ, Ⲛ̄Ⲥ,} *she.*	

Plural.

Coptic.	Sahidic.	Bash.	
Ⲛ̀ⲦⲈⲚ,	Ⲛ̄ⲦⲚ̄,	Ⲛ̀ⲦⲚ̄, *we.*	
Ⲛ̀ⲦⲈⲦⲈⲚ,	Ⲛ̄ⲦⲈⲦⲚ̄,	Ⲛ̀ⲦⲈⲦⲚ̄, *ye.*	
Ⲛ̀ⲦⲞⲨ, Ⲛ̀ⲦⲈ,	Ⲛ̄ⲤⲈ, Ⲛ̄ⲦⲈ,	Ⲛ̀ⲤⲈ, ⲚⲦⲈ, *they.*	

The Optative Mood.

Singular.

Coptic.	Sahidic.	Bash.
ⲙⲁⲣⲓ,	ⲙⲁⲣⲓ,	ⲙⲁⲗⲓ, *I may,*
ⲙⲁⲣⲉⲕ,	ⲙⲁⲣⲉⲕ,	ⲙⲁⲗⲉⲕ, *thou,* m.
ⲙⲁⲣⲉ,	ⲙⲁⲣⲉ,	ⲙⲁⲗⲉ, *thou,* f.
ⲙⲁⲣⲉϥ,} ⲙⲁⲣⲉ,	ⲙⲁⲣⲉϥ,} ⲙⲁⲣⲉ,	ⲙⲁⲗⲉϥ,} ⲙⲁⲗⲉ, *he. he & she. she.*
ⲙⲁⲣⲉⲥ,	ⲙⲁⲣⲉⲥ,	ⲙⲁⲗⲉⲥ,

Plural.

ⲙⲁⲣⲉⲛ,	ⲙⲁⲣⲛ̄,	ⲙⲁⲗⲉⲛ, *we.*
ⲙⲁⲣⲉⲧⲉⲛ,	ⲙⲁⲣⲉⲧⲛ̄,	ⲙⲁⲗⲉⲧⲉⲛ, *ye.*
ⲙⲁⲣⲟⲩ, ⲙⲁⲣⲉ,	ⲙⲁⲣⲟⲩ, ⲙⲁⲣⲉ,	ⲙⲁⲗⲟⲩ, ⲙⲁⲗⲉ, *they.*

The Imperative Mood.

Singular and Plural.

ⲁ; ⲁⲣⲓ or ⲙⲁ, or the root itself.

The Infinitive Mood.

ⲉ̀ or ⲛ̀ or the root itself.

Participles.

ⲡⲁϣⲓⲛ, ⲡⲉⲕϣⲓⲛ, ⲡⲉϥϣⲛ &c. or ⲡϫⲓⲛⲧⲁ, ⲡϫⲓⲛⲧⲉⲕ, ⲡϫⲓⲛⲧϥ &c.

The verb ⲧⲁⲕⲟ, *to destroy,* is given with the aug-
ments, to convey a more clear idea of their position.

Indicative Mood.

The 1st Present Tense.

Singular.

Coptic.	Sahidic.
†-ⲧⲁⲕⲟ,	†-ⲧⲁⲕⲟ, *I am destroying.*
ⲕ-ⲧⲁⲕⲟ, ⲭ-ⲧⲁⲕⲟ,	ⲕ-ⲧⲁⲕⲟ, *thou art destroying*, m.
ⲧⲉ-ⲧⲁⲕⲟ,	ⲧⲉ-ⲧⲁⲕⲟ, *thou art destroying*, f.
ϥ-ⲧⲁⲕⲟ,	ϥ-ⲧⲁⲕⲟ, *he is destroying.*
ⲥ-ⲧⲁⲕⲟ,	ⲥ-ⲧⲁⲕⲟ, *she is destroying.*

Plural.

Coptic.	Sahidic.
ⲧⲉⲛ-ⲧⲁⲕⲟ,	ⲧⲛ̄, or ⲧⲉⲛ-ⲧⲁⲕⲟ, *we are destroying.*
ⲧⲉⲧⲉⲛ-ⲧⲁⲕⲟ,	ⲧⲉⲧⲛ̄, or ⲧⲉⲧⲉⲛ-ⲧⲁⲕⲟ, *ye are destroying.*
ⲥⲉ-ⲧⲁⲕⲟ,	ⲥⲉ-ⲧⲁⲕⲟ, *they are destroying.*

The 2nd Present Tense.

Singular.

Coptic.	Sahidic.	Bashmuric.
ⲉⲓ-ⲧⲁⲕⲟ,	ⲉⲓ-ⲧⲁⲕⲟ,	ⲉⲓ-ⲧⲁⲕⲟ, *I am destroying*, ὤν.
ⲉⲕ-ⲧⲁⲕⲟ,	ⲉⲕ-ⲧⲁⲕⲟ,	ⲉⲕ-ⲧⲁⲕⲟ, *thou,* m.
ⲉⲣⲉ-ⲧⲁⲕⲟ,	ⲉⲣⲉ-ⲧⲁⲕⲟ,	ⲉⲗⲉ-ⲧⲁⲕⲟ, *thou,* f.
ⲉϥ- ⲉⲣⲉ- } ⲧⲁⲕⲟ,	ⲉϥ- ⲉⲣⲉ- } ⲧⲁⲕⲟ,	ⲉϥ- ⲉⲗⲉ- } ⲧⲁⲕⲟ, *he.*
ⲉⲥ- ⲉⲣⲉ- } ⲧⲁⲕⲟ,	ⲉⲥ- ⲉⲣⲉ- } ⲧⲁⲕⲟ,	ⲉⲥ- ⲉⲗⲉ- } ⲧⲁⲕⲟ, *she.*

Plural.

ⲉⲛ-ⲧⲁⲕⲟ,	ⲛ̄, or ⲉⲛ-ⲧⲁⲕⲟ, ⲉⲛ-ⲧⲁⲕⲟ, *we.*	
ⲉⲧⲉⲧⲉⲛ-ⲧⲁⲕⲟ,	ⲉⲧⲉⲧⲛ̄-ⲧⲁⲕⲟ, ⲉⲧⲉⲧⲉⲛ-ⲧⲁⲕⲟ, *ye.*	
ⲉⲩ- ⲟⲩ- ⲉⲣⲉ- } ⲧⲁⲕⲟ,	ⲉⲩ- ⲟⲩ- ⲉⲣⲉ- } ⲧⲁⲕⲟ,	ⲉⲩ- ⲟⲩ- ⲉⲗⲉ- } ⲧⲁⲕⲟ, *they.*

The Imperfect Tense.

Singular.

Coptic.	Sahidic.	Bashmuric.
ⲚⲀⲒ-ⲦⲀⲔⲞ ⲠⲈ,	ⲚⲈⲒ-ⲦⲀⲔⲞ ⲠⲈ,	ⲚⲀⲒ-ⲦⲀⲔⲞ ⲠⲈ, *I was.*
ⲚⲀⲔ-ⲦⲀⲔⲞ ⲠⲈ,	ⲚⲈⲔ-ⲦⲀⲔⲞ ⲠⲈ,	ⲚⲀⲔ-ⲦⲀⲔⲞ ⲠⲈ, *thou,* m.
ⲚⲀⲢⲈ-ⲦⲀⲔⲞ ⲠⲈ,	ⲚⲈⲢⲈ-ⲦⲀⲔⲞ ⲠⲈ,	ⲚⲀⲢⲈ-ⲦⲀⲔⲞ ⲠⲈ, *thou,* f.
ⲚⲀϤ- / ⲚⲀⲢⲈ- } ⲦⲀⲔⲞ ⲠⲈ,	ⲚⲈϤ- / ⲚⲈⲢⲈ- } ⲦⲀⲔⲞ ⲠⲈ,	ⲚⲀϤ- / ⲚⲀⲢⲈ- } ⲦⲀⲔⲞ ⲠⲈ, *he.*
ⲚⲀⲤ- / ⲚⲀⲢⲈ- } ⲦⲀⲔⲞ ⲠⲈ,	ⲚⲈⲤ- / ⲚⲈⲢⲈ- } ⲦⲀⲔⲞ ⲠⲈ,	ⲚⲀⲤ- / ⲚⲀⲢⲈ- } ⲦⲀⲔⲞ ⲠⲈ, *she.*

Plural.

ⲚⲀⲚ-ⲦⲀⲔⲞ ⲠⲈ,	ⲚⲈⲚ-ⲦⲀⲔⲞ ⲠⲈ,	ⲚⲀⲚ-ⲦⲀⲔⲞ ⲠⲈ, *we.*
ⲚⲀⲢⲈⲦⲈⲚ-ⲦⲀⲔⲞ ⲠⲈ,	ⲚⲈⲦⲈⲦⲚ̄-ⲦⲀⲔⲞ ⲠⲈ,	ⲚⲀⲢⲈⲦⲈⲚ-ⲦⲀⲔⲞ ⲠⲈ, *ye.*
ⲚⲀⲨ- / ⲚⲀⲢⲈ- } ⲦⲀⲔⲞ ⲠⲈ,	ⲚⲈⲨ- / ⲚⲈⲢⲈ- } ⲦⲀⲔⲞ ⲠⲈ,	ⲚⲀⲨ- / ⲚⲀⲢⲈ- } ⲦⲀⲔⲞ ⲠⲈ, *they.*

The 1st Perfect Tense.

Singular.

Coptic.	Sahidic.	Bashmuric.
ⲀⲒ-ⲦⲀⲔⲞ,	ⲀⲒ-ⲦⲀⲔⲞ,	ⲀⲒ-ⲦⲀⲔⲞ, *I have.*
ⲀⲔ-ⲦⲀⲔⲞ,	ⲀⲔ-ⲦⲀⲔⲞ,	ⲀⲔ-ⲦⲀⲔⲞ, *thou,* m.
ⲀⲢⲈ-ⲦⲀⲔⲞ,	ⲀⲢⲈ-ⲦⲀⲔⲞ,	ⲀⲢⲈ-ⲦⲀⲔⲞ, *thou,* f.
ⲀϤ- / Ⲁ̀- } ⲦⲀⲔⲞ,	ⲀϤ- / Ⲁ- } ⲦⲀⲔⲞ,	ⲀϤ- / Ⲁ- } ⲦⲀⲔⲞ, *he.*
ⲀⲤ- / Ⲁ̀- } ⲦⲀⲔⲞ,	ⲀⲤ- / Ⲁ- } ⲦⲀⲔⲞ,	ⲀⲤ- / Ⲁ- } ⲦⲀⲔⲞ, *she.*

Plural.

Coptic.	Sahidic.	Bashmuric.
ⲀⲚ-ⲦⲀⲔⲞ,	ⲀⲚ-ⲦⲀⲔⲞ,	ⲀⲚ-ⲦⲀⲔⲞ, *we.*
ⲀⲢⲈⲦⲈⲚ-ⲦⲀⲔⲞ,	ⲀⲦⲈⲦⲚ̅-ⲦⲀⲔⲞ,	ⲀⲦⲈⲦⲚ̅-ⲦⲀⲔⲞ, *ye.*
ⲀⲨ-⎫ ⲦⲀⲔⲞ, ⲁ̀- ⎭	ⲀⲨ-⎫ ⲦⲀⲔⲞ, ⲁ- ⎭	ⲀⲨ-⎫ ⲦⲀⲔⲞ, *they.* ⲁ- ⎭

The 2nd Perfect Tense.

Singular.

Coptic.	Sahidic.	Bashmuric.
Ⲉ̀ⲦⲀⲒ-ⲦⲀⲔⲞ,	Ⲛ̅ⲦⲀⲒ-ⲦⲀⲔⲞ,	ⲈⲦⲀⲒ-ⲦⲀⲔⲞ, *I have.*
Ⲉ̀ⲦⲀⲔ-ⲦⲀⲔⲞ,	Ⲛ̅ⲦⲀⲔ-ⲦⲀⲔⲞ,	ⲈⲦⲀⲔ-ⲦⲀⲔⲞ, *thou,* m.
Ⲉ̀ⲦⲀⲢⲈ-ⲦⲀⲔⲞ,	Ⲛ̅ⲦⲀⲢ-ⲦⲀⲔⲞ,	ⲈⲦⲀⲢⲈ-ⲦⲀⲔⲞ, *thou,* f.
Ⲉ̀ⲦⲀϥ-⎫ ⲦⲀⲔⲞ, Ⲉ̀ⲦⲀ̀- ⎭	Ⲛ̅ⲦⲀϥ-⎫ ⲦⲀⲔⲞ, Ⲛ̅ⲦⲀ- ⎭	ⲈⲦⲀϥ-⎫ ⲦⲀⲔⲞ, *he.* ⲈⲦⲀ- ⎭
Ⲉ̀ⲦⲀⳅ-⎫ ⲦⲀⲔⲞ, Ⲉ̀ⲦⲀ̀- ⎭	Ⲛ̅ⲦⲀⲤ-⎫ ⲦⲀⲔⲞ, Ⲛ̅ⲦⲀ- ⎭	ⲈⲦⲀⲤ-⎫ ⲦⲀⲔⲞ, *she.* ⲈⲦⲀ- ⎭

Plural.

Ⲉ̀ⲦⲀⲚ-ⲦⲀⲔⲞ,	Ⲛ̅ⲦⲀⲚ-ⲦⲀⲔⲞ,	ⲈⲦⲀⲚ-ⲦⲀⲔⲞ, *we.*
Ⲉ̀ⲦⲀⲢⲈⲦⲈⲚ-ⲦⲀⲔⲞ,	Ⲛ̅ⲦⲀⲦⲈⲦⲚ̅-ⲦⲀⲔⲞ,	ⲈⲦⲀⲢⲈⲦⲈⲚ-ⲦⲀⲔⲞ, *ye.*
Ⲉ̀ⲦⲀⲨ-⎫ ⲦⲀⲔⲞ, Ⲉ̀ⲦⲀ̀- ⎭	Ⲛ̅ⲦⲀⲨ-⎫ ⲦⲀⲔⲞ, Ⲛ̅ⲦⲀ- ⎭	ⲈⲦⲀⲨ-⎫ ⲦⲀⲔⲞ, *they.* ⲈⲦⲀ- ⎭

The Pluperfect Tense.

Singular.

Coptic.	Sahidic.
ⲚⲈ ⲀⲒ-ⲦⲀⲔⲞ ⲠⲈ,	ⲚⲈ ⲀⲒ-ⲦⲀⲔⲞ ⲠⲈ, *I had.*
ⲚⲈ ⲀⲔ-ⲦⲀⲔⲞ ⲠⲈ,	ⲚⲈ ⲀⲔ-ⲦⲀⲔⲞ ⲠⲈ, *thou,* m.
ⲚⲈ ⲀⲢⲈ-ⲦⲀⲔⲞ ⲠⲈ,	ⲚⲈ ⲀⲢⲈ-ⲦⲀⲔⲞ ⲠⲈ, *thou,* f.

8

Coptic.	Sahidic.

ⲚⲈ ⲀϤ· ⟩
ⲚⲈ Ⲁ· ⟩ ⲦⲀⲔⲞ ⲠⲈ,   ⲚⲈ ⲀϤ· ⟩
ⲚⲈ Ⲁ· ⟩ ⲦⲀⲔⲞ ⲠⲈ, *he.*

ⲚⲈ ⲀⲤ·
ⲚⲈ Ⲁ· ⟩ ⲦⲀⲔⲞ ⲠⲈ,   ⲚⲈ ⲀⲤ·
ⲚⲈ ⲀⲢⲈ· ⟩   ⲚⲈ Ⲁ·
ⲚⲈ ⲀⲢⲈ· ⟩ ⲦⲀⲔⲞ ⲠⲈ, *she.*

Plural.

Coptic.	Sahidic.
ⲚⲈ ⲀⲚ-ⲦⲀⲔⲞ ⲠⲈ,	ⲚⲈ ⲀⲚ-ⲦⲀⲔⲞ ⲠⲈ, *we.*
ⲚⲈ ⲀⲢⲈⲦⲈⲚ-ⲦⲀⲔⲞ ⲠⲈ,	ⲚⲈ ⲀⲦⲈⲦⲚ̄-ⲦⲀⲔⲞ ⲠⲈ, *ye.*
ⲚⲈ ⲀⲨ-ⲦⲀⲔⲞ ⲠⲈ,	ⲚⲈ ⲀⲨ-ⲦⲀⲔⲞ ⲠⲈ, *they.*

The Present Tense Indefinite.

Singular.

Coptic.	Sahidic.	Bashmuric.
ϢⲀⲒ-ⲦⲀⲔⲞ,	ϢⲀⲒ-ⲦⲀⲔⲞ,	ϢⲀⲒ-ⲦⲀⲔⲞ, *I am.*
ϢⲀⲔ-ⲦⲀⲔⲞ,	ϢⲀⲔ-ⲦⲀⲔⲞ,	ϢⲀⲔ-ⲦⲀⲔⲞ, *thou,* m.
ϢⲀⲢⲈ-ⲦⲀⲔⲞ,	ϢⲀⲢⲈ-ⲦⲀⲔⲞ,	ϢⲀⲖⲈ-ⲦⲀⲔⲞ, *thou,* f.

ϢⲀϤ· ⟩ ⲦⲀⲔⲞ,   ϢⲀϤ· ⟩ ⲦⲀⲔⲞ,   ϢⲀϤ· ⟩ ⲦⲀⲔⲞ, *he.*
ϢⲀⲢⲈ· ⟩   ϢⲀⲢⲈ· ⟩   ϢⲀⲖⲈ· ⟩

ϢⲀⲤ· ⟩ ⲦⲀⲔⲞ,   ϢⲀⲤ· ⟩ ⲦⲀⲔⲞ,   ϢⲀⲤ· ⟩ ⲦⲀⲔⲞ, *she.*
ϢⲀⲢⲈ· ⟩   ϢⲀⲢⲈ· ⟩   ϢⲀⲖⲈ· ⟩

Plural.

ϢⲀⲚ-ⲦⲀⲔⲞ,	ϢⲀⲚ-ⲦⲀⲔⲞ,	ϢⲀⲚ-ⲦⲀⲔⲞ, *we.*
ϢⲀⲢⲈⲦⲈⲚ-ⲦⲀⲔⲞ,	ϢⲀⲦⲈⲦⲚ̄-ⲦⲀⲔⲞ,	ϢⲀⲦⲈⲦⲈⲚ-ⲦⲀⲔⲞ, *ye.*

ϢⲀⲨ· ⟩ ⲦⲀⲔⲞ,   ϢⲀⲨ· ⟩ ⲦⲀⲔⲞ,   ϢⲀⲨ· ⟩ ⲦⲀⲔⲞ, *they.*
ϢⲀⲢⲈ· ⟩   ϢⲀⲢⲈ· ⟩   ϢⲀⲖⲈ· ⟩

The Imperfect Tense Indefinite.

Singular.

Coptic.	Sahidic.
ⲚⲈ ⲰⲀⲒ-ⲦⲀⲔⲞ ⲠⲈ,	ⲚⲈ ⲰⲀⲒ-ⲦⲀⲔⲞ ⲠⲈ, *I was.*
ⲚⲈ ⲰⲀⲔ-ⲦⲀⲔⲞ ⲠⲈ,	ⲚⲈ ⲰⲀⲔ-ⲦⲀⲔⲞ ⲠⲈ, *thou,* m.
ⲚⲈ ⲰⲀⲢⲈ-ⲦⲀⲔⲞ ⲠⲈ,	ⲚⲈ ⲰⲀⲢⲈ-ⲦⲀⲔⲞ ⲠⲈ, *thou,* f.

ⲚⲈ ⲰⲀϤ- }
ⲚⲈ ⲰⲀⲢⲈ-} ⲦⲀⲔⲞ. ⲠⲈ,   ⲚⲈ ⲰⲀϤ- } ⲚⲈ ⲰⲀⲢⲈ-} ⲦⲀⲔⲞ ⲠⲈ, *he.*

ⲚⲈ ⲰⲀⲤ- }
ⲚⲈ ⲰⲀⲢⲈ-} ⲦⲀⲔⲞ ⲠⲈ,   ⲚⲈ ⲰⲀⲤ- } ⲚⲈ ⲰⲀⲢⲈ-} ⲦⲀⲔⲞ ⲠⲈ, *she.*

Plural.

ⲚⲈ ⲰⲀⲚ-ⲦⲀⲔⲞ ⲠⲈ,	ⲚⲈ ⲰⲀⲚ-ⲦⲀⲔⲞ ⲠⲈ, *we.*
ⲚⲈ ⲰⲀⲢⲈⲦⲈⲚ-ⲦⲀⲔⲞ ⲠⲈ,	ⲚⲈ ⲰⲀⲦⲈⲦⲚ̄-ⲦⲀⲔⲞ ⲠⲈ, *ye.*

ⲚⲈ ⲰⲀⲨ- }
ⲚⲈ ⲰⲀⲢⲈ-} ⲦⲀⲔⲞ ⲠⲈ,   ⲚⲈ ⲰⲀⲨ- } ⲚⲈ ⲰⲀⲢⲈ-} ⲦⲀⲔⲞ ⲠⲈ, *they.*

Singular.

Bashmuric.

ⲚⲈ ⲰⲀⲒ-ⲦⲀⲔⲞ ⲠⲈ, *I was.*

ⲚⲈ ⲰⲀⲔ-ⲦⲀⲔⲞ ⲠⲈ, *thou,* m.

ⲚⲈ ⲰⲀⲖⲈ-ⲦⲀⲔⲞ ⲠⲈ, *thou,* f.

ⲚⲈ ⲰⲀϤ- }
ⲚⲈ ⲰⲀⲖⲈ-} ⲦⲀⲔⲞ ⲠⲈ, *he.*

ⲚⲈ ⲰⲀⲤ- }
ⲚⲈ ⲰⲀⲖⲈ-} ⲦⲀⲔⲞ ⲠⲈ, *she.*

Plural.

ⲚⲈ ⲰⲀⲚ-ⲦⲀⲔⲞ ⲠⲈ, *we.*

ⲚⲈ ⲰⲀⲦⲈⲦⲈⲚ-ⲦⲀⲔⲞ ⲠⲈ, *ye.*

ⲚⲈ ⲰⲀⲨ- }
ⲚⲈ ⲰⲀⲢⲈ-} ⲦⲀⲔⲞ ⲠⲈ, *they.*

8*

The 1st Future Tense.

Singular.

Coptic.	Sahidic.	Bashmuric.	
ⲧⲛⲁ-ⲧⲁⲕⲟ,	ⲧⲛⲁ-ⲧⲁⲕⲟ,	ⲧⲛⲁ, ⲧⲛⲉ-ⲧⲁⲕⲟ,	*I shall.*
ⲭⲛⲁ-ⲧⲁⲕⲟ,	ⲕⲛⲁ-ⲧⲁⲕⲟ,	ⲕⲛⲉ-ⲧⲁⲕⲟ,	*thou,* m.
ⲧⲉⲛⲁ-ⲧⲁⲕⲟ,	ⲧⲉⲛⲁ-ⲧⲁⲕⲟ,		*thou,* f.
ⳓⲛⲁ-ⲧⲁⲕⲟ,	ⳓⲛⲁ-ⲧⲁⲕⲟ,	ⳓⲛⲉ-ⲧⲁⲕⲟ,	*he.*
ⲥⲛⲁ-ⲧⲁⲕⲟ,	ⲥⲛⲁ-ⲧⲁⲕⲟ,	ⲥⲛⲉ-ⲧⲁⲕⲟ,	*she.*

Plural.

Coptic.	Sahidic.	Bashmuric.	
ⲧⲉⲛⲛⲁ-ⲧⲁⲕⲟ,	ⲧⲉⲛⲛⲁ- / ⲧⲉⲛⲁ- } ⲧⲁⲕⲟ,	ⲧⲉⲛⲛⲁ- / or / ⲧⲉⲛⲛⲉ- } ⲧⲁⲕⲟ,	*we.*
ⲧⲉⲧⲉⲛⲛⲁ-ⲧⲁⲕⲟ,	ⲧⲉⲧ̄ⲛⲁ- / ⲧⲉⲧ̄ⲁ- } ⲧⲁⲕⲟ,		*ye.*
ⲥⲉⲛⲁ-ⲧⲁⲕⲟ,	ⲥⲉⲛⲁ-ⲧⲁⲕⲟ,	ⲥⲉⲛⲉ-ⲧⲁⲕⲟ,	*they.*

The 2nd Future Tense.

Singular.

Coptic.	Sahidic.	Bashmuric.	
ⲉⲓⲛⲁ-ⲧⲁⲕⲟ,	ⲉⲓⲛⲁ-ⲧⲁⲕⲟ,	ⲁⲓⲛⲁ- / or / ⲁⲓⲛⲉ- } ⲧⲁⲕⲟ,	*I shall.*
ⲉⲕⲛⲁ-ⲧⲁⲕⲟ,	ⲉⲕⲛⲁ-ⲧⲁⲕⲟ,	ⲁⲕⲛⲁ-ⲧⲁⲕⲟ,	*thou,* m.
ⲉⲣⲉⲛⲁ-ⲧⲁⲕⲟ,	ⲉⲣⲉⲛⲁ-ⲧⲁⲕⲟ,	ⲁⲣⲉⲛⲁ-ⲧⲁⲕⲟ,	*thou,* f.
ⲉⳓⲛⲁ- / ⲉⲣⲉⲛⲁ- } ⲧⲁⲕⲟ,	ⲉⳓⲛⲁ- / ⲉⲣⲉⲛⲁ- } ⲧⲁⲕⲟ,	ⲁⳓⲛⲁ- / ⲁⲣⲉⲛⲁ- } ⲧⲁⲕⲟ,	*he.*
ⲉⲥⲛⲁ- / ⲉⲣⲉⲛⲁ } ⲧⲁⲕⲟ,	ⲉⲥⲛⲁ- / ⲉⲣⲉⲛⲁ- } ⲧⲁⲕⲟ,	ⲁⲥⲛⲁ- / ⲁⲣⲉⲛⲁ- } ⲧⲁⲕⲟ,	*she.*

Plural.

Coptic.	Sahidic.	Bashmuric.
ENNA-TAKO,	ENNA- ÑNA- } TAKO,	ANNA- or ANNE- } TAKO, *we*.
EPETENNA-TAKO,	ETETÑNA- ETETÑA- }TAKO,	APETENNA-TAKO, *ye*.
EYNA- OYNA- } TAKO,	EYNA- OYNA- } TAKO,	EYNA-TAKO, *they*.

The 3rd Future Tense.

Singular.

Coptic.	Sahidic.	Bashmuric.
EIÈ-TAKO,	EIE-TAKO,	EIE-TAKO, *I shall*.
EKÈ-TAKO,	EKE-TAKO,	EKE-TAKO, *thou*, m.
EPÈ-TAKO,	EPE-TAKO,	EPE-TAKO, *thou*, f.
EQÈ- EPÈ- } TAKO,	EQE- EPE- } TAKO,	EQE- EPE- } TAKO, *he*.
ECÈ- EPÈ- } TAKO,	ECE- EPE- } TAKO,	ECE- EPE- } TAKO, *she*.

Plural.

ENÈ-TAKO,	ENE-TAKO,	ENE-TAKO, *we*.
EPETENÈ-TAKO,	ETETÑE-TAKO,	ETETNE-TAKO, *ye*.
EYÈ- EPÈ- } TAKO,	EYE- EPE- } TAKO,	EYE- EPE- } TAKO, *they*.

The 4th Future Tense.

Singular.

Coptic.	Sahidic.	Bashmuric.	
ⲧⲁ·ⲧⲁⲕⲟ,	ⲧⲁ- ⲧⲁⲣⲓ- } ⲧⲁⲕⲟ,	ⲧⲁ·ⲧⲁⲕⲟ,	*I shall.*
	ⲧⲁⲣⲉⲕ·ⲧⲁⲕⲟ,		*thou*, m.
ⲧⲉⲣⲁ·ⲧⲁⲕⲟ,	ⲧⲉⲣⲁ·ⲧⲁⲕⲟ,	ⲧⲉⲣⲁ·ⲧⲁⲕⲟ,	*thou*, f.
	ⲧⲁⲣⲉϥ·ⲧⲁⲕⲟ,		*he.*
	ⲧⲁⲣⲉⲥ·ⲧⲁⲕⲟ,	•	*she.*

Plural.

ⲧⲁⲣⲛ̄·ⲧⲁⲕⲟ,		*we.*
ⲧⲁⲣⲉⲧⲛ̄·ⲧⲁⲕⲟ,	ⲧⲁⲗⲉⲧⲉⲛ·ⲧⲁⲕⲟ,	*ye.*
ⲧⲁⲣⲟⲩ·ⲧⲁⲕⲟ,		*they.*

The Imperfect Future.

Singular.

Coptic.	Sahidic.	Bashmuric.	
ⲛⲁⲓⲛⲁ·ⲧⲁⲕⲟ,	ⲛⲉⲓⲛⲁ·ⲧⲁⲕⲟ,	ⲛⲁⲓⲛⲉ- or ⲛⲁⲓⲛⲁ- } ⲧⲁⲕⲟ,	*I should.*
ⲛⲁⲕⲛⲁ·ⲧⲁⲕⲟ,	ⲛⲉⲕⲛⲁ·ⲧⲁⲕⲟ,	ⲛⲁⲕⲛⲉ·ⲧⲁⲕⲟ,	*thou*, m.
ⲛⲁⲣⲉⲛⲁ·ⲧⲁⲕⲟ,	ⲛⲉⲣⲉⲛⲁ·ⲧⲁⲕⲟ,	ⲛⲁⲣⲉⲛⲉ·ⲧⲁⲕⲟ,	*thou*, f.
ⲛⲁϥⲛⲁ- ⲛⲁⲣⲉⲛⲁ- } ⲧⲁⲕⲟ,	ⲛⲉϥⲛⲁ- ⲛⲉⲣⲉⲛⲁ- } ⲧⲁⲕⲟ,	ⲛⲁϥⲛⲉ- ⲛⲁⲣⲉⲛⲉ- } ⲧⲁⲕⲟ,	*he.*
ⲛⲁⲥⲛⲁ- ⲛⲁⲣⲉⲛⲁ- } ⲧⲁⲕⲟ,	ⲛⲉⲥⲛⲁ- ⲛⲉⲣⲉⲛⲁ- } ⲧⲁⲕⲟ,	ⲛⲁⲥⲛⲉ· ⲛⲁⲣⲉⲛⲉ, } ⲧⲁⲕⲟ,	*she.*

Plural.

Coptic.	Sahidic.	Bashmuric.	
NANNA-TAKO,	NENNA-TAKO,	NANNE-TAKO,	*we.*
NAPETENNA-TAKO,	NETETÑA-TAKO,	NAPETENNE-TAKO,	*ye.*
NAYNA- ⎫	NEYNA- ⎫	NEYNE- ⎫	
NAPENA- ⎭ TAKO,	NEPENA- ⎭ TAKO,	NAPENE- ⎭ TAKO, *they.*	

The Subjunctive Mood.

Singular.

Coptic.	Sahidic.	Bashmuric.	
ÑTA-TAKO,	ÑTA-TAKO,	ÑTA-TAKO,	*that I.*
ÑTEK-TAKO,	ÑΓ-TAKO,	ÑΓ-TAKO,	*thou,* m.
ÑTE-TAKO,	ÑTE-TAKO,	ÑTE-TAKO,	*thou,* f.
ÑTEϥ- ⎫ TAKO,	ÑEϥ, Nϥ̄ ⎫ TAKO,	ÑEϥ, Nϥ̄ ⎫ TAKO, *he.*	
ÑTE- ⎭	ÑTE- ⎭	ÑTE- ⎭	
ÑTEC- ⎫ TAKO,	ÑC- ⎫ TAKO,	ÑEC- NC̄- ⎫ TAKO, *she.*	
ÑTE- ⎭	ÑTE- ⎭	ÑTE- ⎭	

Plural.

Coptic.	Sahidic.	Bashmuric.	
ÑTEN-TAKO,	ÑTÑ-TAKO,	ÑTÑ-TAKO,	*we.*
ÑTETEN-TAKO,	ÑTETÑ-TAKO,	ÑTETÑ-TAKO,	*ye.*
ÑTOY- ⎫ TAKO,	ÑCE- ⎫ TAKO,	ÑCE- ⎫ TAKO, *they.*	
ÑTE- ⎭	ÑTE- ⎭	ÑTE- ⎭	

The Optative Mood.

Singular.

Coptic.	Sahidic.	Bashmuric.	
ⲙⲁⲣⲓ-ⲧⲁⲕⲟ,	ⲙⲁⲣⲓ-ⲧⲁⲕⲟ,	ⲙⲁⲗⲓ-ⲧⲁⲕⲟ,	*I may.*
ⲙⲁⲣⲉⲕ-ⲧⲁⲕⲟ,	ⲙⲁⲣⲃⲕ-ⲧⲁⲕⲟ,	ⲙⲁⲗⲉⲕ-ⲧⲁⲕⲟ,	*thou,* m.
ⲙⲁⲣⲉ-ⲧⲁⲕⲟ,	ⲙⲁⲣⲉ-ⲧⲁⲕⲟ,	ⲙⲁⲗⲉ-ⲧⲁⲕⲟ,	*thou,* f.
ⲙⲁⲣⲉϥ-⎫ ⲧⲁⲕⲟ, ⲙⲁⲣⲉ-⎭	ⲙⲁⲣⲉϥ-⎫ ⲧⲁⲕⲟ, ⲙⲁⲣⲉ-⎭	ⲙⲁⲗⲉϥ-⎫ ⲧⲁⲕⲟ, ⲙⲁⲗⲉ-⎭	*he.*
ⲙⲁⲣⲉⲥ-⎫ ⲧⲁⲕⲟ, ⲙⲁⲣⲉ-⎭	ⲙⲁⲣⲉⲥ-⎫ ⲧⲁⲕⲟ, ⲙⲁⲣⲉ-⎭	ⲙⲁⲗⲉⲥ-⎫ ⲧⲁⲕⲟ, ⲙⲁⲗⲉ-⎭	*she.*

Plural.

ⲙⲁⲣⲉⲛ-ⲧⲁⲕⲟ,	ⲙⲁⲣⲛ̄-ⲧⲁⲕⲟ,	ⲙⲁⲗⲉⲛ-ⲧⲁⲕⲟ,	*we.*
ⲙⲁⲣⲉⲧⲉⲛ-ⲧⲁⲕⲟ,	ⲙⲁⲣⲉⲧⲛ̄-ⲧⲁⲕⲟ,	ⲙⲁⲗⲉⲧⲉⲛ-ⲧⲁⲕⲟ,	*ye.*
ⲙⲁⲣⲟⲩ-⎫ ⲧⲁⲕⲟ, ⲙⲁⲣⲉ-⎭	ⲙⲁⲣⲟⲩ-⎫ ⲧⲁⲕⲟ, ⲙⲁⲣⲉ-⎭	ⲙⲁⲗⲟⲩ-⎫ ⲧⲁⲕⲟ, ⲙⲁⲗⲉ-⎭	*they.*

The Imperative Mood.

Singular and Plural.

ⲁ̀-ⲧⲁⲕⲟ,
ⲁ̀ⲣⲓ-ⲧⲁⲕⲟ, ⎫ *destroy.*
ⲙⲁ-ⲧⲁⲕⲟ,
ⲧⲁⲕⲟ,

The Infinitive Mood.

ⲉ̀-ⲧⲁⲕⲟ, ⎫
ⲛ̀-ⲧⲁⲕⲟ, ⎬ *to destroy.*
ⲧⲁⲕⲟ,

Participles.

Coptic.	Sahidic.	Bashmuric.
ϫⲓⲛ,	ϭⲓⲛ,	ϫⲓⲛ,
ⲡⲁϫⲓⲛ or ⲡϫⲓⲛⲧⲁ,	ⲡⲁϭⲓⲛ,	ⲡⲁϫⲓⲛ,
ⲡⲉⲕϫⲓⲛ,	ⲡⲉⲕϭⲓⲛ,	ⲡⲉⲕϫⲓⲛ,
ⲡⲉϥϫⲓⲛ, &c.	ⲡⲉϥϭⲓⲛ, &c.	ⲡⲉϥϫⲓⲛ, &c.

That these are participles is evident from the Arabic, with which they correspond.

Participles.

26. The participles are formed by ⲉ, ⲉⲧ or ⲉⲑ, before the prefixes to the verbs. There are also some peculiar forms of participles, which end in ⲛⲟⲩⲧ, Copt. ⲏⲩⲧ, Sah. ⲱⲟⲩⲧ, Copt. ⲟⲟⲩⲧ, Sah. and ⲗⲟⲩⲧ, Bash. as ⲧⲟⲩⲃⲛⲟⲩⲧ, Copt. ⲙⲱⲟⲩⲧ, Copt. and ⲙⲁⲟⲩⲧ, Bash.

Verbs united with particles expressive of time.

The particles ⲉⲧⲉ, Copt. ⲛⲧⲉⲣⲉ, Sah. *when.*

Singular.

Coptic.	Sahidic.	Bashmuric.
ⲉⲧⲁⲓ,	ⲛⲧⲉⲣⲓ, ⲛⲧⲉⲣⲉⲓ,	ⲉⲧⲁⲓ, ⲛⲧⲉⲗⲉⲓ,
ⲉⲧⲁⲕ,	ⲛⲧⲉⲣⲉⲕ,	
ⲉⲧⲁⲣⲉ,	ⲛⲧⲉⲣⲉ,	ⲉⲧⲁϥ, ⲛⲧⲉⲗⲉϥ,
ⲉⲧⲁϥ ⟩ ⲉⲧⲁⲣⲉ,	ⲛⲧⲉⲣⲉϥ, ⟩ ⲛⲧⲉⲣⲉ,	
ⲉⲧⲁⲥ ⟨	ⲛⲧⲉⲣⲉⲥ, ⟨	

Plural.

Coptic.	Sahidic.	Bashmuric.
ⲈⲦⲀⲚ,	ⲚⲦⲈⲣⲈⲚ,	ⲈⲦⲀⲚ, ⲚⲦⲈⲖⲈⲚ,'
ⲈⲦⲀⲣⲈⲦⲈⲚ,	ⲚⲦⲈⲣⲈⲦⲚ̄,	ⲈⲦⲀⲦⲈⲦⲈⲚ, ⲚⲦⲈⲖⲈⲦⲈⲚ,
ⲈⲦⲀⲨ, ⲈⲦⲀⲣⲈ,	ⲚⲦⲈⲣⲞⲨ,	ⲚⲦⲈⲖⲞⲨ, ⲚⲦⲈⲖⲈⲨ.

Verbs with the particles ⲰⲀⲦⲈ, Copt. ⲰⲀⲚⲦⲈ, Sah. until.

Singular.

Coptic.	Sahidic.	Bashmuric.
ⲰⲀⲦ̀,	ⲰⲀⲚⲦⲈⲒ, ⲰⲀⲚⲦ̀,	ⲰⲀⲚⲦⲈⲒ,
ⲰⲀⲦⲈⲔ,	ⲰⲀⲚⲦⲔ̄,	
ⲰⲀⲦⲈ,	ⲰⲀⲚⲦⲈ,	
ⲰⲀⲦⲈⳊ,} ⲰⲀⲦⲈ,	ⲰⲀⲚⲦⳊ,} ⲰⲀⲚⲦⲈ,	ⲰⲀⲚⲦⲈⳊ,
ⲰⲀⲦⲈⲤ,	ⲰⲀⲚⲦⲤ̄,	

Plural.

ⲰⲀⲦⲈⲚ,	ⲰⲀⲚⲦⲚ̄,	
ⲰⲀⲦⲈⲦⲈⲚ,	ⲰⲀⲚⲦⲈⲦⲚ̄,	
ⲰⲀⲦⲞⲨ, ⲰⲀⲦⲈ,	ⲰⲀⲚⲦⲞⲨ, ⲰⲀⲚⲦⲈ,	ⲰⲀⲚⲦⲞⲨ.

Verbs with the particle ⲈⲚⲈ or ⲈⲚ, if.

Singular.

Coptic.	Sahidic.
ⲈⲚⲀⲒ, ⲈⲚⲈⲀⲒ ⲠⲈ,	ⲈⲚⲈⲒ ⲠⲈ,
ⲈⲚⲀⲔ, ⲈⲚⲈⲀⲔ ⲠⲈ,	ⲈⲚⲈⲔ ⲠⲈ,
ⲈⲚⲀⲣⲈ ⲠⲈ,	ⲈⲚⲈⲣⲈ ⲠⲈ,
ⲈⲚⲀⳊ, ⲈⲚⲀⲣⲈ ⲠⲈ,	ⲈⲚⲈⳊ,} ⲈⲚⲈⲣⲈ ⲠⲈ,
ⲈⲚⲀⲤ, ⲈⲚⲈ Ⲁ ⲠⲈ,	ⲈⲚⲈⲤ,

Plural.

ⲈⲚⲀⲚ ⲠⲈ,	ⲈⲚⲈⲚ ⲠⲈ,
ⲈⲚⲀⲣⲈⲦⲈⲚ ⲠⲈ,	ⲈⲚⲈⲦⲈⲦⲚ̄ ⲠⲈ,
ⲈⲚⲀⲨ, ⲈⲚⲀⲣⲈ ⲠⲈ,	ⲈⲚⲈⲨ, ⲈⲚⲈⲣⲈ ⲠⲈ.

Verbs with the particle ⲱⲁⲛ, if, when.

Singular.

Coptic.	Sahidic.	Bashmuric.
ⲁⲓⲱⲁⲛ,	ⲉⲓⲱⲁⲛ,	
ⲁⲕⲱⲁⲛ,	ⲉⲕⲱⲁⲛ,	
ⲁⲣⲉⲱⲁⲛ,	ⲉⲣⲱⲁⲛ,	ⲁⲗⲉⲱⲁⲛ,
ⲁϥⲱⲁⲛ,⎱ ⲁⲣⲉⲱⲁⲛ,	ⲉϥⲱⲁⲛ,⎱ ⲉⲣⲱⲁⲛ,	
ⲁⲥⲱⲁⲛ,⎰	ⲉⲥⲱⲁⲛ,⎰	

Plural.

ⲁⲛⲱⲁⲛ,	ⲉⲛⲱⲁⲛ,
ⲁⲣⲉⲧⲉⲛⲱⲁⲛ,	ⲉⲧⲉⲧⲛ̄ⲱⲁⲛ,
ⲁⲩⲱⲁⲛ, ⲁⲣⲉⲱⲁⲛ,	ⲉⲩⲱⲁⲛ, ⲉⲣⲱⲁⲛ.

Verbs with the particle ⲙ̀ⲡⲁⲧⲉ, before.

Singular.

Coptic.	Sahidic.
ⲙ̀ⲡⲁϯ,	ⲙ̄ⲡⲁϯ,
ⲙ̀ⲡⲁⲧⲉⲕ,	ⲙ̄ⲡⲁⲧⲕ̄,
ⲙ̀ⲡⲁⲧⲉ,	ⲙ̄ⲡⲁⲧⲉ,
ⲙ̀ⲡⲁⲧⲉϥ,⎱ ⲙ̀ⲡⲁⲧⲉ,	ⲙ̄ⲡⲁⲧϥ̄,⎱ ⲙ̄ⲡⲁⲧⲉ,
ⲙ̀ⲡⲁⲧⲉⲥ,⎰	ⲙ̄ⲡⲁⲧⲥ̄,⎰

Plural.

ⲙ̀ⲡⲁⲧⲉⲛ,	ⲙ̄ⲡⲁⲧⲛ̄,
ⲙ̀ⲡⲁⲧⲉⲧⲉⲛ,	ⲙ̄ⲡⲁⲧⲉⲧⲛ̄,
ⲙ̀ⲡⲁⲧⲟⲩ, ⲙ̀ⲡⲁⲧⲉ,	ⲙ̄ⲡⲁⲧⲟⲩ, ⲙ̄ⲡⲁⲧⲉ.

9*

The Tenses.

The 1st Present Tense.

27. The 1st Present Tense is formed by adding the following prefixes to the root, ϯ *I am,* ⲕ, or ⲭ Copt. before ⲗ, ⲙ, ⲛ, ⲟⲩ, or ⲣ, *thou art,* m.: ⲧⲉ *thou art,* f.: ϥ, *he is;* ⲥ, *she is;* ⲧⲉⲛ, C. ⲧⲉⲛ, ⲧⲛ̄, S. *we are;* ⲧⲉⲧⲉⲛ, C. ⲧⲉⲧⲉⲛ, or ⲧⲉⲧⲛ̄, S. *ye are;* ⲥⲉ, *they are.* Thus, ϯⲥⲱⲟⲩⲛ ⲙ̄ⲡⲉⲕϩⲟϫϩⲉϫ, *I know thy tribulation,* Rev. II, 9. ϥⲟ ⲛ̄ⲛⲟⲉⲓⲕ, *is an adulterer,* Luke XVI, 18. Sah. ϫⲉ ϥ ⲛ̄ⲙⲁⲩ *that he is there.* John XII, 9. Sah.

The 2nd Present Tense.

28. The 2nd Present Tense has the following prefixes, as, ⲉⲓ, *I am;* ⲉⲕ, *thou art,* m. ⲉⲣⲉ, *thou art,* f.; ⲉϥ or ⲉⲣⲉ, *he is;* ⲉⲥ or ⲉⲣⲉ, *she is;* ⲉⲛ, Copt. ⲉⲛ or ⲛ̄, Sah. *we are;* ⲉⲧⲉⲧⲉⲛ, ⲉⲧⲉⲧⲛ̄, *ye are;* ⲉⲩ, ⲟⲩ or ⲉⲣⲉ, *they are.*

29. The second person f. is ⲉⲣⲉ, (Bash. ⲉⲗⲉ,) but before vowels it is written ⲉⲣ, and occasionally, ⲉⲣⲁ, as ⲉⲣⲉⲓⲣⲉ, *thou doest;* S. Ming. 258. ⲉⲣⲟⲩⲉϣ, *thou wilt;* S. Zoeg. p. 509. Sometimes it is written ⲡ̄ ⲡ̄ⲗⲟⲃⲉ, *thou art mad;* S. Acts XII, 15. The Bash. corresponds as ⲉⲗⲥⲟⲟⲩⲛ, *thou knowest,* Zoeg. 151. ⲉⲣⲉ the prefix of the third persons sing. and plur. is always separated from the verb, by the noun or some other word, as ⲉⲣⲉ ⲡⲟⲩϩⲏⲧ ⲙⲟⲕϩ, *their heart was afflicted,* Matt. XXVI, 22. ⲉⲣⲉ ⲟⲩⲛⲓϣϯ ⲅⲁⲣ ⲛ̄ϩⲟϫϩⲉϫ ϣⲱⲡⲓ, *for great tribulation shall be.* Matt. XXIV, 21.

30. The Prefix ⲉⲣⲉ appears to be almost indefinite as to time.

31. The third person plural is ⲉⲩ, but after ⲧ it is written ⲟⲩ, as ⲫⲏⲉⲧ ⲟⲩⲙⲟⲩϯ ⲉⲣⲟϥ, *when they call.* Matt. XXVII, 22.

ⲉ̀ is the sign of the participle present as ⲉ̀ⲥⲱ ⲉ̀ ⲁⲛⲟⲕ ⲟⲩⲥϩⲓⲙⲓ ⲛ̀ⲥⲁⲙⲁⲣⲓⲧⲏⲥ, *to drink, I being* (οὖσα) *a woman of Samaria*, John IV, 9. ⲉ ⲁⲛⲟⲛ ϩⲉⲛⲣⲱⲙⲉ ⲛ̄ϩⲣⲱⲙⲁⲓⲟⲥ. ⲉ ⲙⲛ̄ ⲛⲟⲃⲉ ⲉⲣⲟⲛ, *we being men Romans, not being a fault in us.* Sah. Acts XVI, 37.

32. The following examples will serve to show the prefixes of the 2nd present tense, as, ⲁⲛⲟⲕ ⲇⲉ ⲉⲓ ϩⲛ̄ ⲧⲉⲧⲛ̄ⲙⲏⲧⲉ, *but I am among you*, Luke XXII, 27. Sah. ⲉⲕ ϩⲓ ⲧⲉϩⲓⲏ ⲛⲙ̄ⲙⲁϥ, *thou art in the way with him.* Matt. V, 25. Sah. ⲉϥ ϩⲛ̄ ⲧⲡⲉ, *is in heaven.* Matt. VI, 10. Sahidic.

33. The prefixes of this tense also express the present participle, as, ⲁϥⲛⲁⲩ ⲉ̀ⲟⲩⲣⲱⲙⲓ ⲉϥϩⲉⲙⲥⲓ, *he saw a man sitting*, Matt. IX, 9. ⲛⲓⲃ ⲇⲉ ⲛⲁⲩϯϩⲟ ⲉ̀ⲣⲟϥ ⲡⲉ ⲉⲩⲭⲱⲙ̀ⲙⲟⲥ, *and the devils besought him saying*, Matt. VIII, 31.

Imperfect Tense.

34. The Imperfect Tense is formed by prefixing the following particles to the root, ⲛⲁⲓ. *I was;* ⲛⲁⲕ, *thou wast*, m. ⲛⲁⲣⲉ, *thou wast*, f. ⲛⲁϥ or ⲛⲁⲣⲉ, *he was;* ⲛⲁⲥ or ⲛⲁⲣⲉ, *she was.* Plur. ⲛⲁⲛ, *we were;* ⲛⲁⲣⲉⲧⲉⲛ, *ye were;* ⲛⲁⲩ or ⲛⲁⲣⲉ, *they were.* The Sahidic is ⲛⲉⲓ, ⲛⲉⲕ, ⲛⲉⲣⲉ, ⲛⲉϥ or ⲛⲉⲣⲉ, ⲛⲉⲥ or ⲛⲉⲣⲉ. Plur. ⲛⲉⲛ, ⲛⲉⲧⲉⲧⲛ̄, ⲛⲉⲩ or ⲛⲉⲣⲉ. Sometimes the Sahidic is written without the ⲉ, as, ⲛϥ, ⲛⲥ̄, ⲛⲛ̄, etc.

35. The Imperfect Tense has ⲡⲉ frequently following the verb, as, ⲟⲩⲟⲅ ⲛⲁ϶ⲧⲥⲃⲱ ⲡⲉ, *and taught*, John VII, 14. ⲛⲉϥϣⲟⲟⲡ ⲡⲉ ⲛ϶ⲓ ⲡⲗⲟⲅⲟⲥ, *the word was*, John I, 1. Sah. ⲛⲁϥⲃⲱⲛⲧ ⲇⲉ ⲡⲉ ⲡⲓⲡⲁⲥⲭⲁ, *and the Passover was near*, John XI, 55. ⲇⲉ ⲛⲉϥⲁⲅϩⲣⲁⲧ϶ ⲡⲉ ⲛ̄ⲃⲟⲗ, *but he stood without*, John XVII, 16 Sah.

ⲛⲁⲣⲉ or ⲛⲉⲣⲉ Sah. is generally separated from the verb, and usually occurs before the nominative preceding it, as ⲛⲁⲣⲉ ⲛⲓⲙⲁⲑⲏⲧⲏⲥ ⲑⲟⲩⲏⲧ, *the disciples were assembled*, John XX, 19. S. ⲛⲉⲣⲉ ⲡⲉϥⲛⲟ϶ ⲇⲉ ⲛ̄ϣⲏⲣⲉ ϩⲛ̄ ⲧⲥⲱϣⲉ, *and his greater son was in the field*, Luke XXII, 25. Sah. The Bashmuric will probably be written occasionally ⲛⲁⲗⲉ.

The 1st Perfect Tense.

36. The Prefixes to the 1st Perfect Tense are ⲁⲓ, *I;* ⲁⲕ, *thou,* m. ⲁⲣⲉ or ⲁⲣ, *thou,* f. ⲁϥ or ⲁ̀, *he;* ⲁⲥ or ⲁ̀, *she;* Plur. ⲁⲛ, *we;* ⲁⲣⲉⲧⲉⲛ, ⲁⲧⲉⲧⲛ̄, Sahidic, *ye;* ⲁⲩ or ⲁ̀, *they.*

37. When ⲁ occurs in composition it is usually found before the nominative to the verb, as ⲓ̄ⲏ̄ⲥ ⲁ̀ ⲡⲓⲡ̄ⲛ̄ⲁ̄ ⲟⲗϥ, *the spirit took Jesus*, Matt. IV, 1. ⲁ ⲓ̄ⲥ̄ ϫⲟⲟⲥ ⲛⲁϥ, *Jesus said to him.* Sah. Mark XIV, 72. ⲁ ⲛ̄ⲓⲟⲩⲇⲁⲓ ⲧⲱⲟⲩⲛ, *the Jews rose*, Acts XVIII, 12. Sah. ⲛⲏⲉ̀ⲧ ⲁ̀ ⲛⲓⲡⲣⲟⲫⲏⲧⲏⲥ ϫⲟⲧⲟⲩ, *those things which the Prophets said*, Acts XXVI, 22.

38. Although ⲁ is used instead of the Prefixes ⲁϥ, ⲁⲥ and ⲁⲩ, yet it occurs also with them; as, ⲁ̀ ⲧⲁϣⲉⲣⲉ ⲁⲥⲃⲱⲛⲧ ⲉ̀ⲫⲙⲟⲩ, *my daughter hath approached to death*,

Mark. V, 23. ⲁ̀ ⲡⲥⲁⲧⲁⲛⲁⲥ ⲁϥϣⲉⲛⲁϥ ⲉ̀ⲃⲟⲩⲛ ⲉ̀ⲡϩⲏⲧ
ⲛ̄ⲓⲟⲩⲇⲁⲥ, *Satan entered into the heart of Judas.* Luke
XXII, 3. ⲭⲉ ⲁ ϩⲏⲗⲓⲁⲥ ⲟⲩⲱ ⲁϥⲉⲓ, *that Elias hath now
come.* Matt. XVII, 12. Sah.

The 2nd Perfect Tense.

39. The 2nd Perfect Tense is distinguished by ⲉⲧ
Copt. and ⲛ̄ⲧ Sah. being added to the first perfect, in
all the persons, except that the 2 pers. fem. is ⲛ̄ⲧⲁⲣ,
instead of ⲛ̄ⲧⲁⲣⲉ.

40. The ⲛ̄ⲧⲁ, is found in the same position in composition as the ⲁ̀ in the first perfect, thus; ⲛ̄ⲧ ⲁ ⲓ̅ⲥ̅
ⲇⲉ ⲭⲟⲟⲥ ⲉⲧⲃⲉ, *but Jesus spoke concerning,* John XI, 13.
Sah. ⲉⲛⲉ̀ⲙⲓ ⲭⲉ ⲡⲭ̅ⲥ̅ ⲉⲧⲁϥⲧⲱⲛϥ ⲉ̀ⲃⲟⲗϩⲉⲛ ⲛⲏⲉⲧⲙⲱⲟⲩⲧ,
we know that Christ hath risen from the dead. Rom. VI, 9.

41. The Prefixes are often found after the particle
ⲭⲉ, *that,* and sometimes after ⲉⲛⲉ, *if;* and ⲁⲗⲗⲁ, *but.*
But the ⲛ̄ⲧ must not be confounded with ⲛ̄ⲧ, *who, which.*

The Pluperfect Tense.

42. The Pluperfect Tense is formed by adding the
auxiliary verb ⲛⲉ ⲡⲉ to the prefixes of the perfect, as
ⲛⲉ ⲁⲓ ⲡⲉ, *I;* ⲛⲉ ⲁⲕ ⲡⲉ, *thou,* m.; ⲛⲉ ⲁⲣⲉ ⲡⲉ, *thou,* f.;
ⲛⲉ ⲁϥ or ⲁ ⲡⲉ, *he;* ⲛⲉ ⲁⲥ or ⲁ ⲡⲉ, *she;* Plur. ⲛⲉ ⲁⲛ
ⲡⲉ, *we;* ⲛⲉ ⲁⲣⲉⲧⲉⲛ or ⲁⲧⲉⲧⲛ̄, ⲡⲉ, *ye.* S. ⲛⲉ ⲁⲩ or ⲁ
ⲡⲉ, *they;* as, ⲛⲉ ⲁϥⲉⲣϩⲏⲧⲥ ⲛ̀ⲣⲓⲕⲓ ⲡⲉ, *had begun to de-
cline,* Luke IX, 12: ⲛ̄ⲓⲟⲩⲇⲁⲓ ⲛⲉ ⲁⲩⲉⲓ ⲡⲉ ϣⲁ ⲙⲁⲣⲑⲁ,
the Jews had come to Martha, John XI, 19 Sah. ⲛⲉ ⲁⲩ-
ⲛⲁⲩ ⲅⲁⲣ ⲉ̀ⲣⲟϥ ⲧⲏⲣⲟⲩ ⲡⲉ, *for all had seen him,* Mark

VI, 50. This Tense is also found without the ⲡⲉ, as,
ⲒⲎⲤ ⲆⲈ Ⲁϥⲓ ⲉⲃⲟⲗ, *Jesus had gone out*, John V, 13. ⲧⲀⲓ
ⲆⲈ ⲚⲈ ⲀⲥⲟⲩⲀϩⲊ̄ ⲚⲤⲀ ⲡⲀⲩⲗⲟⲥ, *and this had followed
Paul.* Acts XVI, 17. Sah.

The Present Tense Indefinite.

43. This Tense is formed by adding ⲱ, and sometimes
ⲉⲱ in the Sahidic to the Perfect Tense, as ⲱⲀⲓ, *I;*
ⲱⲀⲕ, *thou,* m.; ⲱⲀⲣⲉ or ⲱⲀⲣ, *thou,* f. ⲱⲀⲗⲉ, B. ⲱⲀϥ
or ⲱⲀⲣⲉ, ⲱⲀⲗⲉ, B. *he;* ⲱⲀⲥ or ⲱⲀⲣⲉ, ⲱⲀⲗⲉ, B. *she;*
Plur. ⲱⲀⲚ, *we;* ⲱⲀⲣⲉⲧⲉⲚ, ⲱⲀⲧⲉⲧⲚ̄, S. *ye;* ⲱⲀⲩ or
ⲱⲀⲣⲉ, ⲱⲀⲗⲉ, Bash. *they.*

This Tense sometimes expresses the present, and
sometimes the perfect.

The Imperfect Tense Indefinite.

44. The Imperfect Tense Indefinite is formed from
the preceding by adding ⲚⲈ to it, as ⲟⲩⲟϩ ⲚⲈ ⲱⲀⲩⲤ-
ⲟⲚϩϥ ⲡⲉ, *and they had bound him*, or *he was bound.*
Luke VIII, 29. ⲚⲈ ⲱⲀϥⲟⲩⲱⲙ ⲡⲉ Ⲛⲉⲙ Ⲛⲓⲉⲑⲙⲟⲥ, *he
did eat with the gentiles.* Galat. II, 12.

The 1st Future Tense.

45. The Prefixes to the first Future are ⲚⲀ or ⲚⲈ
Bash. with the Prefixes of the first Present Tense, as,
ϯⲚⲀ, *I;* ⲕ or ⲭⲚⲀ. *thou,* m.; ⲧⲉⲚⲀ. *thou,* f.; ϥⲚⲀ. *he;*
ⲥⲚⲀ, *she;* Plur. ⲧⲉⲚⲚⲀ. ⲧⲉⲚⲀ, Sah. *we;* ⲧⲉⲧⲉⲚⲚⲀ, ⲧⲉ-
ⲧⲚ̄ⲚⲀ, Sah. *ye;* ⲥⲉⲚⲀ, *they;* thus: ⲉⲥⲉ ⲡⲓⲀ̀ⲫⲟⲧ ⲉ̀ⲧⲚⲀ-
ⲥⲟϥ. *to drink the cup which I shall drink?* Matt. XX, 22.

ⲦⲈⲦⲚⲀⲄⲘⲞⲞⲤ ⲄⲰⲦⲦⲎ•ⲨⲦⲚ̄, *ye also shall sit.* Matt. XIX, 28. Sahidic.

The 2nd Future Tense.

46. The characteristics of the second Future are ⲚⲀ or ⲚⲈ Bash. united with the Prefixes of the second Present Tense, ⲈⲒⲚⲀ, *I;* ⲈⲔⲚⲀ, *thou,* m.; ⲈⲢⲈⲚⲀ, *thou,* f.; ⲈϤⲚⲀ or ⲈⲢⲈⲚⲀ, *he;* ⲈⲤⲚⲀ or ⲈⲢⲈⲚⲀ, *she;* Plur. ⲈⲚⲚⲀ or Ⲛ̄ⲚⲀ, Sah. *we;* ⲈⲢⲈⲦⲈⲚⲚⲀ or ⲈⲦⲈⲦⲚ̄ⲚⲀ, ⲈⲦⲈⲦⲚ̄Ⲁ, Sah.*ye;* ⲈⲨⲚⲀ or ⲞⲨⲚⲀ, *they;* thus: ⲈϤⲚⲀⲘⲞⲞϢⲈ Ⲛ̄ⲦⲞⲦϤ Ⲛ̄ⲢⲀⲦϤ, *he will go on foot.* Acts XX, 13. Sah. ϪⲈⲔⲀⲤ ⲄⲰⲦⲦⲎ•ⲨⲦⲚ̄ ⲈⲦⲈⲦⲚⲀⲠⲒⲤⲦⲈⲨⲈ, *that ye might believe.* John XIX, 35. Sah. ⲞⲨⲞⲄ ⲠⲒϢⲖⲞⲖ ⲈⲦ ⲞⲨⲚⲀⲈⲢⲂⲰⲔ, *and the nation that they shall serve,* Acts VII, 7.

47. The second person fem. sing. Sah. occurs thus, ⲈⲢⲚⲀ. These Prefixes do not always express the Future, for instance they express the present participle, ⲠⲈⲦⲢⲞⲤ ⲘⲚ̀ ⲒⲰⲄⲀⲚⲚⲎⲤ ⲈⲨⲚⲀⲂⲰⲔ ⲈⲄⲞⲨⲚ Ⲉ ⲠⲈⲢⲠⲈ, *Peter and John entering into the Temple,* Acts III, 3. Sah. and with ⲄⲒⲚⲀ they express the Subjunctive Mood.

The Coptic has sometimes ⲀⲒⲚⲀ, ⲀⲔⲚⲀ, ⲀⲢⲈⲚⲀ etc. as, ⲄⲀⲢⲀ ⲀϤⲚⲀϪⲈⲘ ⲄⲖⲒ ⲄⲒⲰⲦⲤ, *if he might find any thing upon it,* Mark XI, 13.

The 3rd Future Tense.

48. The Prefixes of the third Future.

The Prefixes of this Tense are ⲈⲒⲈ̀, *I;* ⲈⲔⲈ̀, *thou,* m.; ⲈⲢⲈ̀, *thou,* f.; ⲈϤⲈ̀ or ⲈⲢⲈ̀, *he;* ⲈⲤⲈ̀ or ⲈⲢⲈ̀, *she;* Plur. ⲈⲚⲈ̀, *we;* ⲈⲢⲈⲦⲈⲚⲈ̀, ⲈⲦⲈⲦⲚ̄Ⲉ, Sah. *ye;* ⲈⲨⲈ̀, ⲈⲢⲈ̀, *they;* thus:

10

ⲉⲥⲉⲙⲓⲥⲓ ⲛ̄ⲟⲩϣⲏⲣⲓ ⲉⲩⲉ̀ⲙⲟⲩϯ ⲉ̀ⲡⲉϥⲣⲁⲛ, *she shall bring
forth a son and they shall call his name.* Matt. I, 23. ⲉⲣⲉ̀
ⲡⲓⲣⲱⲙⲓ ⲭⲁ ⲡⲉϥⲓⲱⲧ ⲛⲉⲙ ⲧⲉϥⲙⲁⲩ ⲛ̄ⲥⲱϥ ⲟⲩⲟϩ ⲉϥⲉ̀-
ⲧⲟⲙϥ ⲉ̀ⲧⲉϥⲥϩⲓⲙⲓ, *a man shall leave his father and his
mother, and shall cleave to his wife.* Matt. XIX, 5.

This Tense sometimes expresses the Optative Mood,
as, ⲧⲉⲭⲁⲣⲓⲥ ⲉⲥⲉϣⲱⲡⲉ ⲛⲏ̄ⲙⲁⲛ, *grace be with us,* 2. John
5. Sah. ϫⲉⲕⲁⲥ ⲉⲣⲉ̀ ⲟⲩⲣⲱⲙⲓ ⲛ̀ⲟⲩⲱⲧ ⲙⲟⲩ, *that one man
should die,* John XI, 50.

The 4th Future Tense.

49. The Prefixes to this Tense are very seldom
met with, but we may note a few examples, as, ⲡⲥⲁϩ
ⲧⲁⲟⲩⲁϩⲧ̄ ⲛ̄ⲥⲱⲕ, *Master, I will follow thee.* Matt. VIII,
19. Sah. ⲟⲩⲟϩ ϩⲏⲡⲡⲉ ⲧⲉⲣⲁⲉⲣⲃⲟⲕⲓ, *and behold thou shalt
conceive,* Luke I, 31. ⲧⲉⲣⲁⲛⲁⲩ ⲉ̀ⲡⲱⲟⲩ ⲙ̀ⲫϯ, *thou shalt
see the glory of God.* John XI, 40. ⲧⲁⲣⲛ̄ⲣⲛⲟⲃⲉ ϫⲉ ⲛ̄ⲧ-
ⲛ̄ϣⲟⲟⲡ ⲁⲛ ϩⲁ ⲡⲛⲟⲙⲟⲥ. *shall we sin because we are not
under the law?* Rom. VI, 15. Sah. ϣⲓⲛⲉ ⲧⲁⲣⲉⲧⲛ̄ϭⲓⲛⲉ.
ⲧⲱϩⲙ̄ ⲧⲁⲣⲟⲩⲟⲩⲱⲛ ⲛⲏⲧⲛ̄, *seek, ye shall find; knock,
they shall open to you.* Luke XI, 9. Sah.

The Imperfect Future Tense.

50. This Tense contains the Prefixes to the imperfect, and ⲛⲁ the characteristic of the future, as,
ⲛⲁⲓⲛⲁ, ⲛⲉⲓⲛⲁ, *I;* ⲛⲁⲕⲛⲁ, ⲛⲉⲕⲛⲁ, Sah. *thou,* m.; ⲛⲁⲣⲉⲛⲁ,
ⲛⲉⲣⲉⲛⲁ, Sah. *thou,* f.; etc. often with ⲡⲉ, ⲟⲩⲟϩ ⲑⲁⲓ ⲛⲁⲥ-
ⲛⲁⲙⲟⲩ ⲡⲉ, *and she was about to die,* Luke VIII, 42.
ⲛⲁⲣⲉ ⲡⲓϫⲟⲓ ⲅⲁⲣ ⲛⲁϩⲓⲟⲩⲓ̀ ⲙ̀ⲡⲉϥⲁⲟⲩⲓⲛ ⲉ̀ⲙⲙⲁⲩ, *for*

the ship was to cast out her burden there. Acts XXI, 3.
ⲚⲀⲢⲈⲦⲈⲚⲚⲀⲦⲎⲓⲦⲞⲨ ⲚⲎⲓ ⲠⲈ, *ye would have given them to
me.* Galat. IV, 15. ⲚⲈⲨⲚⲀⲘⲓϢⲈ ⲠⲈ Ⲛ̄ϬⲒ ⲚⲀⲦⲨⲠⲈⲢⲎⲦⲦⲎⲤ,
my servants would fight, John XVIII, 36. Sah.

The Subjunctive Mood.

51. The Prefixes to this Mood are Ⲛ̀ⲦⲀ, *I;* Ⲛ̀ⲦⲈⲔ,
Ⲛ̄ⲅ, Sah. *thou,* m.; Ⲛ̀ⲦⲈ, *thou,* f.; Ⲛ̀ⲦⲈϥ, Ⲛ̀ⲦⲈ, Ⲛϥ̄, ⲚⲈϥ,
Ⲛ̄ⲦⲈ, Sah. *he;* Ⲛ̀ⲦⲈⲤ, Ⲛ̀ⲦⲈ, ⲚⲤ̄, Ⲛ̄ⲦⲈ. Sah. *she;* Plur. Ⲛ̀ⲦⲈⲚ,
Ⲛ̄ⲦⲚ̄, Sah. *we;* Ⲛ̀ⲦⲈⲦⲈⲚ, Ⲛ̄ⲦⲈⲦⲚ̄. Sah. *ye;* Ⲛ̀ⲦⲞⲨ, Ⲛ̀ⲦⲈ, ⲚⲤⲈ,
Ⲛ̄ⲦⲈ, Sah. *they.*

This Mood follows the tense of the verb that precedes it, whether of the present Tense, the Imperfect,
the Perfect, or the Future, as, ⲚⲈⲨⲤⲰⲦⲘ̄ ⲘⲚ̄ ⲈⲦⲈⲤⲘⲎ
Ⲛ̄ⲤⲈⲚⲞⲒ ⲀⲚ, *they heard a voice, but they understood not,*
Sah. Acts IX, 7. ⲤⲈⲚⲀⲠⲀⲢⲀⲆⲒⲆⲞⲨ Ⲙ̄ⲘⲞϥ Ⲉ ⲦⲞⲞⲦⲞⲨ Ⲛ̄Ⲛ̄-
ⲢⲰⲘⲈ Ⲛ̄ⲤⲈⲘⲞⲞⲨⲦϥ̄: *they shall deliver him into the hands
of men, they shall kill him.* Matt. XVII, 22. Sah.

Also ⲈⲦⲢⲈϥⲀⲖⲈ ⲚϥⲌⲘⲞⲞⲤ ⲌⲒⲦⲞⲨⲰⲦϥ, *that he would
ascend and sit with him.* Sah. Acts VIII, 31. ⲈⲐⲢⲞⲨϢⲈ
ⲉ̀ⲃⲞⲨⲚ, *that they went in,* Acts XIV, 1. ⲌⲘ̄ ⲠⲦⲈⲨⲤⲰⲦⲘ̄
ⲈⲢⲞϥ ⲀⲨⲰ Ⲛ̄ⲤⲈⲚⲀⲨ Ⲙ̄ⲘⲀⲈⲒⲚ ⲈⲚⲈϥⲈⲒⲢⲈ Ⲙ̄ⲘⲰⲞⲨ, *when
they heard and saw the miracles which he did.* Acts IX, 6.
Sah. ⲌⲘ̄ ⲠⲦⲢⲀⲰϢ, *when I cry.* Ps. IV, 3. Sah.

After the Particles ⲌⲒⲚⲀ, ϢⲀⲚ, ⲌⲰⲤⲦⲈ, ⲬⲈ, ⲬⲈⲔⲀⲤ,
ⲘⲎⲠⲞⲦⲈ etc., it is the Subjunctive; as, ⲌⲒⲚⲀ Ⲛ̀ⲦⲈⲦⲈⲚ
ⲉ̀ⲘⲒ, *that ye may know.* Matt. IX, 6.

10*

The Optative Mood.

52. This Mood has ⲙⲁⲣ added to the Prefixes of
the second Present Tense, as, ⲙⲁⲣⲓ, *I;* ⲙⲁⲣⲉⲕ, *thou,* m.;
ⲙⲁⲣⲉ, *thou,* f.; ⲙⲁⲣⲉϥ, ⲙⲁⲣⲉ, *he;* ⲙⲁⲣⲉⲥ. ⲙⲁⲣⲉ, *she;*
Plur. ⲙⲁⲣⲉⲛ, ⲙⲁⲣⲛ̄, Sah. *we;* ⲙⲁⲣⲉⲧⲉⲛ, ⲙⲁⲣⲉⲧⲛ̄, Sah. *ye;*
ⲙⲁⲣⲟⲩ, ⲙⲁⲣⲉ, *they;* thus, ⲙⲁⲣⲉ ⲡⲁⲓ ⲁ̀ⲫⲟⲧ ⲥⲉⲛⲧ, *this
cup pass from me.* Matt. XXVI, 39. ⲙⲁⲣⲉϥⲛⲁⲍⲙⲉϥ ⲙⲁ-
ⲣⲉϥⲧⲟⲩϫⲟϥ, *let him deliver him, let him save him,* Psalm
XXII, 8.   The Bashmuric has ⲙⲁⲗⲉϥ, ⲙⲁⲗⲉⲛ, etc.

The Imperative Mood.

53. The Imperative Mood is expressed by the root
itself without any Prefix, as, ⲥⲱⲧⲉⲙ, *hear thou, hear ye;*
ⲥⲙⲟⲩ, *praise thou, praise ye;* or it takes ⲁ, ⲁⲣⲓ, or ⲙⲁ
before the root, as, ⲁ̀ⲛⲁⲩ ⲟⲩⲟⲍ ⲁ̀ⲣⲉⲍ ⲉ̀ⲣⲱⲧⲉⲛ, *see, and
keep you,* Luke XII, 15. ⲛⲏⲉⲧϣⲱⲛⲓ ⲁ̀ⲣⲓⲫⲁⲃⲣⲓ ⲉ̀ⲣⲱⲟⲩ,
heal the sick, Matt. X, 8. ⲁⲣⲓⲙⲛ̄ⲧⲣⲉ ⲍⲁ ⲡⲁⲡⲉⲑⲟⲟⲩ,
bear witness of the evil, John XVIII, 23. Sah. ⲁ̀ⲣⲓⲫⲙⲉⲩⲓ̀
ⲙ̀ⲫⲣⲏϯ ⲉ̀ⲧⲁϥⲥⲁϫⲓ ⲛⲉⲙⲱⲧⲉⲛ, *remember, as he spoke with
you,* Luke XXIV, 6. ⲫⲁⲓ ⲇⲉ ⲁ̀ⲣⲓⲉ̀ⲙⲓ, *and know this,* Luke
XII, 39. ⲁ̀ϫⲟⲥ, Copt. ⲁϫⲓⲥ, Sah. *say, say ye;* ⲁ̀ⲙⲟⲩ, *come;*
ⲁ̀ⲗⲓ, *take,* from ⲉⲗ; ⲁⲗⲟⲕ, Zoeg. p. 520. ⲁⲗⲱⲧⲛ̄, *suffer
ye her,* John XII, 7. Sah. from ⲗⲟ. ⲁ̀ⲛⲓ, *bring,* from ⲉⲛ etc.

The Infinitive Mood.

54. The Infinitive Mood is sometimes expressed
by the root itself, but more frequently it has ⲉ̀ or ⲛ̀ prefixed, as, ⲉⲩⲕⲱϯⲛ̀ⲥⲁ ⲥⲁϫⲓ ⲛⲉⲙⲁϥ, *seeking to speak*

with him, Luke XII, 46. thus, ⲁϥⲧⲁⲟⲩⲟϥ ⲉⲥⲙⲟⲩ ⲉⲣⲱⲧⲉⲛ, *he sent him to bless you,* Acts III, 26. ⲟⲩⲟⲥ ⲁⲓⲓ ⲉⲡⲉⲥⲏⲧ ⲉⲛⲁⲥⲙⲟⲩ, *and I have come down to deliver them,* Acts VII, 34. ⲁϥⲉⲣⲥⲏⲧⲥ ⲛⲅⲓⲟⲩⲓ ⲉⲃⲟⲗ, *he began to cast out,* Luke XIX, 45. ⲟⲩⲟⲥ ⲙⲡⲉ ⲥⲗⲓ ϣⲝⲉⲙⲭⲟⲙ ⲛⲉⲣⲟⲩⲱ, *and no one could answer,* Matt. XXII, 46. ⲁⲩⲱ ⲁⲩⲁⲣⲭⲉⲓ ⲛϣⲁⲝⲉ, *and began to speak,* Acts II, 4. Sahidic.

The Coptic takes ⲡ before the verb as a sign of the Infinitive, as ⲉ ⲡⲕⲟⲥⲧ, πρὸς τὸ ἐνταφιάσαι με, *to my burial,* Sah. Matt. XXVI, 12. ⲡⲥⲟⲩⲱⲛⲅ̄, τὸ ἐπίστασθαί σε, Sap. 793.

ⲉ is also used to express the Infinitive with the verbs ⲑⲣⲉ, ⲧⲣⲉ, Sah. as, ⲁⲣⲉⲧⲉⲛⲉⲣⲉⲧⲉⲛ ⲉⲑⲣⲟⲩⲭⲁ ⲟⲩⲣⲱⲙⲓ ⲛⲱⲧⲉⲛ ⲉⲃⲟⲗ ⲛⲣⲉϥϧⲱⲧⲉⲃ, *ye have asked them to release a murderer to you,* or *that they would etc.,* Acts III, 14. ⲉⲧⲣⲉⲩⲥⲁⲣⲉⲥ ⲉⲣⲟϥ, *to keep him,* or *that they should keep etc.,* Acts XII, 4. ⲉⲑⲣⲉⲕⲁⲓⲧⲟⲩ, *to do them,* σοι ποιῆσαι, Acts XXII, 10. ⲉⲧⲣⲉϥϯ ⲛⲟⲩⲙⲉⲧⲁⲛⲉⲁ ⲙ̄ⲡⲓⲏ̄ⲗ, *to give repentance to Israel,* Sah. Acts V, 31. ⲛⲁⲛⲟⲩⲥ ⲛⲁⲛ ⲉⲧⲣⲉⲛϭⲱ ⲙ̄ⲡⲓ ⲙⲁ, ὧδε εἶναι, *good for us to remain here,* or *that we should remain,* Mark. IX, 5. Sah. ⲉⲑⲣⲉ ⲛⲓⲉⲑⲛⲟⲥ ⲥⲱⲧⲉⲙ ⲉⲡⲓⲥⲁⲝⲓ, ἀκοῦσαι τὰ ἔθνη, *the gentiles to hear the word,* or *should hear the word,* Acts XV, 7.

We may here remark that ⲝⲓⲛ the sign of action and ⲑⲣⲉ are thus construed, ⲉⲡⲭⲓⲛⲧⲟⲩⲥⲱⲧⲉⲙ ⲛⲥⲱⲛ, πρὸς τὸ πείθεσθαι αὐτούς, Copt. ⲉⲧⲣⲉⲩⲥⲱⲧⲙ̄ ⲛⲁⲛ, *to obey us,* or *that they may obey us,* James III, 3. ϧⲉⲛ ⲡⲭⲓⲛⲧⲟⲩⲧⲁⲥⲑⲟ, ἐν τῷ ὑποστρέφειν αὐτούς, *in their returning,* Luke II, 43.

The Participles.

55. The Participles of the Present Tense are expressed by the Prefixes of the 2nd Present Tense, as,
ⲁϥⲧⲱⲃⲅ ⲉϥⲭⲱⲙ̄ⲙⲟⲥ, *he prayed, saying,* Matt. XXVI, 39.
ⲉⲅⲕⲓⲙ ⲛ̄ⲧⲟⲅⲁ̀ⲫⲉ ⲉⲅⲭⲱⲙ̄ⲙⲟⲥ, *wagging their heads, saying,* Matt. XXVII, 39. ⲉϥⲙⲟⲟⲱⲉ ⲁⲅⲱ ⲉϥⲭⲓϥⲟⲟ̅ⲥ ⲉϥⲥⲙⲟⲅ
ⲉⲡⲛⲟⲅⲧⲉ, *walking and leaping, praising God,* Acts III, 8. S.

Participles are also expressed by the Prefixes of
the Perfect and the Future with the relative pronoun
prefixed, as, ⲛ̀ⲑⲱⲟⲅ ⲁⲉ ⲉ̀ⲧⲁⲅⲥⲱⲧⲉⲙ ⲁⲅⲧⲱ̀ⲟⲅ ⲙ̀ⲫⲧ̀,
οἱ δὲ ἀκύσαντες, ἐδόξαζον τὸν κύριον, *and they hearing,*
or *(when they heard) glorified God,* Acts XXI, 20. ⲉⲧⲁϥϥⲁⲓ
ⲁⲉ ⲛ̀ⲛⲉϥⲃⲁⲗ ⲉ̀ⲡⲱⲱⲓ, *and lifting up his eyes,* John VI, 5.
ⲟⲅⲟⲅ ⲛⲏⲉⲑⲛⲁⲥⲱⲧⲉⲙ ⲉⲅⲉ̀ⲱⲛⲃ, *and those hearing* (οἱ
ἀκούσαντες) *shall live,* John V, 25. ⲉⲑⲛⲁⲧⲁⲕⲟ, *perituram,*
John VI, 27.

Participles are also formed by prefixing ⲉ̀ to the
signs of the Perfect Tense, as, ⲉ̀ⲁϥⲅⲟⲛⲅⲉⲛ, παραγγείλας,
Matt. X, 5. ⲉ̀ⲁⲅⲧⲅⲁⲡ, κρίναντες, Acts XIII, 27.
ⲉ̀ⲁⲧⲉⲧⲉⲛⲉⲣⲅ̄ⲧⲥ ⲓⲥⲭⲉⲛ ⲓⲗ̄ⲏ̄ⲙ̄, ἀρξάμενοι, *beginning from
Jerusalem,* Luke XXIV, 47.

The Potential Mood.

56. The Letter ⲱ̀, (ⲉⲱ Sahitic.) is often met with
between the Prefixes and verbs, being the sign of the
Potential Mood. It is found connected with the pre-
formants of the Indicative Mood, and the Negative Prefixes, but is most frequently united with those of the

Future Tenses, thus: ⲚⲀⲨⲤⲟϬⲚⲓ ⲭⲉ ⲁ̀ⲣⲏⲟⲩ ⲤⲉⲚⲀⲱ̀Ⲛⲟ-
ⲅⲉⲙ ⲙ̀ⲡⲓⲭⲟⲓ ⲉ̀ⲙⲀⲨ, *they took counsel whether they could
save the vessel there*, Acts XXVII, 39. ⲦⲉϥⲄⲉⲚⲉⲀ Ⲛⲓⲙ
ⲡⲉⲦⲚⲀⲉⲱ̄ⲦⲀⲄⲟⲤ, *who can declare his generation*, Acts
VIII, 33. Sah. ⲚⲚⲀⲉⲱⲟⲩⲭⲀⲓ̈ Ⲛ̄ⲅⲏⲦϥ, δεῖ σωθῆναι, *by
which we can be saved*, Acts IV, 12. Sah. ⲉⲨⲭⲱⲙ̀ⲙⲟⲤ
ⲚⲀϥ ⲭⲉ Ⲛⲓⲙ ⲉⲐⲚⲀⲱⲚⲟⲅⲉⲙ, *saying to him, who can be
saved?* Mark X, 26.

Of the Prefix ⲱⲟⲩ.

57. M. Quatremère says that ⲱⲟⲩ, when placed before verbs serves to indicate that a thing ought to be
done, — that it merits to be done; as "ⲀϥⲦⲟⲩⲦⲱⲚ Ⲧⲉϥ-
ⲭⲓⲭ ⲉ̀ⲃⲟⲗ Ⲛ̀ⲱⲟⲩⲤⲟⲗⲡⲤ, *It étendit sa main, qui eût mérité
d'être coupée.*" In composition it appears to express di-
gnus, as, ⲅⲱⲤ ⲅⲀⲚⲱⲟⲩⲙⲉⲚⲣⲓⲦⲟⲩ Ⲛⲉ ⲚⲉⲕⲙⲀⲚ̀ⲱⲱⲡⲓ,
how worthy to be loved (lovely) are thy tabernacles, Psalm
LXXXIII, 1. ⲀⲀⲨⲓⲀ ⲡⲓⲟⲩⲣⲟ ⲡⲓⲱⲟⲩⲦⲀⲓⲟϥ, *David the king,
very worthy to be honoured.* Prec. Copt. MS. p. 277, 284 etc.
ⲅⲱⲃ Ⲛⲱⲟⲩⲣ̄ⲱⲡⲏⲣⲉ ⲙ̄ⲙⲟϥ, *things worthy to be admired*,
Zoeg. 619. Sahidic.

The Negative Prefixes.

The Negative Prefix Ⲛ.

58. The negative Prefixes to verbs are ⲀⲚ, Ⲛ̀, with
ⲀⲚ, Ⲛ, ⲙ, ⲙ̀ⲡⲉ, ⲙ̀ⲡⲀⲦⲉ, Ⲧⲙ̄, ⲱⲦⲉⲙ, which are thus used.

The 1st Present Tense Negative.

Singular.

Coptic.	Sahidic.	Bashmuric.	
Ⲛ̀ⲧ ⲀⲚ,	Ⲛ̄ⲧ ⲀⲚ,	ⲈⲚ or Ⲛ̀ⲧ ⲈⲚ,	*I.*
Ⲛ̀Ⲕ ⲀⲚ,	Ⲛ̄ⲅ ⲀⲚ,		*thou,* m.
Ⲛ̀ⲦⲈ ⲀⲚ,	Ⲛ̄ⲦⲈ ⲀⲚ,		*thou,* f.
Ⲛ̀ⳡ ⲀⲚ,	Ⲛ̄ⳡ ⲀⲚ,	ⲈⲚⳡ ⲈⲚ,	*he.*
Ⲛ̀Ⲥ ⲀⲚ,	Ⲛ̄Ⲥ ⲀⲚ,		*she.*

Plural.

Coptic.	Sahidic.	Bashmuric.	
Ⲛ̀ⲦⲈⲚ ⲀⲚ,	Ⲛ̄ⲦⲚ̄ ⲀⲚ,		*we.*
Ⲛ̀ⲦⲈⲦⲈⲚ ⲀⲚ,	Ⲛ̄ⲦⲈⲦⲚ̄ ⲀⲚ,		*ye.*
Ⲛ̀ⲤⲈ ⲀⲚ,	Ⲛ̄ⲤⲈ ⲀⲚ,	ⲈⲚⲤⲈ ⲈⲚ,	*they.*

The 2nd Present Tense Negative.

Singular.

Coptic.		Sahidic.		
ⲚⲀⲒ ⲀⲚ,		ⲚⲈⲒ ⲀⲚ, *I.*		
ⲚⲀⲔ ⲀⲚ,		ⲚⲈⲔ ⲀⲚ, *thou,* m.		
ⲚⲀⲠⲈ ⲀⲚ,			*thou,* f.	
ⲚⲀⳡ ⲀⲚ, }	ⲚⲀⲠⲈ ⲀⲚ,	ⲚⲈⳡ ⲀⲚ, }	ⲚⲀⲠⲈ ⲀⲚ,	*he.* *he & she.*
ⲚⲀⲤ ⲀⲚ, }		ⲚⲈⲦ ⲀⲚ, }		*she.*

Plural.

Coptic.	Sahidic.
ⲚⲀⲚ ⲀⲚ,	ⲚⲈⲚ ⲀⲚ, *we.*
ⲚⲀⲠⲈⲦⲈⲚ ⲀⲚ,	ⲚⲈⲦⲈⲦⲚ̄ ⲀⲚ, *ye.*
ⲚⲀⲨⲀⲚ ⲀⲚ, ⲚⲀⲠⲈ ⲀⲚ,	ⲚⲈⲨ ⲀⲚ, *they.*

The Perfect Tense Negative.

Singular.

Coptic.

ⲚⲈⲦⲀⲒ ⲀⲚ, *I.*

ⲚⲈⲦⲀⲔ ⲀⲚ, *thou,* m.

ⲚⲈⲦⲀⲠⲈ ⲀⲚ, *thou,* f.

ⲚⲈⲦⲀϥ ⲀⲚ, *he.*

ⲚⲈⲦⲀⲤ ⲀⲚ, *she.*

Plural.

ⲚⲈⲦⲀⲚ ⲀⲚ, *we.*

ⲚⲈⲦⲀⲠⲈⲦⲈⲚ ⲀⲚ, *ye.*

ⲚⲈⲦⲀⲨ ⲀⲚ, ⲚⲈⲦⲀ ⲀⲚ, *they.*

The 1st Future Tense Negative.

Singular.

Coptic.	Sahidic.	Bashmuric.
Ⲛ̀ϯⲚⲀ ⲀⲚ,	Ⲛ̄ϯⲚⲀ, ⲚⲈⲒⲚⲀ ⲀⲚ,	Ⲛ̀ϯⲚⲈ ⲈⲚ, *I.*
Ⲛ̀ⲬⲚⲀ ⲀⲚ,	Ⲛ̄ⲅⲚⲀ ⲀⲚ,	*thou,* m.
Ⲛ̀ⲦⲈⲚⲀ ⲀⲚ,	Ⲛ̄ⲦⲈⲚⲀ ⲀⲚ,	*thou,* f.
Ⲛ̀ϥⲚⲀ ⲀⲚ, } ⲚⲀⲠⲈⲚⲀ ⲀⲚ,	Ⲛ̄ϥⲚⲀ ⲀⲚ,	ⲚϥⲚⲀ ⲈⲚ, *he.*
Ⲛ̀ⲤⲚⲀ ⲀⲚ, }	Ⲛ̄ⲤⲚⲀ ⲀⲚ,	*she.*

Plural.

Coptic.	Sahidic.	Bashmuric.
Ⲛ̀ⲦⲈⲚⲚⲀ ⲀⲚ,	Ⲛ̄Ⲧ̄ⲚⲀ ⲀⲚ,	*we.*
Ⲛ̀ⲦⲈⲦⲈⲚⲚⲀ ⲀⲚ,	Ⲛ̄ⲦⲈⲦ̄ⲚⲀ ⲀⲚ,	*ye.*
Ⲛ̀ⲤⲈⲚⲀ ⲀⲚ,	Ⲛ̄ⲤⲈⲚⲀ ⲀⲚ,	*they.*

11

The 2nd Future Tense Negative.

Singular.

Coptic.	Sahidic.	
Ⲛ̀ⲚⲀ,	Ⲛ̅ⲚⲀ, *I.*	
Ⲛ̀ⲚⲈⲔ,	Ⲛ̅ⲚⲈⲔ, *thou,* m.	
Ⲛ̀ⲚⲈ,	Ⲛ̅ⲚⲈ, *thou,* f.	
Ⲛ̀ⲚⲈϤ, } Ⲛ̀ⲚⲈ,	Ⲛ̅ⲚⲈϤ,} Ⲛ̅ⲚⲈ, *he* and *she.*	*he.*
Ⲛ̀ⲚⲈⳠ,	Ⲛ̅ⲚⲈⳠ,	*she.*

Plural.

Ⲛ̀ⲚⲈⲚ,	Ⲛ̅ⲚⲈⲚ, *we.*
Ⲛ̀ⲚⲈⲦⲈⲚ,	Ⲛ̅ⲚⲈⲦⲚ̅, *ye.*
Ⲛ̀ⲚⲞⲨ,	Ⲛ̅ⲚⲈⲨ, *they.*

The 1st Present Tense Negative.

59. The first Present Tense Negative and Participle
are thus expressed Ⲛ̀ϮⲤⲰⲞⲨⲚ Ⲙ̀ⲠⲒⲢⲰⲘⲒ ⲀⲚ, *I know not
the man,* Mat. XXVI, 72. ⲀⲨⲰ Ⲛ̅ⲦⲚ̅ⲈⲒⲢⲈ ⲀⲚ Ⲛ̅ⲦⲘⲈ, *and
we do not the truth,* 1 John I, 8. Sah. ⲚϤⲤⲞⲞⲨⲚ ⲀⲚ,
knoweth not, 1 John II, 11. Sah.

The Prefixes of the present Tense also express the
Participle present, but the Coptic and Bashmuric often
add ⲉ to the Prefixes, as ⲈⲚϤ̅ⲆⲒⲀⲕⲢⲒⲚⲈ ⲀⲚ Ⲙ̅ⲠⲤⲰⲘⲀ,
not discerning the body. 1 Cor. IX, 29. Sah. ⲈⲚⲅ̅ⲚⲀⲨ ⲀⲚ
ⲈⲂⲞⲖ Ⲉ ⲠⲢⲎ, *not seeing the sun,* Acts XII, 11. Sah. ⲈⲚ-
ϮⲈⲘⲠϢⲎ ⲈⲚ, *I am not worthy,* 1 Cor. XV, 9. Bash. ⲈⲚ-
ⲤⲈⲀⲢⲒⲤⲔⲈ ⲈⲚ Ⲙ̀ⲫϮ, *they please not God.* 1 Thes. II, 15.
Bashmuric.

The 2nd Present Tense Negative.

60. The second Present Tense Negative is thus formed, ⲛⲁϥⲟⲩⲏⲟⲩ ⲁⲛ ⲙ̄ⲡⲓⲟⲩⲁⲓ ⲡⲓⲟⲩⲁⲓ ⲙ̄ⲙⲟⲛ, *he is not far from each one of us,* Acts XVII, 27. ⲛⲉⲕϭⲱϣⲧ ⲅⲁⲣ ⲁⲛ ⲉ̀ϩⲟ ⲛ̄ⲣⲱⲙⲉ, *for thou regardest not the face of men.* Mat. XXII, 16. Sah. ⲙ̄ⲡⲉⲧⲉ ⲛⲉϥⲕⲣⲓⲛⲉ ⲙ̄ⲙⲟϥ ⲁⲛ, *who condemneth not himself,* Rom. XIV, 22. Sah.

The Perfect Tense Negative.

61. This Tense in the Coptic is thus presented to us. ⲛⲉⲧⲁⲓⲓ̀ ⲅⲁⲣ ⲁⲛ ⲉ̀ⲑⲁϩⲉⲙ ⲛⲓⲑⲙⲏⲓ, *I came not to call the just,* Mark II, 17. ⲟⲩ ⲅⲁⲣ ⲡϣⲏⲣⲓ ⲙ̄ⲫⲣⲱⲙⲓ ⲛⲉⲧⲁϥⲓ̀ ⲁⲛ, *for the son of man hath not come,* Mark X, 45.

The 1st Future Tense Negative.

62. The following are specimens of the first Future Tense negative, ⲛ̄ϥⲛⲁⲭⲁ ⲑⲏⲛⲟⲩ ⲁⲛ, *he will not leave you,* 1 Cor. X, 13. ⲉⲣⲉ ⲡⲣⲱⲙⲉ ⲛⲁⲱⲛϩ ⲁⲛ ⲉ ⲟⲉⲓⲕ ⲙ̄ⲙⲁⲧⲉ, *man shall not live by bread alone,* Mat. III, 4. Sah. ⲛⲁⲣⲉ ϯⲙⲉⲧⲟⲩⲣⲟ ⲛ̄ⲧⲉ ⲫϯ ⲛⲁⲓ̀ ⲁⲛ, *the kingdom of God will not come.* Luke XVII, 20. ⲛ̄ⲥⲉⲛⲁⲃⲟⲗϥ ⲉ̀ⲃⲟⲗ ⲁⲛ, *which shall not be thrown down.* Mat. XXIV, 2.

The 2nd Future Tense Negative.

63. This future occurs without the ⲁⲛ, as ⲡⲁⲛⲁⲓ ⲇⲉ ⲛ̄ⲛⲁⲟⲗϥ ⲉ̀ⲃⲟⲗ ϩⲁⲣⲟϥ, *my mercy I will not take from him.* Ps. LXXXIX, 33. ⲟⲩⲁⲓ ⲉ̀ⲃⲟⲗ ⲛ̄ⲃ̄ⲏⲧⲟⲩ ⲛ̄ⲛⲉϥⲗⲟϥⲗⲉϥ, *one of them shall not be broken,* Ps. XXXIV, 20. ⲛ̄ⲛⲉⲧⲉⲛⲫⲟϩ ⲉ̀ⲙⲉϣⲧ ⲛⲓⲃⲁⲕⲓ ⲛ̄ⲧⲉ ⲡⲓⲥⲗ̄, *ye shall not have gone over*

the cities of Israel, Mat. X, 23. When these Prefixes
follow the Particles ⲭⲉ, ⲭⲉⲕⲁⲥ, ϩⲟⲡⲱⲥ, &c., they express the Subjunctive.

It may perhaps be hardly necessary to observe that
the Prefix is sometimes written ⲉⲛ instead of ⲛ̄.

The Negative Prefix ⲙ.

64. The following form of this Prefix is only found
in the Sahidic and Bashmuric Dialects. viz.

The Present Tense.

Singular.

Sahidic.

ⲙⲉⲓ, *I*.

ⲙⲉⲕ, *thou*, m.

ⲙⲉⲣⲉ, *thou*, f.

ⲙⲉϥ,   *he*.
       } ⲙⲉⲣⲉ, *he* and *she*.
ⲙⲉⲥ,   *she*.

Plural.

ⲙⲉⲩ, ⲙⲉⲣⲉ, *they*.

The Imperfect Tense.

ⲛⲉⲙⲉϥ, *he*.

The Perfect Tense.

ⲙⲁⲕ, *thou*, m.

ⲙⲁϥ, *he*.

ⲉ is found prefixed to this form as the sign of the
Participle, as ⲉⲙⲉϥ, ⲉⲙⲉⲥ, ⲉⲙⲉⲩ, &c.

The Negative Prefix Ⲙ̀ⲠⲈ.

The Present Tense.

Singular.   Plural.

Coptic.   Coptic.

Ⲙ̀ⲠⲀⲒ, *I.*   Ⲙ̀ⲠⲀⲚ, *we.*

Ⲙ̀ⲠⲀⲔ, *thou,* m.   Ⲙ̀ⲠⲀⲦⲈⲦⲈⲚ, *ye.*

Ⲙ̀ⲠⲀⲢⲈ, *thou,* f.   Ⲙ̀ⲠⲀⲨ, Ⲙ̀ⲠⲀⲢⲈ, *they.*

Ⲙ̀ⲠⲀϥ,⎫   ⟩ *he.*
Ⲙ̀ⲠⲀⲤ,⎭ Ⲙ̀ⲠⲀⲢⲈ, *he* and *she.*
            she.

The Perfect Tense.

Singular.

Coptic.	Sahidic.		Bashmuric.	
Ⲙ̀ⲠⲒ,	Ⲙ̄ⲠⲈⲒ, Ⲙ̄ⲠⲒ,			*I.*
Ⲙ̀ⲠⲈⲔ,	Ⲙ̄ⲠⲈⲔ,		ⲈⲘⲠⲈⲔ,	*thou,* m.
Ⲙ̀ⲠⲈ,	Ⲙ̄ⲠⲈ,			*thou,* f.
Ⲙ̀ⲠⲈϥ,	Ⲙ̄ⲠⲈϥ,	⎱Ⲙ̄ⲠⲈ, *he.*	ⲈⲘⲠⲈϥ,	*he.*
Ⲙ̀ⲠⲈⲤ,	Ⲙ̄ⲠⲈⲤ,	⎰and *she.*	ⲈⲘⲠⲈⲤ,	*she.*

Plural.

Ⲙ̀ⲠⲈⲚ,	Ⲙ̄ⲠⲚ̄, Ⲙ̄ⲠⲈⲚ,			*we.*
Ⲙ̀ⲠⲈⲦⲈⲚ,	Ⲙ̄ⲠⲈⲦⲚ̄,			*ye.*
Ⲙ̀ⲠⲞⲨ,	Ⲙ̄ⲠⲞⲨ, Ⲙ̄ⲠⲈ,		ⲈⲘⲠⲞⲨ,	*they.*

Ⲉ before the Ⲙ is a sign of the Participle.

The Subjunctive.

The Imperfect and Perfect Tenses.

Singular.

Coptic.

ⲈⲦⲈⲘ̀ⲠⲒ, *I.*

ⲈⲦⲈⲘ̀ⲠⲈⲔ, *thou,* m.

ⲈⲦⲈⲘ̀ⲠⲈ, *thou,* f.

ⲈⲦⲈⲘ̀ⲠⲈϤ,⎫   *he.*
ⲈⲦⲈⲘ̀ⲠⲈⲤ,⎭ ⲈⲦⲈⲘ̀ⲠⲈ, *he* and *she.*
       she.

Plural.

ⲈⲦⲈⲘⲠⲈⲚ, *we.*

ⲈⲦⲈⲘ̀ⲠⲈⲦⲈⲚ, *ye.*

ⲈⲦⲈⲘ̀ⲠⲞⲨ, *they.*

These Prefixes in Coptic correspond with ⲚⲦⲈⲢⲒⲦⲘ̅ in Sahidic.

The Negative Prefix Ⲙ̀ⲠⲀⲦⲈ.

The Indicative and Subjunctive.

Singular.

Coptic.   Sahidic.

Ⲙ̀ⲠⲀϮ,   Ⲙ̅ⲠⲀϮ, *I.*

Ⲙ̀ⲠⲀⲦⲈⲔ,   Ⲙ̅ⲠⲀⲦⲔ̅, *thou,* m.

Ⲙ̀ⲠⲀⲦⲈ,   Ⲙ̅ⲠⲀⲦⲈ, *thou,* f.

Ⲙ̀ⲠⲀⲦⲈϤ, ⎫ Ⲙ̀ⲠⲀⲦⲈ. Ⲙ̅ⲠⲀⲦϤ̅,⎫ *he.*
Ⲙ̀ⲠⲀⲦⲈⲤ, ⎭   Ⲙ̅ⲠⲀⲦⲤ̅,⎭ Ⲙ̅ⲠⲀⲦⲈ, *he & she.*
           she.

Plural.

Coptic.	Sahidic.
ⲘⲠⲀⲧⲉⲚ,	ⲘⲠⲀⲦⲚ, *we.*
ⲘⲠⲀⲦⲉⲦⲉⲚ,	ⲘⲠⲀⲦⲉⲦⲚ, *ye.*
ⲘⲠⲀⲦⲞⲨ, ⲘⲠⲀⲦⲉ,	ⲘⲠⲀⲦⲞⲨ, ⲘⲠⲀⲦⲉ, *they.*

The Imperfect and Pluperfect Tenses.

Singular.

Coptic.	Sahidic.
Ⲛⲉ ⲘⲠⲀⲦ Ⲡⲉ,	Ⲛⲉ ⲘⲠⲀⲦ Ⲡⲉ, *I.*
Ⲛⲉ ⲘⲠⲀⲦⲉⲕ Ⲡⲉ,	Ⲛⲉ ⲘⲠⲀⲦⲔ Ⲡⲉ, *thou,* m.
Ⲛⲉ ⲘⲠⲀⲦⲉ Ⲡⲉ,	Ⲛⲉ ⲘⲠⲀⲦⲉ Ⲡⲉ, *thou,* f.
Ⲛⲉ ⲘⲠⲀⲦⲉϥ Ⲡⲉ,	Ⲛⲉ ⲘⲠⲀⲦϥ Ⲡⲉ, *he.*
Ⲛⲉ ⲘⲠⲀⲦⲉⲥ Ⲡⲉ,	Ⲛⲉ ⲘⲠⲀⲦⲤ Ⲡⲉ, *she.*

&c. &c.

The Negative Prefixes ⲰⲦⲉⲘ Copt. and ⲦⲘ Sah.

Singular.

Coptic.	Sahidic.
ⲚⲦⲀⲰⲦⲉⲘ,	ⲚⲦⲀⲦⲘ, *I.*
ⲚⲦⲉⲕⲰⲦⲉⲘ,	ⲚⲅⲦⲘ, *thou,* m.
ⲚⲦⲉⲰⲦⲉⲘ,	ⲚⲦⲉⲦⲘ, *thou,* f.
ⲚⲦⲉϥⲰⲦⲉⲘ, } ⲚⲦⲉⲰⲦⲉⲘ,	ⲚϥⲦⲘ, } ⲚⲦⲉⲦⲘ, *he.* *he & she.*
ⲚⲦⲉⲥⲰⲦⲉⲘ,	ⲚⲤⲦⲘ, *she.*

Plural.

ⲚⲦⲉⲚⲰⲦⲉⲘ,	ⲚⲦⲚⲦⲘ, *we.*
ⲚⲦⲉⲦⲉⲚⲰⲦⲉⲘ,	ⲚⲦⲉⲦⲚⲦⲘ, *ye.*
ⲚⲦⲞⲨⲰⲦⲉⲘ, ⲚⲤⲉⲰⲦⲉⲘ,	ⲚⲤⲉⲦⲘ, *they.*

The Subjunctive.

The Imperfect and Pluperfect Tenses.

Singular.

Sahidic.

ⲚⲦⲈⲢⲈⲒⲦⲘ̄, *I.*

ⲚⲦⲈⲢⲈⲔⲦⲘ̄, *thou,* m.

ⲚⲦⲈⲢⲈⲦⲘ̄, *thou,* f.

ⲚⲦⲈⲢⲈϤⲦⲘ̄, *he.*

ⲚⲦⲈⲢⲈⲤⲦⲘ̄, *she.*

Plural.

ⲚⲦⲈⲢⲞⲨⲦⲘ̄, *they.*

Conditional.

Singular.

Coptic.	Sahidic.	Bashmuric.
ⲀⲒϢⲦⲈⲘ,	ⲈⲒⲦⲘ̄,	*I.*
ⲀⲔϢⲦⲈⲘ,	ⲈⲔⲦⲘ̄,	*thou,* m.
ⲀⲢⲈϢⲦⲈⲘ,	ⲈⲢⲈⲦⲘ̄,	*thou,* f.
ⲀϤϢⲦⲈⲘ, } ⲀⲢⲈϢⲦⲈⲘ,	ⲈϤⲦⲘ̄, } ⲈⲢⲈⲦⲘ̄, ⲀⲖⲈϢⲦⲈⲘ,	*he.* *he & she.*
ⲀⲤϢⲦⲈⲘ, }	ⲈⲤⲦⲘ̄, }	*she.*

Plural.

ⲀⲚϢⲦⲈⲘ,	ⲈⲚⲦⲘ̄,	*we.*
ⲀⲢⲈⲦⲈⲚϢⲦⲈⲘ,	ⲈⲦⲈⲦⲚ̄ⲦⲘ̄,	*ye.*
ⲀⲨϢⲦⲈⲘ,	ⲈⲨⲦⲘ̄,	*they.*

Another particle with this Prefix in the Sahidic is ϢⲀⲚ, *if,* as ⲈⲒϢⲀⲚⲦⲘ̄, ⲈⲔϢⲀⲚⲦⲘ̄, etc.

The Imperative.

Coptic.	Sahidic.	Bashmuric.
ⲘⲡⲈⲣ,	Ⲙ̅ⲡⲣ̅,	ⲘⲡⲈⲗ,
ⲘⲡⲈⲛⲐⲢⲈ,	Ⲙ̅ⲡⲣ̅ⲧⲢⲈ,	ⲘⲡⲈⲗⲧⲢⲈ.

These take the Pronoun Suffixes, as Ⲙ̇ⲡⲈⲛⲐⲢⲓ, for which see the auxiliary verb ⲐⲢⲈ, Coptic. ⲦⲢⲈ, Sahidic which are below.

The Infinitive.

Coptic.	Sahidic.	Bashmuric.
Ⲉ̇ⲱⲦⲈⲘ,	ⲈⲦⲘ̅,	ⲈⲱⲦⲘ̅,
and	and	
Ⲉ̇ⲱⲦⲈⲘⲐⲢⲈ,	ⲈⲦⲘ̅ⲧⲢⲈ,	
Ⲉ̇ⲱⲦⲈⲘⲈⲐⲢⲈ,	ⲈⲦⲘ̅ⲈⲦⲢⲈ.	

These like the above take the Pronoun Suffixes to the verb ⲐⲢⲈ, Coptic and ⲦⲢⲈ, Sahidic.

The Auxiliary verb ⲐⲢⲈ, ⲦⲢⲈ, Sah. to be, to do.

Singular.

Coptic.	Sahidic.	Bashmuric.
ⲐⲢⲓ,	ⲦⲢⲀ,	*I.*
ⲐⲢⲈⲕ,	ⲦⲢⲈⲕ,	*thou,* m.
ⲐⲢⲈ,	ⲦⲢⲈ,	*thou,* f.
ⲐⲢⲈϥ, } ⲐⲢⲈ,	ⲦⲢⲈϥ, } ⲦⲢⲈ,	*he.* *he* and *she.*
ⲐⲢⲈⲥ,	ⲦⲢⲈⲥ,	*she.*

Plural.

Coptic.	Sahidic.	Bashmuric.
ⲐⲢⲈⲛ,	ⲦⲢⲈⲛ,	*we.*
ⲐⲢⲈⲦⲈⲦⲈⲛ, ⲐⲢⲈⲦⲈⲛ,	ⲦⲢⲈⲦⲈⲦⲛ̅, ⲦⲢⲈⲧⲛ̅,	*ye.*
ⲐⲢⲟⲨ, ⲐⲢⲈ,	ⲦⲢⲈⲨ, ⲦⲢⲈ,	ⲦⲢⲟⲨ, *they.*

12

65. The Auxiliary is thus used ⲛⲏ ⲇⲉ ⲉ̀ⲧⲁⲩⲉ̀ⲣⲓϫⲱⲛⲧ, *and have made me angry*, or *have provoked me.* Num. XV, 23. ⲁϥⲉ̀ⲣⲟ ⲙ̀ⲙⲟⲥ ⲉ̀ϫⲫⲉ ⲛⲱⲓⲕ, *causeth her to commit adultery.* Matt. XIX, 9. ⲁⲩⲧⲣⲉ ⲡϫⲟⲓ ⲁⲥⲁⲓ, *they made the vessel that it should be lightened,* or *they lightened the vessel.* Acts XXVII, 38. Sahidic. ϯⲛⲁⲧⲣⲉⲧⲉⲧⲛ̄ⲣ̄ⲡⲙⲉⲉⲩⲉ ⲛ̄ⲛⲉϥϩⲃⲏⲩⲉ, *I will cause that you remember his works, I will remind you of his works,* 1 John 10. Sah. ⲙⲛ̄ⲛ̄ⲥⲁ ⲧⲣⲁⲃⲱⲕ, *after my departure.* Acts XX, 29. Sahidic. ⲡⲟ̅ⲥ̅ ⲫⲏⲉ̀ⲧⲉ̀ⲣⲟ ⲛ̀ⲛⲁⲓ, *the Lord who doeth these things,* Acts XV, 17. ⲉⲑⲣⲟⲩⲛⲁⲩ ⲉ̀ⲣⲱⲟⲩ ⲛ̀ϫⲉ ⲛⲓⲣⲱⲙⲓ, *that men may see them,* Matt. XXIII, 5. ⲉ̀ⲑⲣⲉⲧⲉⲛⲱϣ ⲉ̀ⲧⲁⲓ ⲉ̀ⲡⲓⲥⲧⲟⲗⲏ, *that ye read this epistle,* 1 Thes. V, 26.

66. ⲑⲣⲉ and ⲧⲣⲉ are signs of the Subjunctive with ⲉ, or some sign of the Subjunctive before them, as ⲉⲑⲣⲉⲕⲁⲓⲧⲟⲩ, *that thou mayest do them,* or *to do them.* Acts XXII, 10. ⲉⲑⲣⲉϥϣⲱⲡⲓ ⲛ̀ⲓⲱⲧ ⲛ̀ⲟⲩⲙⲏϣ ⲛ̀ⲉⲑⲛⲟⲥ, *that he might be the father of many nations,* Rom. IV, 18. ⲉ̀ⲑⲣⲟⲩⲥⲁϫⲓ ⲛⲁϩⲣⲁⲕ, *that they might speak before thee,* Acts XXIII, 30. ϩⲁⲡⲥ ⲟⲛ ⲉⲧⲣⲁⲛⲁⲩ ⲉⲧⲕⲉϩⲣⲱⲙⲏ, *it is necessary also that I should see Rome.* Acts XIX, 21. Sah. ⲛⲁⲛⲟⲩⲥ ⲛⲁⲛ ⲉⲧⲣⲉⲛϭⲱ ⲙ̄ⲡⲁⲓ ⲙⲁ, *it is good for us that we should remain here,* or *to remain here.* Mark IX, 5. Sah. ⲉ̀ⲑⲣⲉ ⲛⲓⲉⲑⲛⲟⲥ ⲥⲱⲧⲉⲙ ⲉ̀ⲡⲓⲥⲁϫⲓ, *that the gentiles should hear the word,* Acts XV, 7. ⲉⲧⲙ̄ⲧⲣⲉϥⲃⲱⲕ ⲉϩⲟⲩⲛ, *that he would not go in,* Acts XIX, 31. Sah. ⲙ̄ⲛ̄ⲛ̄ⲥⲁ ⲧⲣⲉ ⲡⲉϣⲧⲟⲣⲧⲣ̄ ⲗⲟ, *after the tumult ceased,* Acts XX, 1. Sah. ⲉⲧⲣⲉⲩϩⲁⲣⲉϩ ⲉⲣⲟϥ, *to keep him,* or *that they should keep him.* Acts XII, 4. Sah.

It will be seen that ⲉⲑⲣⲉ and ⲉⲧⲣⲉ with the suffixes express also the infinitive.

We may also observe that these auxiliaries, taking the Pronoun suffixes, often lose their distinctive signification, which is absorbed by the following verb.

The Auxiliary Verb ⲉⲣ, ⲣ̄, Sah. ⲉⲗ, Bash. to be, to do.

67. When the verb ⲉⲣ, ⲣ̄ or ⲉⲗ, is joined to a noun, it is a verb, as ⲟⲩⲱⲓⲛⲓ, *light;* ⲉⲣⲟⲩⲱⲓⲛⲓ, *to enlighten* or *to make light;* ⲙⲉⲑⲣⲉ, *a witness;* ⲉⲣⲙⲉⲑⲣⲉ, *to bear witness.*

ⲉⲣ is prefixed to verbs, and nouns used verbally, derived from the Greek, as ⲛⲁⲩⲉⲣⲁⲥⲡⲁⲍⲉⲥⲑⲉ ⲙ̄ⲙⲟϥ, *they saluted him,* Mark IX, 15. ⲉⲩⲉⲣϩⲉⲗⲡⲓⲥ ⲉⲡⲉϥⲣⲁⲛ, *they shall hope in his name,* Mat. XII, 21. — But ⲣ̄ in Sah. is very seldom prefixed to words derived from the Greek.

ϯ, *to give,* is also an auxiliary, and is joined to ⲱⲟⲩ, Copt. ⲉⲟⲟⲩ, Sah. ⲉⲁⲩ, Bash. *glory.* ϯⲱⲟⲩ, ϯⲉⲟⲟⲩ, Sah. *to give glory, to glorify.* ⲧⲟⲧ, Copt. ⲧⲟⲟⲧ, Sahidic. ⲧⲁⲁⲧ, Bash., *the hand,* ϯⲧⲟⲧ, ϯⲧⲟⲟⲧ, *to give the hand, to help.* ⲙ̄ⲕⲁϩ, *sorrow, grief,* ϯⲙ̄ⲕⲁϩ, *to give sorrow, to afflict.*

Of Irregular and defective Verbs.

68. Of the verb ⲡⲉ, *to be,* which is generally accompanied with a personal Pronoun, as ⲁⲛⲟⲕ ⲡⲉ, *I am.* Psalm XLIX, 7. ⲛ̄ⲧⲟⲕ ⲡⲉ, *thou art,* Ezech. XXXVIII, 17. ⲛ̄ⲑⲟϥ ⲡⲉ, *he is,* John XIII, 26. ⲁⲛⲟⲛ ⲡⲉ, *we are,* 1. John III, 1. Sah. ⲛ̄ⲧⲱⲧⲛ̄ ⲡⲉ, *ye are,* Matt. V, 14. Sahidic.

ⲌⲀⲚⲔⲞⲨⲌⲒ ⲡⲉ, *few are*, Mat. XXII, 14. ⲚⲀⲒ ⲡⲉ, *these are*, John XX, 18. ⲧⲉ is construed with feminine nouns in the same way, as ⲧⲀⲤⲀⲢⲌ ⲧⲉ, John VI, 55.

The Present Tense.
Singular.

Masc.	Fem.
ⲡⲉ, *I am*, m.	ⲧⲉ, *I am*, f.
ⲡⲉ, *thou art*, f.	ⲧⲉ, *thou art*, f.
ⲡⲉ, *he* or *it is*.	ⲧⲉ, *she* or *it is*.

Plural.

ⲚⲈ, $\left.\begin{matrix} we \\ ye \\ they \end{matrix}\right\}$ *are*.
ⲡⲉ,

The Imperfect Tense.
Sing. and Plural.

ⲚⲈ ⲡⲉ, *was* or *were*, m.

ⲚⲈ ⲧⲉ, *was* or *were*, f.

ⲚⲈⲨ, *were*.

The Irregular Verb ⲬⲈ, ⲬⲞ, ⲬⲰ, or ⲬⲞⲞ, Sah. ⲬⲀ, Bash. to say.

The Present Tense.
Singular.
Coptic.

ϯⲬⲰ ⲘⲘⲞⲤ, $\left.\begin{matrix} \\ \\ \end{matrix}\right\}$ *I say*.
ϯⲬⲞⲤ,

ⲔⲬⲰ ⲘⲘⲞⲤ, *thou sayest*, m.

ⲈϥⲬⲰ ⲘⲘⲞⲤ, $\left.\begin{matrix} \\ \\ \end{matrix}\right\}$ ⲈⲢⲈⲬⲰ ⲘⲘⲞⲤ, *he* or *she says*.
ⲬⲰ ⲘⲘⲞⲤ,

ⲈⲤⲬⲰ ⲘⲘⲞⲤ, *she says*.

Singular.

Sahidic.

ϯⲭⲟⲟⲥ, *I say.*

ⲉⲕⲭⲱ, *thou sayest,* m.

ⲭⲱ ⲙ̄ⲙⲟⲥ, }
ϥ̄ⲭⲱ ⲙ̄ⲙⲟⲥ, } ⲉⲣⲉⲭⲱ ⲙ̄ⲙⲟⲥ, *he or she says.*

he says.

ⲉⲥⲭⲱ ⲙ̄ⲙⲟⲥ, *she says.*

Plural.

Coptic and Sahidic.

ⲧⲉⲛⲭⲱ ⲙ̀ⲙⲟⲥ, *we say.*

ⲧⲉⲧⲉⲛⲭⲱ & ⲧⲉⲧⲛ̄ⲭⲱ ⲙ̀ⲙⲟⲥ, *ye say.*

ⲉⲩⲭⲱ ⲙ̀ⲙⲟⲥ, }
ⲥⲉⲭⲱ ⲙ̀ⲙⲟⲥ, } *they say.*

The Imperfect Tense.
Singular.

Coptic.	Sahidic.
ⲛⲁⲓⲭⲱ ⲙ̀ⲙⲟⲥ,	ⲛⲉⲓⲭⲱ ⲙ̄ⲙⲟⲥ, *I did say.*
ⲛⲁϥⲭⲱ ⲙ̀ⲙⲟⲥ,	ⲛⲉϥⲭⲱ ⲙ̄ⲙⲟⲥ, *he did say.*

Plural.

ⲛⲁⲩⲭⲱ ⲙ̀ⲙⲟⲥ,	ⲛⲉⲩⲭⲱ ⲙ̄ⲙⲟⲥ, *they did say.*

The Perfect Tense.
Singular.

Coptic.	Sahidic.
ⲁⲓⲭⲱⲧⲟⲩ,	ⲡⲉⲭⲁⲓ, *I have said.*
ⲁⲕⲭⲟⲥ,	ⲁⲓⲭⲟⲧⲟⲩ, } *thou,* m.
ⲁϥⲭⲟⲥ,	ⲁⲕⲭⲟⲟⲥ, }
	ⲁϥⲭⲉ, *he.*
	ⲁϥⲭⲟⲥ, ⟨ ⲁϥⲭⲁⲥ, *he.*
ⲁⲥⲭⲟⲥ,	ⲁϥⲭⲟⲟⲥ, ⟨ ⲁⲭⲟⲟⲥ, *he or she.*
	ⲁⲥⲭⲟⲟⲥ, *he and she.*

Plural.

Coptic.	Sahidic.
ⲀⲢⲦⲈⲚⲬⲰ ⲘⲘⲞⲤ, *ye.*	
ⲠⲈⲬⲰⲞⲨ ⲘⲘⲞⲤ, *they.*	ⲀⲨⲬⲨⲞⲤ, *they.*
ⲀⲨⲬⲞⲤ,	

The Future Tense.
Singular.

Coptic.	Sahidic.
ⲈⲔⲈ̀ⲬⲞⲤ,	ⲈⲔⲈⲬⲞⲞⲤ, *thou shalt,* etc.
ⲈⳓⲚⲀⲬⲞⲤ,	ⳓⲚⲀⲬⲨⲞⲤ, } *he.*
	ⲈⳓⲚⲀⲬⲞⲞⲨ, }

Plural.

Coptic.	Sahidic.
ⲦⲈⲚⲚⲀⲬⲈ, *we.*	ⲦⲈⲚⲀⲬⲞⲤ, *we.*
ⲈⲨⲈ̀ⲬⲰⲞⲨ, *they.*	ⲤⲈⲚⲀⲬⲞⲞⲨ, *they.*

The Imperative Mood.

Coptic.	Sahidic.
ⲀⲬⲞⲤ,	ⲀⲬⲓⲤ, *say.*

The Infinitive.

Coptic.	Sahidic.
ⲀⲬⲞⳓ,	ⲀⲬⲓⲤ, *to say.*

The Perfect Tense.
Singular.

Coptic.	Sahidic.	Bashmuric.
ⲠⲈⲬⲎⲓ,	ⲠⲈⲬⲀⲓ, ⲠⲈⲬⲎⲓ,	*I said.*
ⲠⲈⲬⲀⲔ,	ⲠⲈⲬⲀⲔ,	*thou,* m.
ⲠⲈⲬⲀⳓ, } ⲠⲈⲬⲈ,	ⲠⲈⲬⲀⳓ, } ⲠⲈⲬⲈ,	ⲠⲈⲬⲈⳓ, *he.*
ⲠⲈⲬⲀⲤ, }	ⲠⲈⲬⲀⲤ, } *he and she.*	ⲠⲈⲬⲈⲤ, *she.*

Plural.

Coptic.	Sahidic.	Bashmuric.
ⲠⲈϪⲀⲚ,		*we.*
ⲠⲈϪⲰⲦⲈⲚ,		*ye.*
ⲠⲈϪⲀⲨ, ⲠⲈϪⲈ,	ⲠⲈϪⲀⲨ, ⲠⲈϪⲈ,	ⲠⲈϪⲈⲨ, *they.*

69. ⲞⲨⲞⲚ, and ⲞⲨⲚ̄, Sah. ⲞⲨⲀⲚ, Bash. are used for the verb *to have* or *to be*, and Ⲙ̇ⲘⲞⲚ, ⲘⲚ̄Ϯ, Sah. *not to have,* or *to be.* But when they take the Personal Suffixes after them, they always represent the verb *to have*, with Ⲙ̇ⲘⲀⲨ, which is very often added.

Singular.

Coptic:	Sahidic.
ⲞⲨⲞⲚⲦⲎⲒ, ⲞⲨⲞⲚϮ,	ⲞⲨⲚ̄ⲦⲀⲒ, ⲞⲨⲚ̄Ϯ, *I.*
ⲞⲨⲞⲚⲦⲀⲔ, ⲞⲨⲞⲚⲦⲈⲔ,	ⲞⲨⲚ̄ⲦⲀⲔ, ⲞⲨⲚ̄ⲦⲔ̄, *thou,* m.
ⲞⲨⲞⲚⲦⲈ,	ⲞⲨⲚ̄ⲦⲈ, *thou,* f.
ⲞⲨⲞⲚⲦⲀϥ, ⲞⲨⲞⲚⲦⲈϥ,	ⲞⲨⲚ̄ⲦⲀϥ, ⲞⲨⲚ̄Ⲧϥ̄, *he.*
ⲞⲨⲞⲚⲦⲀⲤ, ⲞⲨⲀⲚⲦⲈⲤ,	ⲞⲨⲚ̄ⲦⲀⲤ, ⲞⲨⲚ̄ⲦⲤ̄, *she.*

Plural.

ⲞⲨⲞⲚⲦⲀⲚ, ⲞⲨⲞⲚⲦⲈⲚ,	ⲞⲨⲚ̄ⲦⲀⲚ, *we.*
ⲞⲨⲞⲚⲦⲈⲦⲈⲚ, ⲞⲨⲞⲚⲦⲰⲦⲈⲚ,	ⲞⲨⲚ̄ⲦⲈⲦⲚ̄, ⲞⲨⲚ̄ⲦⲎⲦⲚ̄, *ye.*
ⲞⲨⲞⲚⲦⲞⲨ, ⲞⲨⲞⲚⲦⲰⲞⲨ,	ⲞⲨⲚ̄ⲦⲀⲨ, ⲞⲨⲚ̄ⲦⲈⲨ, *they.*

Singular.

Bashmuric.

ⲞⲨⲀⲚⲦⲎⲒ, *I.*

ⲞⲨⲀⲚⲦⲎϥ, ⲞⲨⲀⲚⲦⲈϥ, *he.*

ⲞⲨⲀⲚⲦⲎⲤ, *she.*

Plural.

ⲞⲨⲀⲚⲦⲎⲚ, *we.*

ⲞⲨⲀⲚⲦⲎⲞⲨ, *they.*

The Participle is formed by adding ε, as ⲉⲟⲩⲟⲛⲧⲉⲕ, *thou having*. The above are also written ⲟⲩⲟⲛⲛ̀ⲑⲓ, ⲟⲩⲟⲛⲛ̀ⲧⲁⲕ, ⲟⲩⲟⲛⲛ̀ⲧⲁϥ, etc.

The Negative *not to have*, is thus expressed, and generally with ⲙ̄ⲙⲁⲩ.

The Present Tense.
Singular.

Coptic.	Sahidic.	Bashmuric.
ⲙ̀ⲙⲟⲛⲑⲓ, ⲙ̀ⲙⲟⲛ†,	ⲙ̄ⲙⲛ̄†, ⲙⲛ̄†,	ⲙⲉⲛⲑⲓ, *I.*
ⲙ̀ⲙⲟⲛⲧⲉⲕ,	ⲙ̄ⲙⲛ̄ⲧⲕ̄, ⲙⲛ̄ⲧⲕ̄,	*thou*, m.
ⲙ̀ⲙⲟⲛⲧⲉ,	ⲙⲛ̄ⲧⲉ,	*thou*, f.
ⲙ̀ⲙⲟⲛⲧⲉϥ, ⲙ̀ⲙⲟⲛⲧⲁϥ,	ⲙ̄ⲙⲛ̄ⲧⲁϥ, ⲙⲛ̄ⲧϥ̄,	ⲙⲉⲛⲑⲓϥ, *he.*
ⲙ̀ⲙⲟⲛⲧⲉⲥ, ⲙ̀ⲙⲟⲛⲧⲁⲥ,	ⲙ̄ⲙⲛ̄ⲧⲁⲥ, ⲙⲛ̄ⲧⲥ̄,	*she,*

Plural.

Coptic.	Sahidic.	Bashmuric.
ⲙ̀ⲙⲟⲛⲧⲉⲛ, ⲙ̀ⲙⲟⲛⲧⲁⲛ,	ⲙⲛ̄ⲧⲁⲛ,	ⲙⲉⲛⲑⲛ, *we.*
ⲙ̀ⲙⲟⲛⲧⲉⲧⲉⲛ, ⲙ̀ⲙⲟⲛⲧⲱⲧⲉⲛ,	ⲙⲛ̄ⲑⲏⲧⲛ̄,	*ye.*
ⲙ̀ⲙⲟⲛⲧⲟⲩ, ⲙ̀ⲙⲟⲛⲧⲱⲟⲩ,	ⲙⲛ̄ⲧⲁⲩ, ⲙⲛ̄ⲧⲟⲩ,	ⲙⲉⲛⲧⲉⲩ, *they.*

The Imperfect Tense.

Coptic.	Sahidic.
ⲛⲉ ⲙ̀ⲙⲟⲛⲧⲉϥ ⲡⲉ, *he.*	ⲛⲉ ⲙⲛ̄ⲧⲕ̄, *thou,* m.
ⲛⲉ ⲙ̀ⲙⲟⲛⲧⲟⲩ ⲡⲉ, *they.*	ⲛⲉ ⲙⲛ̄ⲧϥ̄, *he.*
	ⲛⲉ ⲙⲛ̄ⲧⲥ̄, *she.*

These are sometimes written ⲙ̀ⲙⲟⲛ ⲛ̀† or ⲛ̀ⲑⲓ, ⲙ̀ⲙⲟⲛⲛ̀ⲧⲁⲛ, ⲙ̀ⲙⲟⲛⲛ̀ⲧⲱⲧⲉⲛ, etc.

Of Verbs Passive.

70. To what has been said of verbs Passive under Chap. V, we may add the following.

Verbs active are made passive by changing the vowels of the root, as ⲕⲱ, *to put,* ⲕⲏ, *to be put,* Sah. ⲙⲟⲩⲣ, *to bind,* ⲙⲏⲣ, *to be bound,* ⲥⲁⲍ, *to write,* ⲥⲏⲍ, *to be written,* Sah. ⲧⲱⲍ, *to mix,* ⲧⲏⲍ, *to be mixed,* Sah. ϣⲱϥ, *to lay waste,* ϣⲏϥ, *to be laid waste,* Sah.

Verbs active ending in ⲟ and in the passive in ⲛⲟⲩⲧ, Copt. and in ⲏⲩ in Sah. as ⲧⲁⲗⲟ, *to put on,* ⲧⲁⲗⲛⲟⲩⲧ, Copt. ⲧⲁⲗⲏⲩ, Sah. *to be put on,* etc.

71. The Participles are formed by adding ⲉⲧ, as ⲉⲧⲧⲁⲕⲏⲟⲩⲧ, from ⲧⲁⲕⲟ, and ⲉⲧⲧⲁⲕⲧⲏⲟⲩⲧ. from ⲧⲁⲕⲧⲟ; and sometimes by suffixing ⲧ also to the end as ⲉⲧ-ⲥⲍⲟⲩⲟⲣⲧ, from ⲥⲍⲟⲩⲣ, Sah.

Of Suffixes to Verbs.

The following are the Pronoun Suffixes to Verbs.

Singular.

Coptic.		Sahidic.
ⲓ or ⲧ,		ⲓ or ⲧ, *me.*
ⲕ,		ⲕ or ⲅ, *thee,* m.
ϯ, ⲓ,		ⲧⲉ or ⲉ, *thee,* f.
ϥ,		ϥ, *him.*
ⲥ,		ⲥ, *her.*

Plural.

ⲛ, ⲧⲉⲛ,		ⲛ, ⲧⲛ̄, *us.*
ⲧⲉⲛ,		ⲧⲛ̄, *you.*
ⲟⲩ,		ⲟⲩ, *them.*

The first Person singular.

72. The ι is suffixed to verbs ending in o, as ΜΑ-
ΤΟΥΧΟΙ, *deliver me,* Ps. CXXXIX, 1. ϩⲀ ⲪⲎⲈⲦⲀϥⲦⲀⲞⲨⲞⲒ,
to him that sent me, John VII, 33. The τ is suffixed to
other verbs as, ⲞⲨⲞϨ ⲦⲈⲦⲈⲚⲚⲀϪⲈⲘⲦ ⲀⲚ, *and ye shall
not find me,* John VII, 36. ⲈⲔⲈⲚⲀϨⲘⲈⲦ, *thou shalt save
me,* Ps. XLII, 1.

The second Person singular.

73. ⲠⲈϪⲈ ⲒⲎⲤ ⲚⲀϥ ⲦⲰⲚⲔ, *Jesus said unto him rise,*
John V, 8. ⲚⲔⲀⲀⲔ ⲈⲂⲞⲖ, *to release thee,* John XIX, 10.
Sah. ⲦⲰⲞⲨⲚⲄ ⲠⲈⲦⲢⲈ, *rise Peter,* Acts X, 13. Sah. Ⲉϥ-
ϪⲰⲘⲘⲞⲤ ϪⲈ ⲦⲰⲞⲨⲚⲄ, *saying arise,* Acts X, 26. Sahidic.
ⲞⲨⲞϨ ⲤⲈⲚⲀϥⲒ† ⲈⲂⲞⲖ, Copt. ⲀⲨⲰ ⲤⲈⲚⲀϥⲒⲦⲈ ⲈⲂⲞⲖ, Sah. *and
shall carry thee out,* f. Acts V, 9. ⲠⲈⲔⲚⲀϨ† ⲠⲈⲦⲀϥⲚⲀϨⲘⲒ,
thy faith hath saved thee, f. Mat. IX, 22. †ⲀⲖⲞⲨ ⲦⲰⲞⲨⲚⲒ,
maid arise, f. Luke VIII, 54.

The first Person plural.

74. ⲀⲖⲖⲀ ⲚⲀϨⲘⲈⲚ ⲈⲂⲞⲖϨⲀ ⲠⲒⲠⲈⲦϨⲰⲞⲨ, *but deliver
us from evil,* Mat. VI, 13. ϥⲚⲀⲦⲀⲘⲞⲚ ⲈϨⲰⲂⲚⲒⲘ, *he will
show us all things,* John IV, 25. Sah. ⲀⲔⲪⲀⲤⲦⲈⲚ ⲘⲪⲢⲎ†
ⲘⲠⲒϨⲀⲦ, *thou hast tried us as silver,* Psalm LXVI, 10.
ⲈϢϪⲈ Ⲁ ⲠⲚⲞⲨⲦⲈ ⲘⲈⲚⲢⲈⲦⲚ, *if God hath loved us,* 1. John
IV, 11. Sahidic.

The second Person plural.

75. ЄЦЀΤΑΜѠΤЄΝ, *he shall make known unto you,*
John XVI, 13. ΑЧΜЄΡΙΤΝ̄, *hath loved us,* Rom VIII. 37.
Sahidic.

The third Person plural.

76. ΑЧΤΑΜѠΟΥ ЀΝЄЧΧΙΧ, *he showed them his hands,*
John XX, 20. ЀⲂⲞⲐⲂⲞΥ, Copt. ЄⲌⲞΤⲂⲞΥ, Sahidic. *to kill
them,* Deut. IX, 28. ΧЄΚΑⳌ ЄЧЄΧΙΤΟΥ ЄΥΜΗΡ, *that he
might lead them bound,* Acts IX, 21. Sah.

Of Adverbs.

77. A few adverbs are formed from nouns by prefixing the letter Є to them, with the article, as ЄⲌⲞⲞΥ,
a day, Sah. ЄⲠⲌⲞⲞΥ, *daily,* ЀⲫⳍⲎⲞΥ, *in vain.*

But most often adverbs are formed thus ⳠЄΝ ΟΥ-
ⳠⲰⲞΥΤЄΝ, ὀρθῶς, *rightly,* Luke XX, 21. ⳠЄΝ ΟΥΜЄⲐΜΗΙ,
truly, Luke XX, 21.

The other adverbs will be easily discovered in the
course of reading.

Of the Conjunction ΧЄ.

78. The conjunction ΧЄ frequently answers to the
word *quod,* and generally follows the verbs of seeing,
hearing, saying, and declaring; as ΟΥⲞⳌ ΑЧΝΑΥ ЀⲠΟΥ-
ⲰΙΝΙ ΧЄ ΝΑΝЄЧ, *and he saw the light that it was good.*
Gen. I, 4. ΧЄ ⲐⲰⲞΥ ΤЄ ⳨ΜЄΤΟΥΡⲞ Ν̄ΤЄ ΝΙⲫΝⲞΥΙ, *for
theirs is the kingdom of heaven,* Mit. V, 3.

13·

It is often united with prepositions, as ⲉⲑⲃⲉ ϫⲉ, ⲉ̀ⲃⲏⲗ ϫⲉ, ⲉ̀ϥⲙⲁ ϫⲉ, etc.

Of Prepositions.

79. 1) Prepositions abound in the Egyptian Language, two or more of them being frequently united in composition; as ⲉ̀ⲃⲟⲩⲛ ⲉ̀, ⲉⲍⲟⲩⲛ ⲉ, Sah. *in;* ⲉ̀ⲃⲣⲏⲓ ⲉϫⲉⲛ, *above;* ⲉ̀ⲃⲟⲗⲃⲉⲛ, ⲉⲃⲟⲗ ⲍⲛ̄, Sah. *out of;* ⲛ̀ⲃⲣⲏⲓ ⲃⲉⲛ, *in;* ⲥⲁ ⲡⲉⲥⲏⲧ, ⲍⲓ ⲡⲉⲥⲏⲧ, and ⲉ̀ ⲡⲉⲥⲏⲧ, *beneath, under.* The Preposition ⲉ̀ is frequently found united with others: as ⲉ̀ⲃⲟⲩⲛ ⲉ̀, *in, into;* ⲉ̀ⲍⲣⲏⲓ ⲉ̀, *to, towards;* ϣⲁ ⲉ̀ⲍⲣⲏⲓ ⲉ̀, *to* etc.

2) Prepositions are sometimes prefixed to Substantives, which then have the force of Prepositions only, as has been already shown, as ⲍⲁⲣⲟ, *to;* ⲍⲁⲣⲟⲓ, *to me;* from ⲍⲁ, *to* and ⲣⲟ, *the mouth;* ⲉ̀ⲍⲣⲁ, *to, before;* from ⲉ̀ *to,* and ⲍⲣⲁ, *the face;* etc.

3) The Prepositions are also used in composition with verbs, to express the idea conveyed by the verb and preposition when separated; as ϣⲉ ⲉ̀ⲡϣⲱⲓ, *to ascend;* from ϣⲉ, *to go,* and ⲉ̀ⲡϣⲱⲓ, *above;* ⲓ̀ⲉⲡⲉⲥⲏⲧ, *to descend;* from ⲓ *to go,* and ⲉ̀ⲡⲉⲥⲏⲧ, *beneath;* ϣⲉ ⲉ̀ⲃⲟⲩⲛ, *to enter;* from ϣⲉ, *to go,* and ⲉ̀ⲃⲟⲩⲛ, *in.*

4) The preposition ⲉ̀ⲃⲟⲗ, very often occurs in connection with verbs; as ϥⲓⲉ̀ⲃⲟⲗ, *to bear, to carry out;* ⲭⲁ ⲉ̀ⲃⲟⲗ, *to remit;* ⲥⲱⲣ ⲉ̀ⲃⲟⲗ, *to disperse;* ϭⲱⲣⲡ ⲉ̀ⲃⲟⲗ, *to reveal,* &c.

5) The Preposition ⲉ̀ⲃⲟⲗ is used with nouns in the same way, as ϣⲏⲗ ⲉ̀ⲃⲟⲗ, *a paralytic;* ⲭⲟⲩϣⲧ ⲉ̀ⲃⲟⲗ, *expectation;* ⲭⲱⲣ ⲉ̀ⲃⲟⲗ, *a dispersion;* ⲃⲱⲗ ⲉ̀ⲃⲟⲗ, *a dissolu-*

tion; &c. It is also used with the same words when used verbally.

6) A considerable number of Prepositions take the Pronoun suffixes, as ⲀⲦϬⲚⲈ, Copt. *without,* ⲀⲦϬⲚⲞⲄⲒ, *without me,* ⲀⲦϬⲚⲞⲨⲔ, *without thee,* m., ⲈⲐⲂⲈ, Copt., ⲈⲦⲂⲈ, Sah. *of* or *concerning,* ⲈⲐⲂⲎⲦ, Copt. ⲈⲦⲂⲎⲎⲦ, Sah. *concerning me;* ⲈⲐⲂⲎⲦϥ, Copt. ⲈⲦⲂⲎⲎⲦϥ. Sah. *concerning him;* &c. ⲚⲈⲘ, Copt. ⲚⲘ̄, Sah. *with,* ⲚⲈⲘⲎⲒ, Copt. ⲚⲘ̄ⲘⲀⲒ, Sah. *with me;* ⲚⲈⲘⲀⲔ, Coptic. ⲚⲘ̄ⲘⲀⲔ, Sah. *with thee;* m. ⲚⲀⲅⲣⲈⲚ, Coptic. ⲚⲀⲅⲣⲚ̄, Sahidic. *with, before.* ⲚⲀⲅⲣⲀⲒ, *with me,* &c.

7) The following list of Prepositions is given, as they very frequently occur in Coptic, Sahidic and Bashmuric.

Coptic.	Sahidic.
ⲀⲦϬⲚⲈ, *without.*	ⲀϪⲚ̄, *without.*
ⲈⲂⲞⲖ, *from, out of.*	ⲈⲂⲞⲖ, *from, out of.*
ⲈⲂⲞⲖϧⲈⲚ, *from, out of.*	ⲈⲂⲞⲖⲅⲘ̄, } *from, out of.*
ⲈⲂⲞⲖⲞⲨⲦⲈ, *before.*	ⲈⲂⲞⲖⲅⲚ̄, }
ⲈⲂⲞⲖⲅⲀ, *from.*	ⲈⲂⲞⲖⲅⲒⲦⲘ̄, } *of, from.*
ⲈⲂⲞⲖⲅⲒⲦⲈⲚ, *from, out of.*	ⲈⲂⲞⲖⲅⲒⲦⲚ̄, }
ⲈⲂⲞⲖⲅⲒⲦⲞⲦ, *from.*	ⲈⲂⲞⲖⲅⲒⲦⲞⲞⲦ, *from.*
ⲈⲂⲞⲖⲅⲒⲱⲦ, *from.*	ⲈⲂⲞⲖⲅⲒⲭⲘ̄, } *of, from.*
ⲈⲂⲞⲖⲅⲒⲭⲈⲚ, *of, from.*	ⲈⲂⲞⲖⲅⲒⲭⲚ̄, }
ⲈⲘⲎⲣ, *beyond, over.*	ⲈⲄ, *in, to.*
ⲈⲠⲈⲤⲎⲦ, *beneath, under.*	ⲈⲅⲞⲨⲚ, *in, within.*
ⲈⲤⲔⲈⲚ, *by, near.*	ⲈⲅⲣⲀⲒ, *in, to.*
ⲈⲄ, *in, to.*	ⲈⲅⲣⲀⲒ ⲈϪⲘ̄, *to.*
ⲈϧⲞⲨⲚ, *in, within.*	ⲈⲅⲣⲀⲒ ⲅⲘ̄, *of, from.*

Coptic.	Sahidic.
ⲉⲃⲣⲏⲓ, *in, to.*	ⲙⲛ̄ⲛ̄ⲥⲁ, *after.*
ⲉⲃⲣⲏⲓ, ⲉⲅⲣⲏⲓ, } ⲉⲝⲉⲛ, *in, above, upon.*	ⲙ̄ⲡⲙ̄ⲧⲟ, ⲙ̄ⲡⲙ̄ⲧⲟ ⲉⲃⲟⲗ, } *before.*
ⲉⲅⲣⲏⲓ ⲉⲁ, *upon.*	ⲙ̄ⲡⲕⲱⲧⲉ, *about.*
ⲉⲝⲉⲛ, *upon, above.*	ⲛⲁⲅⲣⲙ̄, ⲛⲁⲅⲣⲛ̄, } *to.*
ⲓⲝⲱ, *above.*	
ⲓⲥⲝⲉⲛ, *from.*	ⲛⲙ̄, *with.*
ⲙⲉⲛⲉⲛⲥⲁ, *after.*	ⲛ̄ⲅⲟⲩⲛ, ⲥⲁⲅⲟⲩⲛ, } *within.*
ⲙ̄ⲡⲉⲙⲑⲟ, *before.*	
ⲛⲁⲅⲣⲁ, *before.*	ⲛ̄ⲅⲏⲧ, *in.*
ⲛⲉⲙ, *with.*	ⲡⲁⲅⲟⲩ, *behind.*
ⲛ̄ⲟⲩⲉϣⲉⲛ, *without.*	ⲅⲁⲣⲟ, *of, from.*
ⲛ̄ⲥⲁ, *after.*	ⲅⲁⲧⲙ̄, ⲅⲁⲧⲛ̄, } *nigh to.*
ⲛ̄ⲧⲉⲛ, *from.*	
ⲛ̄ⲃⲏⲧ, *in.*	ⲅⲁⲑⲏ, ⲅⲁⲧⲅⲏ, } *before.*
ⲛ̄ⲃⲟⲩⲛ, *within.*	
ⲛ̄ⲃⲣⲏⲓ, *in.*	ⲅⲙ̄, ⲅⲛ̄, } *in.*
ⲟⲩⲃⲉ, *against.*	
ⲟⲩⲧⲉ, *between.*	ⲅⲓⲣⲛ̄, *before.*
ⲫⲁⲅⲟⲩ, *after, behind.*	ⲅⲓⲧⲙ̄, ⲅⲓⲧⲛ̄, } *from.*
ϣⲁ, *to.*	
ⲃⲁ, *towards.*	ⲅⲓⲝⲙ̄, *on, in.*
ⲃⲁⲑⲟⲩⲟ, *nigh to.*	
ⲃⲁⲣⲁⲧ, *under.*	
ⲃⲁⲣⲟ, *of, from.*	
ⲃⲁⲧⲉⲛ, *nigh to.*	
ⲃⲁⲧⲟⲧ, *nigh to, to.*	
ⲃⲁⲧⲅⲏ, *before.*	

Coptic.

ⲃⲁϫⲉⲛ,⎫
⎬ *before*.
ⲃⲁϫⲱ, ⎭

ⲃⲉⲛ, *in*.

ⲃⲉⲛⲧ, *near to*.

ⲅⲁ, *to*.

ⲅⲓ, *upon, in*.

ⲅⲓⲙⲏⲣ, *beyond*.

ⲅⲓⲡⲉⲛ, *before*.

ⲅⲓⲧⲉⲛ, *by, from*.

ⲅⲓⲱⲧ, *from, of*.

ⲅⲓϫⲉⲛ, *upon, in*.

ⲅⲓϫⲱ, *upon, in*.

Of Conjunctions.

80. 8) The conjunction ⲟⲩⲟⲅ, *and*, is frequently omitted in composition, as ⲟⲩⲟⲅ ⲁⲩⲟⲩⲱⲙ ⲧⲏⲣⲟⲩ ⲁⲩⲥⲓ, *and they all ate (and) were satisfied*. Mat. XV, 37. Copt. ⲟⲩⲟⲅ ⲓⲥ ⲅⲁⲛⲁⲅⲅⲉⲗⲟⲥ ⲁⲩⲓ ⲁⲩϣⲉⲙϣⲓ ⲙⲙⲟϥ, *and behold angels came, (and) ministered to him*, Mat. IV, 11. Copt.

9) The Conjunction ⲕⲉ, *and, also*, is placed between the article and the noun; as ⲛ̄ⲧⲉⲛⲅⲓⲟⲩⲓ ⲙ̄ⲡⲟⲩ ⲕⲉ ⲛⲁⲅ-ⲃⲉϥ ⲉⲃⲟⲗ ⲅⲓϫⲱⲛ, *that we may cast away also their yoke from us*. Ps. II, 2. ⲙ̄ⲡⲓ ⲕⲉ ⲓⲱⲧ ⲉ̀ⲧⲁϥⲧⲁⲟⲩⲟϥ, *the Father also, who hath sent him*.

Of Interjections.

81. The principal interjections in Egyptian are ⲓⲥ, or ⲅⲏⲡⲡⲉ ⲓⲥ, Copt. ⲅⲏⲏⲧⲉ ⲓⲥ; Sah. *behold!* ⲟⲩⲟⲓ, *alas! woe to;* and ⲱ̀, *oh!*

CHAP. VIII.

Of the Formation of words.

82. In treating of the formation of Egyptian words it is by no means intended to enter upon the controversy, whether nouns or verbs were the original words in language, but to give a simple statement of what the Egyptian presents to us.

83. Primitive words were no doubt short, and generally of one syllable, as ⲣⲏ, *the sun;* ⲫⲉ, *heaven;* ⲭⲱ, *the lead;* ⲃⲣⲉ, *food;* &c.

84. Compound words are formed by uniting two or more words, as ϥⲧⲉⲫⲁⲧ, *a quadruped,* from ϥⲧⲉ, *four* and ⲫⲁⲧ, *a foot;* ⲟⲩⲱⲙⲛ̀ϩⲏⲧ, *to repent,* from ⲟⲩⲱⲙ, *to consume,* and ϩⲏⲧ, *the heart,* &c. ⲙⲁⲓ̈ⲛⲟⲩⲧⲉ, *religious,* from ⲙⲁⲓ̈, *loving,* ⲛⲟⲩⲧⲉ, *God,* Sah.

Some words are composed of ⲙⲁ, Copt., Sah. and Bash., *a place,* and ⲛ̀, the sign of the genitive, united with other words, as ⲙⲁⲛ̀ⲙⲟⲛⲓ, *a pasture, a place to feed;* from ⲙⲁ, and ⲙⲟⲛⲓ, *to feed,* ⲙⲁⲛ̀ⲫⲱⲧ, *a refuge, a place to flee to;* from ⲙⲁ, and ⲫⲱⲧ, *a flight.* ⲙⲁⲛ̀ϣⲱⲡⲓ, *a habitation;* from ⲙⲁ, and ϣⲱⲡⲓ, *to dwell.* ⲙⲁⲛ̀ϯϩⲁⲡ, *a tribunal;* from ⲙⲁ, and ϯ, *to give,* and ϩⲁⲡ, *judgment.*

Some words are composed of ⲙⲉ or ⲙⲁⲓ̈, *loving,* united with other words, as ⲙⲁⲓϩⲁⲧ, *covetous;* from ⲙⲁⲓ, and ϩⲁⲧ. *silver,* ⲙⲁⲓⲧⲁⲓⲟ, *ambitious;* from ⲙⲁⲓ, and ⲧⲁⲓⲟ, *honour.*

ⲘⲈⲦ or ⲘⲈⲐ, Copt. and ⲘⲚⲦ. Sah. are often prefixed to nouns and also to words derived from the Greek;
as ⲘⲈⲦⲞⲨⲢⲞ, *a kingdom;* from ⲘⲈⲦ and ⲞⲨⲢⲞ, *a king;*
ⲘⲈⲦⲘⲀⲦⲞⲒ, *an army;* from ⲘⲈⲦ and ⲘⲀⲦⲞⲒ, *a soldier;*
ⲘⲚⲦⲘⲚⲦⲢⲈ, *a testimony;* from ⲘⲚⲦ and ⲘⲚⲦⲢⲈ, *a witness;* Sah. &c.

The word ⲢⲈⲘ, Copt. and ⲢⲘ̄, Sah. ⲖⲈⲘ. Bash. *a
native, an inhabitant,* or *belonging to,* and the sign of the
genitive prefixed to nouns; as ⲢⲈⲘⲚ̀ⲎⲒ, *a domestic;* from
ⲢⲈⲘ and ⲎⲒ, *a house;* ⲢⲈⲘⲘ̀ⲪⲈ, *heavenly;* from ⲢⲈⲘ and
ⲪⲈ, *heaven;* ⲢⲈⲘⲚ̀ⲬⲎⲘⲒ, *an Egyptian;* ⲢⲈⲘⲦⲀⲢⲤⲞⲤ, *a
native of Tarsus.*

ⲢⲈϤ, Copt. and Sah. ⲖⲈϤ, Bash. added to verbs
form compound nouns, as ⲢⲈϤⲚⲀⲨ, *an inspector,* from
ⲚⲀⲨ, *to see.* ⲢⲈϤϢⲘ̄ϢⲈ, Sah. *a minister,* from ϢⲘϢⲈ,
to minister, ⲖⲈϤϯ̇ϨⲈⲡ, Bash. *a judge;* from ϯϨⲀⲡ, *to judge.*

ⲤⲀ, Copt. and Sah. *an artificer,* is used in the formation of some words, as ⲤⲀⲚϬ̇ⲎⲬⲒ, *a maker or seller
of purple;* from ϬⲎⲬⲒ, *purple.* ⲤⲀⲚ̀ⲰⲒⲔ, *a baker;* from
ⲰⲒⲔ, *bread.* ⲤⲀⲚ̄ϨⲞⲘⲚⲦ, Sah. *an artificer in brass;* from
ϨⲞⲘⲚ̄Ⲧ, *brass.*

ⲬⲒⲚ, Copt. and Bash. ϬⲒⲚ, Sah. prefixed to verbs
often denote the presence of the action, so that they
then correspond with the infinite of the Greek, with the
article; as ⲬⲒⲚⲘⲞϢⲒ, Copt. ϬⲒⲚⲘⲞⲞϢⲈ, Sah. *the action of
going, ⲧⲟ go.* With these prefixes verbs are frequently
used as nouns; as ⲬⲒⲚⲬⲪⲞ, *possession,* from ⲬⲪⲞ, *to possess.*
ⲬⲒⲚϬⲞⲂϯ. *a preparation,* from ϬⲞⲂϯ, *to prepare.*

ϢⲞⲨ. Copt. and Sah. when prefixed to verbs "serves

to indicate" Quatremère says, "that a thing merits to be done, — that it ought to be done." It consequently expresses *worthiness;* as ϩⲱⲥ ϩⲁⲛϣⲟⲩⲙⲉⲛⲡⲓⲧⲟⲩ ⲛⲉ ⲛⲉⲕⲙⲁⲛ̀ϣⲱⲡⲓ, *How worthy to be loved are thy tabernacles.* Ps. LXXXIII, 1. from ⲙⲉⲛⲡⲓⲧ, *beloved.*

ϩⲁ, Copt., Sah. and Bash. appears to express *a person, master* or *chief;* as ϩⲁⲛϣⲉ, Sah. *a centurion,* or *chief of a hundred men,* from ϣⲉ, *a hundred.* ϩⲁⲙ̅ϣⲉ, Sah. *a carpenter, an artificer in wood.* &c.

ⲁⲧ or ⲁⲑ, Copt., Sah. and Bash. which is a negative prefix to nouns.

ⲗⲁ, Copt. *much, greatly,* as ⲗⲁⲭⲁⲗ, *very shady.*

Some nouns are formed from verbs by adding a Letter at the end, as ⲥϩⲟⲩⲟⲣⲧ, *a curse,* from ⲥϩⲟⲩⲟⲣ, *to curse.* ⲣⲁⲃⲧ, *a fuller;* from ⲣⲁⲃ, *to wash;* ⲭⲁⲣⲟϥ, *silence;* from ⲭⲁⲣⲱ, *to silence.*

Part IV.

Of the Dialects.

1. We know very little of the ancient Language of Egypt, and nearly all the remains of it we now possess, have been transmitted to us through the medium of the Coptic, Sahidic and Bashmuric Dialects. The Coptic Dialect was spoken in Lower Egypt, of which Memphis was the capital, hence it has been called with great propriety the Memphitic Dialect. The Sahidic derived its name from the Arabic word صعيد or الصعيد, *the Upper or Superior;* and was the Dialect of Upper Egypt,

of which Thebes was the capital; it has therefore been called the Thebaïc. It is impossible to say which of these two dialects was the more ancient. Georgius, Valperga, Munter, and others have decided in favour of the Coptic; and Macrizy, Renaudotius, Lacroze, and Jablonsky, with much more appearance of reason, have contended for the Sahidic. Still, however, the question must be very much left to conjecture, as we have not at present sufficient evidence to enable us to decide. Besides these two dialects, which have long been known, there is a third, which was spoken in Baschmour, a Province of the Delta.

The existence of three Dialects in Egypt has been so satisfactorily proved by Quatremère, Engelbreth and other writers, and so fully confirmed by the Bashmouric Fragments which have been discovered and published, that no more need be added to establish the fact. If however any doubt should remain on the mind of any one, the following quotation from a Manuscript work of Athanasius, a Prelate of the Coptic Church, who was Bishop of Kous, will entirely remove it.* "The Coptic Language," says he, "is divided into three dialects, the Coptic dialect of Misr, the Bahiric, and the Bashmuric: these different dialects are derived from the same language."

The introduction of Greek words into the Egyptian language commenced, no doubt, from the time of the

---

* Coptic MS. Royal Library Paris, quoted by Quatremèro.

Macedonian conquest, which the introduction of Christianity tended to confirm and extend. The Christian Religion contained so many new ideas, that new words would be found necessary to express them. These words the Greek Language would readily supply, having been previously used by the Apostles of Christ, for a similar object: and it is probable that the Egyptians adopted the terms required, from the Greek writings of the Apostles. But we find in the Coptic and Sahidic Versions of the Scriptures, that the Translators often used Greek words in the Translation when they possessed Egyptian words, which fully expressed the same idea, which proves that the Greek and Egyptian Language were both extensively used at that period.

The Coptic Dialect.

2. The Coptic,*) or as it has been called the Bahiric, but more properly the Memphitic, was the Dialect of Lower Egypt, the מצור Mizur of the Scriptures. This Dialect is more free from Greek than the Sahidic.

Manuscripts exist in Coptic of nearly the whole of the Sacred Scriptures, of which the Pentateuch, the Book of Job, the Psalms, the Major and Minor Prophets, and the New Testament, with translations, have been published. Liturgies also of the Coptic Church exist in MSS. and the works of some of the early Fathers, the

---

*) The word Coptic was evidently derived from the word ⲄⲨⲠⲦⲤ as pronounced by the Egyptians.

Acts of the Council of Nice, and also the lives of a considerable number of Saints and Martyrs.

The Sahidic Dialect.

3. The Sahidic, or more correctly the Thebaic Dialect, was spoken in Upper Egypt. As has been hinted before, it has adopted a greater number of Greek words than the Coptic. The vowels in this dialect are more frequently expressed by lines above the consonants than in the Coptic or Bashmouric; as ⲘⲚⲚⲤⲀ, *after*, Sahidic. ⲘⲈⲚⲈⲚⳓⲀ, Copt. ⲘⲠⲘⲦⲞ, Sah. *before*, ⲘⲠⲈⲘⲦⲞ, Copt.

Fragments of nearly every part of the Old and New Testament exist in Sahidic, but only fragments of the New Testament have as yet been published, and fragments of some of the Lives of Saints and Martyrs.

The Bashmouric Dialect.

4. The Bashmouric Dialect was spoken in Bashmour, a Province of the Delta, and agrees in some respects with the Coptic, and in others more nearly resembles the Sahidic.

The inhabitants of the Delta were described by ancient writers* as wild beasts, leading a wandering life, and living by robbery and plunder, whom the Persians, Greeks and Romans could hardly subdue. This will account in a great measure for the Bashmouric being more rude than the Sahidic.

A few Fragments only of this Dialect exist, and have been published.

* Thucydid. l. I. c. 110. and Diod. Sicul. l. II. c. 77.

Praxis.

Of the first Chapter of St. John's Gospel.

1. ϧⲉⲛ ⲧⲁⲣⲭⲏ ⲛⲉ ⲡⲥⲁϫⲓ ⲡⲉ ⲟⲩⲟϩ ⲡⲓⲥⲁϫⲓ ⲛⲁϥⲭⲏ ϧⲁⲧⲉⲛ ⲫϯ ⲟⲩⲟϩ ⲛⲉ ⲟⲩⲛⲟⲩϯ ⲡⲉ ⲡⲓⲥⲁϫⲓ.

In the beginning was the Word, and the Word was with God, and God was the Word.

ϧⲉⲛ, prepos. ⲧⲁⲣⲭⲏ, noun f. with ⲧ the defin. art. f. prefixed ⲛⲉ....ⲡⲉ, verb. irreg. imper. 3 pers. sing. ⲡⲥⲁϫⲓ, noun m. with ⲡ the defin. art. m. prefixed. ⲟⲩⲟϩ conjunct. ⲛⲁϥⲭⲏ verb indic. imper. 3. pers. sing. from ⲭⲏ. ϧⲁⲧⲉⲛ, prepos. ⲫϯ noun sing. m. ⲟⲩⲛⲟⲩϯ, noun masc. sing. with ⲟⲩ indef. art. prefixed.

2. ⲫⲁⲓ ⲉ̀ⲛⲁϥⲭⲏ ⲓⲥϫⲉⲛ ϩⲏ ϧⲁⲧⲉⲛ ⲫϯ.

This was from the beginning with God.

ⲫⲁⲓ, pron. demonstr. sing. m. ⲉ̀ⲛⲁϥⲭⲏ, verb. imperf. (see above) with ⲉ̀ pron. rel. ⲓⲥϫⲉⲛ, prepos. ϩⲏ, noun sing.

3. ϩⲱⲃⲛⲓⲃⲉ̀ⲛ ⲁⲩϣⲱⲡⲓ ⲉ̀ⲃⲟⲗϩⲓⲧⲟⲧϥ ⲟⲩⲟϩ ⲁⲧϭⲛⲟϥ ⲙ̀ⲡⲉ ϩⲗⲓ ϣⲱⲡⲓ ϧⲉⲛ ⲫⲏⲉ̀ⲧ ⲁϥϣⲱⲡⲓ.

All things were made by him, and without him was not anything made, among that which was made.

ϩⲱⲃⲛⲓⲃⲉⲛ, compound adject. from ϩⲱⲃ and ⲛⲓⲃⲉⲛ.. ⲁⲩϣⲱⲡⲓ, verb. perfect 3. pers. plur. from ϣⲱⲡⲓ. ⲉ̀ⲃⲟⲗϩⲓⲧⲟⲧϥ, prepos. with ϥ the pron. suff. 3. pers. sing. ⲁⲧϭⲛⲟϥ, prepos. with ϥ pron. suff. ⲙ̀ⲡⲉ, neg. pref. 3. pers. m. to verb. ϣⲱⲡⲓ, ϩⲗⲓ, adject. neut. ⲫⲏⲉ̀ⲧ, pron. demonst. and relat. sing. ⲁϥϣⲱⲡⲓ, verb. perf. 3. pers. sing. see above.

4. ⲛⲉ ⲡⲱⲛⲃ ⲡⲉ ⲉ̀ⲧⲉ ⲛ̀ⲃⲏⲧϥ ⲟⲩⲟⲍ ⲡⲱⲛⲃ ⲡⲉ ⲫⲟⲩⲱⲓⲛⲓ ⲛ̀ⲛⲓⲣⲱⲙⲓ ⲡⲉ.

In Him was life, and the life was the light of men.

ⲡⲱⲛⲃ, noun sing. with ⲡ, the defin. artic. m. pref.
ⲉ̀ⲧⲉ, pron. relat. sing. ⲛ̀ⲃⲏⲧϥ, prep. with ϥ suff. ⲛⲉ...
ⲡⲉ, verb. irreg. imperf. 3. pers. sing. ⲫⲟⲩⲱⲓⲛⲓ, noun
sing. with ⲫ def. art. m. pref. ⲛ̀ⲛⲓⲣⲱⲙⲓ, noun pl. with
ⲛ̀ sign of gen. and ⲛⲓ def. art. plur. m. prefixed.

5. ⲟⲩⲟⲍ ⲡⲓⲟⲩⲱⲓⲛⲓ ⲁϥⲉⲣⲟⲩⲱⲓⲛⲓ ⲃⲉⲛ ⲡⲓⲭⲁⲕⲓ ⲟⲩⲟⲍ
ⲙ̀ⲡⲉ ⲡⲓⲭⲁⲕⲓ ϣ̀ⲧⲁⲍⲟϥ.

*And the light shined in the darkness, and the dark-
ness did not comprehend it.*

ⲁϥⲉⲣⲟⲩⲱⲓⲛⲓ, verb. perf. 3. pers. sing. from ⲟⲩⲱⲓⲛⲓ
with ⲉⲣ prefixed. ⲡⲓⲭⲁⲕⲓ, noun sing. with ⲡⲓ def. art.
m. sing. pref. ϣ̀ⲧⲁⲍⲟϥ, verb perf. 3. pers. sing. with
ⲙ̀ⲡⲉ, (see above) and ϣ intensive prefixed, and ϥ suff.
from ⲧⲁⲍⲟ.

6. ⲁϥϣⲱⲡⲓ ⲛ̀ⲭⲉ ⲟⲩⲣⲱⲙⲓ ⲉ̀ⲁⲩⲟⲩⲟⲣⲡϥ ⲉ̀ⲃⲟⲗⲍⲓⲧⲉⲛ
ⲫϯ ⲉ̀ⲡⲉϥⲣⲁⲛ ⲡⲉ ⲓⲱⲁⲛⲛⲏⲥ.

*There was a man who was sent by God, whose name
was John.*

ⲛ̀ⲭⲉ, a sign of the nominative. ⲟⲩⲣⲱⲙⲓ, noun sing.
m. with ⲟⲩ indef. art. sing. prefixed. ⲉ̀, pron. relat. sing.
ⲁⲩⲟⲩⲟⲣⲡϥ, verb. perf. 3. pers. plur. for the pass. sing.
(see pass. v.) and ϥ 3. pers. sing. suff. ⲉ̀ⲃⲟⲗⲍⲓⲧⲉⲛ, prep.
ⲉ̀ⲡⲉϥⲣⲁⲛ, ⲉ̀ rel. pron. ⲡⲉϥ, his m. ⲣⲁⲛ, noun sing. m.
ⲡⲉ, verb irreg. imperf.

7. ⲫⲁⲓ ⲁϥⲓ̀ ⲉⲩⲙⲉⲧⲙⲉⲑⲣⲉ ⲍⲓⲛⲁ ⲛ̀ⲧⲉϥⲉⲣⲙⲉⲑⲣⲉ ⲃⲁ
ⲡⲓⲟⲩⲱⲓⲛⲓ ⲍⲓⲛⲁ ⲛ̀ⲧⲉ ⲟⲩⲟⲛⲛⲓⲃⲉⲛ ⲛⲁⲍϯ ⲉ̀ⲃⲟⲗⲍⲓⲧⲟⲧϥ.

*This (man) came for a witness, that he might witness
to the light, that every one might believe through him.*

ⲁϥⲓ̀, verb perf. 3. pers. sing. from ⲓ̀. ⲉⲩⲘⲉⲧⲘⲉⲑⲣⲉ,
noun sing. with ⲉⲩ for ⲉⲟⲩ, ⲉ prepos. ⲟⲩ, indef. art.
contract. into ⲉⲩ. ⲅⲓⲛⲁ, conjunct. ⲚⲧⲉϥⲉⲣⲘⲉⲑⲣⲉ, verb.
subjunct. 3. pers. sing. from Ⲙⲉⲑⲣⲉ with ⲉⲣ prefixed.
ⲃⲁ, prepos. ⲟⲩⲟⲛⲚⲓⲃⲉⲛ, adj. Ⲛⲧⲉ ⲛⲁⲅϯ, verb subjunct.
3. pers. sing.

8. ⲛⲉ Ⲛ̀ⲑⲟϥ ⲁⲛ ⲡⲉ ⲡⲓⲟⲩⲱⲓⲛⲓ ⲁⲗⲗⲁ ⲅⲓⲛⲁ Ⲛⲧⲉϥⲉⲣ-
Ⲙⲉⲑⲣⲉ ⲃⲁ ⲡⲓⲟⲩⲱⲓⲛⲓ.

*He was not the light, but that he might witness to
the light.*

Ⲛ̀ⲑⲟϥ, pron. 3. pers. m. ⲁⲛ, adv. ⲁⲗⲗⲁ, conj.

9. ⲛⲁϥ̀ⲱⲟⲡ Ⲛⲭⲉ ⲡⲓⲟⲩⲱⲓⲛⲓ Ⲛⲧⲁ̀ϥⲘⲎⲓ ⲫⲎⲉ̀ⲧ ⲉⲣⲟⲩⲱⲓⲛⲓ ⲉ̀ⲣⲱⲘⲓ ⲛⲓⲃⲉⲛ ⲉⲑⲛⲎⲟⲩ ⲉ̀ⲡⲓⲕⲟⲥⲙⲟⲥ.

*He was the true light, which enlighteneth every man
who cometh into the world.*

ⲛⲁϥ̀ⲱⲟⲡ, verb imperf. 3. pers. sing. from ϣⲟⲡ.
Ⲛⲧⲁ̀ϥⲘⲎⲓ, adject. sing. with Ⲛ, prefixed forming the
adjective. ⲉ̀ⲣⲟⲘⲓ, noun sing. with ⲉ̀ prep. ⲛⲓⲃⲉⲛ, adj.
ⲉⲑⲛⲎⲟⲩ, verb. pres. 3. pers. sing. with ⲉⲑ pron. relat.
from ⲛⲎⲟⲩ. ⲉ̀ⲡⲓⲕⲟⲥⲙⲟⲥ, noun sing. with ⲉ̀ prep. and
ⲡⲓ, defin. art. prefixed.

10. ⲛⲁϥⲭⲎ ⲃⲉⲛ ⲡⲓⲕⲟⲥⲙⲟⲥ ⲡⲉ ⲟⲩⲟⲅ ⲡⲓⲕⲟⲥⲙⲟⲥ
ⲁϥϣⲱⲡⲓ ⲉ̀ⲃⲟⲗⲅⲓⲧⲟⲧϥ ⲟⲩⲟⲅ Ⲙ̀ⲡⲉ ⲡⲓⲕⲟⲥⲙⲟⲥ ⲥⲟⲩⲱⲛϥ.

*He was in the world, and the world was made by Him,
and the world knew Him not.*

Ⲙ̀ⲡⲉ...ⲥⲟⲩⲱⲛϥ, verb. with neg. and ϥ suffix.

11. ⲁϥ̀ ⲍⲀ ⲚⲈⲦⲈⲚⲞⲨϥ ⲞⲨⲞⲌ ⲚⲈⲦⲈⲚⲞⲨϥ ⲘⲠⲞⲨ-
ϣⲟⲡϥ ⲉ̀ⲣⲱⲞⲨ.

*He came to his own, and his own received him not
to them.*

ⲌⲀ, prep. ⲚⲈⲦⲈⲚⲞⲨϥ, adj. plur. with ϥ suff. ⲘⲠⲞⲨ-
ϣⲟⲡϥ, verb. neg. with ϥ suff. 3. pers. plur. ⲉ̀ⲣⲱⲞⲨ, Dat.
pron. plur.

12. ⲚⲎ ⲆⲈ Ⲉ̀Ⲧ ⲀⲨϣⲟⲡϥ ⲉ̀ⲣⲱⲞⲨ Ⲁϥϯ Ⲉⲣϣⲓϣⲓ ⲚⲰⲞⲨ
ⲉ̀Ⲉⲣ ϣⲎⲣⲓ Ⲛ̀ⲚⲞⲨϯ ⲚⲎⲈⲐ ⲚⲀⲌϯ Ⲉ̀ⲠⲈϥⲢⲀⲚ.

*But those who received him to them, he gave them
power to become sons of God, (to) those who believe in
his name.*

ⲚⲎ, pron. demon. plur. ⲆⲈ, conj. Ⲉ̀Ⲧ, pron. rel. pl.
ⲀⲨϣⲟⲡϥ, verb. perf. 3. pers. pl. Ⲁϥϯ, verb. perf. 3. pers.
sing. from ϯ. Ⲉⲣϣⲓϣⲓ, noun sing. masc. ⲚⲰⲞⲨ, pron.
dat. Ⲉ̀Ⲉⲣ, verb. infin. with ⲉ̀ pref. the sign of the infin.
ϣⲎⲣⲓ, noun plur.

13. ⲚⲎⲈ̀ⲦⲈ Ⲉ̀ⲂⲞⲖⲂⲈⲚ ⲤⲚⲞϥ ⲀⲚ ⲚⲈ ⲞⲨⲆⲈ Ⲉ̀ⲂⲞⲖⲂⲈⲚ
ⲫⲞⲨⲰϣ Ⲛ̀ⲤⲀⲢⲌ ⲀⲚ ⲚⲈ ⲞⲨⲆⲈ Ⲉ̀ⲂⲞⲖⲂⲈⲚ ⲫⲞⲨⲰϣ Ⲛ̀ⲢⲰⲘⲒ
ⲀⲚ ⲚⲈ ⲀⲖⲖⲀ Ⲉ̀Ⲧ ⲀⲨⲘⲀⲤⲞⲨ Ⲉ̀ⲂⲞⲖⲂⲈⲚ ⲫϯ.

*Those who were not of blood, neither of the will of
flesh, nor of the will of man, but who were born of God.*

ⲤⲚⲞϥ. noun sing. m. ⲀⲚ. adv. negat. ⲞⲨⲆⲈ, conj.
Ⲛ̀ⲤⲀⲢⲌ, noun sing. m. with Ⲛ̀ sign of gen. ⲀⲨⲘⲀⲤⲞⲨ,
verb perf. 3. pers. plur. with ⲞⲨ, plur. suff. from ⲘⲀⲤ.

14. ⲞⲨⲞⲌ ⲠⲒⲤⲀϪⲒ ⲀϥⲈⲢ ⲞⲨⲤⲀⲢⲌ ⲞⲨⲞⲌ ⲀϥϣⲱⲠⲒ
Ⲛ̀ⲂⲢⲎⲒ Ⲛ̀ⲂⲎⲦⲈⲚ ⲞⲨⲞⲌ ⲀⲚⲚⲀⲨ Ⲉ̀ⲠⲈϥⲰ̀ⲞⲨ Ⲙ̀ⲪⲢⲎϯ Ⲙ̀Ⲡⲱ̀ⲞⲨ
Ⲛ̀ⲞⲨϣⲎⲢⲒ Ⲙ̀ⲘⲀⲨⲀⲦϥ Ⲛ̀ⲦⲞⲦϥ Ⲙ̀ⲠⲈϥⲒⲰⲦ ⲈϥⲘⲈⲌ Ⲛ̀ⲌⲘⲞⲦ
ⲚⲈⲘ ⲘⲈⲐⲘⲎⲒ.

15

*And the word was made flesh, and dwelt among us,
and we saw his glory, as the glory of the only son of his
Father, full of grace and truth.*

ⲁϥⲉⲣ, verb perf. 3. pers. sing. from ⲉⲣ. ⲛ̅ⲃⲣⲏⲓ
ⲛ̅ⲃⲏⲧⲉⲛ, 2 prepos. the last ⲉⲛ suff. ⲁⲛⲛⲁⲩ, verb perf.
1. pers. plur. from ⲛⲁⲩ. ⲉ̇ⲡⲉϥⲱ̀ⲟⲩ, noun sing. m. with
ⲉ̇ sign of acc. and ⲡⲉϥ, pref. ⲙ̇ⲫⲣⲏϯ, adv. ⲛ̀ⲟⲩϣⲏⲣⲓ,
noun m. sing. with ⲛ̀ sign of gen. and ⲟⲩ indef. art.
prefixed. ⲙ̇ⲙⲁⲩⲁⲧϥ, adj. sing. ⲛ̅ⲧⲟⲧϥ, pron. partic. gen.
from ⲧⲟⲧ, see pronouns. ⲙ̇ⲡⲉϥⲓⲱⲧ, noun sing. with ⲙ̇
sign of gen. and ⲡⲉϥ prefixed. ⲉϥⲙⲉⲍ, verb present or
part. 3. pers. sing. ⲛ̀ⲍⲙⲟⲧ, noun sing. m. with ⲛ̀ sign
of gen. ⲛⲉⲙ, conj. ⲙⲉⲑⲙⲏⲓ, noun sing. f.

15. ⲓⲱⲁⲛⲛⲏⲥ ⲉϥⲉⲣⲙⲉⲑⲣⲉ ⲉⲑⲃⲏⲧϥ ⲟⲩⲟⲍ ⲉϥⲱϣ
ⲉ̇ⲃⲟⲗ ⲉϥϫⲱⲙ̇ⲙⲟⲥ, ϫⲉ ⲫⲁⲓ ⲡⲉ ⲫⲏⲉⲧ ⲁⲓϫⲟϥ ϫⲉ ⲫⲏⲉⲑ
ⲛⲏⲟⲩ ⲙⲉⲛⲉⲛⲥⲱⲓ ⲁϥⲉⲣϣⲟⲣⲡ ⲉ̇ⲣⲟⲓ ϫⲉ ⲛⲉ ⲟⲩϣⲟⲣⲡ ⲉ̇ⲣⲟⲓ
ⲣⲱ ⲡⲉ.

*John witnesseth concerning him, and crieth out, say-
ing, that this is he of whom I spake, he who cometh after
me hath been before me, for he was before me.*

ⲉⲑⲃⲏⲧϥ, prepos. with ϥ suff. ⲉϥⲱϣ ⲉ̇ⲃⲟⲗ, verb
pres. 3. pers. sing. with ⲉ̇ⲃⲟⲗ, prepos. joined. ⲉϥϫⲱⲙ̇ⲙⲟⲥ,
particip. from ϫⲱ, and ⲙ̇ⲙⲟⲥ particle postfixed. ϫⲉ,
conjunct. but often expletive. ⲁⲓϫⲟϥ, verb perfect. 1. pers.
sing. with ϥ suffixed. ⲙⲉⲛⲉⲛⲥⲱⲓ, prepos. with 1. pers.
sing. suffixed. ⲁϥⲉⲣϣⲟⲣⲡ, verb perf. 3. pers. sing. from
ⲉⲣ and ϣⲟⲣⲡ, ⲉ̇ⲣⲟⲓ, particle used for pronoun. 1. pers.
sing. ⲣⲟ, *he, the same.*

16. ⲭⲉ ⲁⲛⲟⲛ ⲧⲏⲣⲉⲛ ⲁⲛϭⲓ ⲉⲃⲟⲗϧⲉⲛ ⲡⲉϥⲙⲟϩ ⲛⲉⲙ
ⲟⲩϩⲙⲟⲧ ⲛ̀ⲧϣⲉⲃⲓⲱ̀ ⲛ̀ⲟⲩϩⲙⲟⲧ.

*Because we all have received out of his fulness, and
grace for grace.*

ⲁⲛⲟⲛ, pron. plur. 1. pers. ⲧⲏⲣⲉⲛ, adject. with ⲉⲛ,
1. pers. plur. suffixed. ⲁⲛϭⲓ, verb perf. 1. pers. plur.
from ϭⲓ. ⲡⲉϥⲙⲟϩ, noun sing. m. with ⲡⲉϥ prefixed.
ⲟⲩϩⲙⲟⲧ, noun sing. with ⲟⲩ indefin. artic. prefixed.
ⲛ̀ⲧϣⲉⲃⲓⲱ̀, prepos.: from ϣⲉⲃⲓⲱ̀, with ⲧ the art. f. and
ⲛ̀ prefixed.

17. ⲭⲉ ⲡⲓⲛⲟⲙⲟⲥ ⲁⲩⲧⲏⲓϥ ⲉⲃⲟⲗϩⲓⲧⲉⲛ ⲙⲱⲩⲥⲏⲥ
ⲡⲓϩⲙⲟⲧ ⲇⲉ ⲛⲉⲙ ϯⲙⲉⲑⲙⲏⲓ ⲁⲩϣⲱⲡⲓ ⲉⲃⲟⲗϩⲓⲧⲉⲛ ⲓⲏⲥ ⲡⲭⲥ.

*For the law was given by Moses, but the grace and
the truth were by Jesus Christ.*

ⲡⲓⲛⲟⲙⲟⲥ, noun sing. with ⲡⲓ defin. art. m. ⲁⲩⲧⲏⲓϥ,
verb perf. 3. pers. plur. with ϥ suff. ϯⲙⲉⲑⲙⲏⲓ, noun
sing. with ϯ, defin. art. f.

18. ⲫϯ ⲙ̀ⲡⲉ ϩⲗⲓ ⲛⲁⲩ ⲉ̀ⲣⲟϥ ⲉ̀ⲛⲉϩ ⲡⲓⲙⲟⲛⲟⲅⲉⲛⲏⲥ
ⲛ̀ⲛⲟⲩϯ ⲫⲏⲉⲧ ⲭⲏ ϧⲉⲛ ⲕⲉⲛϥ ⲙ̀ⲡⲉϥⲓⲱⲧ ⲛ̀ⲑⲟϥ ⲡⲉⲧ
ⲁϥⲥⲁⲭⲓ.

*Not any one hath ever seen God; the only begotten
of God, he who is in the bosom of his Father, he hath de-
clared him.*

ⲙ̀ⲡⲉ..ⲛⲁⲩ, verb 3. pers. sing. negat. prefixed.
ⲉ̀ⲛⲉϩ, adv. ⲕⲉⲛϥ, noun sing. with ϥ suffixed. ⲛ̀ⲑⲟϥ,
pron. 3. pers. sing. ⲡⲉⲧ, pron. relat. ⲁϥⲥⲁⲭⲓ, verb perf.
3. pers. sing.

19. ⲟⲩⲟϩ ⲑⲁⲓ ⲧⲉ ϯⲙⲉⲧⲙⲉⲑⲣⲉ ⲛ̀ⲧⲉ ⲓⲱⲁⲛⲛⲏⲥ
ϩⲟⲧⲉ ⲉⲧ ⲁⲩⲟⲩⲱⲣⲡ ϩⲁⲣⲟϥ ⲛ̀ⲭⲉ ⲛⲓⲓⲟⲩⲇⲁⲓ ⲉ̀ⲃⲟⲗϧⲉⲛ

ⲒⲎ̅Ⲙ̅ ⲚⲊⲀⲚⲞⲨⲎⲂ ⲚⲈⲘ ⳍⲀⲚⲖⲈⲨⲒⲦⲎⲤ ⳍⲒⲚⲀ Ⲛ̀ⲦⲞⲨ ϢⲈⲚϤ
ⲬⲈ Ⲛ̀ⲐⲞⲔ ⲚⲒⲘ.

*And this is the testimony of John, when the Jews, who
sent to him from Jerusalem Priests and Levites that they
might ask him, who art thou?*

ⲐⲀⲒ, pron. def. fem. sing. ⲦⲈ, verb. irreg. pres. 3. pers.
sing. fem. Ⲛ̀ⲦⲈ, sign of gen. ⳍⲞⲦⲈ, adv. ⳍⲀⲢⲞϤ, prep.
joined with ⲢⲞϤ, a particle representing the pronoun.
ⲚⲒⲞⲨⲆⲀⲒ, noun with ⲚⲒ defin. art. plur. prefixed. Ⲛ̀ⳍⲀⲚ-
ⲞⲨⲎⲂ, noun plur. with Ⲛ̀ gen. and ⳍⲀⲚ, indef. art. pl.
prefixed. Ⲛ̀ⲦⲞⲨϢⲈⲚϤ. verb subjunct. 3. pers. plur. with
ϥ suffixed. Ⲛ̀ⲐⲞⲔ, pron. 2. pers. sing. ⲚⲒⲘ, pron. sing.

20. ⲞⲨⲞⳍ ⲀϤⲞⲨⲰⲚⳍ Ⲙ̀ⲠⲈϤⲬⲰⲖ ⲈⲂⲞⲖ ⲞⲨⲞⳍ ⲀϤⲞⲨⲰⲚⳍ
ⲬⲈ ⲀⲚⲞⲔ ⲀⲚ ⲠⲈ Ⲡ̅Ⲭ̅Ⲥ̅.

*And he confessed and denied not; and confessed that
I am not the Christ.*

ⲀϤⲞⲨⲰⲚⳍ, verb perf. 3. pers. sing. Ⲙ̀ⲠⲈϤⲬⲰⲖ ⲈⲂⲞⲖ,
verb. negat. perf. 3. pers. sing. from ⲬⲰⲖ ⲈⲂⲞⲖ. ⲀⲚⲞⲔ,
pron. 1. pers. sing.

From the Hymns for the Principal Feasts.

ⲠⲀⲖⲒⲚ ⲞⲚ ⲀϤⲘⲞϢⲒ
Again he walked
ϢⲀ ϢⲘⲞⲨⲚ ⲤⲚⲀⲨ*)
To Shmoun the second;
ⲀϤⲬⲰⲢ ⲈⲂⲞⲖ Ⲛ̀ⲚⲒⳍⲀⲬⲒ
He dispersed the enemies
ⲂⲈⲚ ⲠⲒⲘⲀ Ⲉ̀ⲦⲈⲘⲘⲀⲨ.
In that place.

---

*) The name of a city of ancient Egypt.

ⲠⲒⲬⲰⲔ.

Index

of the

Prefixes, Suffixes, &c.

ⲀⲦⲉⲦⲚ, Pref. 1. Perf. 2. p. plur. p. 48.

ⲀⲨ, Pref. 1. Perf. 3. p. plur. 48.

ⲀⲨ, Suff. 3. pers. plur. p. 37.

ⲀⲨⲚⲀ, Pref. 2. Fut. 3. p. plur. p. 51.

Ⲁϥ, Pref. 1. Perf. 3. p. sing. m. p. 47.

ⲀϥⲚⲀ, Pref. 2. Fut. 3. p. sing. m. p. 51.

ⲀⲭⲠ, Ordinal for hours. p. 43.

Ⲅ, Suff. to verbs. 2. p. sing. m. for Ⲕ p. 97.

ⲉ, Pref. Infinit. p. 54.

ⲉ, Suff. 2. p. f. p. 36, 45, 97.

ⲉ, Sign of the Dative, Accus. and Ablat. p. 21, 22, 23.

ⲉ, Sign of the Participle. p. 65. 96.

ⲉ, Forms Adjectives. p. 24.

ⲉⲑ, Forms Adjectives. p. 24.

ⲉⲑ, Forms Participles. p. 65.

ⲉⲑⲡⲉ, Auxiliary verb. p. 90, 91.

ⲉⲓ, Pref. 2. Pres. 1. p. sing. p. 46.

ⲉⲓⲉ, Pref. 3. Fut. 1. p. sing. p. 51.

ⲉⲓⲚⲀ, Pref. 2. Fut. 1. p. sing. p. 51.

ⲉⲔ, Pref. 1. Pres. 2. p. masc. sing. p. 46.

ⲉⲔⲉ, Pref. 3. Fut. 2. p. sing. m. p. 51.

ⲉⲔⲚⲀ, Pref. 2. Fut. 2. p. sing. m. p. 51.

ⲉⲗ, The Auxiliary verb. Bash. p. 91.

ⲉⲗⲉ, Pref. 2. Fut. 2. p. sing. f. and 3. p. sing. and plur. p. 47. Bash.

ⲉⲚ, Pref. 2. Pres. 1. p. plur. p. 47.

ⲉⲚ, Suff. 1. p. plur. p. 36.

ⲉⲚ, *if,* with the Prefixes to verbs. p. 66.

ⲉⲚⲉ, *if,* with the Prefixes to verbs. p. 66.

ⲉⲚⲉ, Pref. 3. Fut. 1. p. plur. p. 51.

ⲉⲚⲚⲀ, Pref. 2. Fut. 1. p. plur. p. 51.

ⲉⲞⲨ, Suff. 3. pers. plur. p. 37.

ⲉⲣ, Auxiliary verb. p. 91.

ⲉⲣⲉ, Pref. 2. Fut. 2. p. sing. f. and 3. p. sing. and plur. p. 47.

ⲈⲡⲈ, Pref. 3. Ful. 2. p. sing. f. and 3. p. sing. and plur. p. 51.

ⲈⲢⲈⲚⲀ, Pref. 2. Fut. 2. p. sing. f. p. 51.

ⲈⲡⲈⲦⲈⲚⲈ, Pref. 3. Fut. 2. p. plur. p. 51.

ⲈⲡⲈⲦⲈⲚⲚⲀ, Pref. 2. Fut. 2. p. plur. p. 51.

ⲈⲤ, Pref. 2. Pres. 3. p. sing. f. p. 47.

ⲈⲤⲈ, Pref. 3. Fut. 3. p. sing. f. p. 51.

ⲈⲤⲚⲀ, Pref. 2. Fut. 3. p. sing. f. p. 51.

ⲈⲦ, Forms Adjectives. p. 24.

ⲈⲦ, Forms Participles. p. 65.

ⲈⲦⲀ, Pref. 2. Perf. 3. p. sing. and plur. m. and f. p. 48.

ⲈⲦⲀⲓ, Pref. 2. Perf. 1. p. sing. p. 48, 65.

ⲈⲦⲀⲔ, Pref. 2. Perf. 2. p. sing. m. p. 48, 65.

ⲈⲦⲀⲚ, Pref. 2. Perf. 1. p. plur. p. 48, 66.

ⲈⲦⲀⲡⲈ, Pref. 2. Perf. 2. p. sing. f. p. 48, 65.

ⲈⲦⲀⲡⲈⲦⲈⲚ, Pref. 2. Pres. 2. p. plur. p. 48, 66.

ⲈⲦⲀⲤ, Pref. 2. Perf. 3. p. sing. f. p. 48, 65.

ⲈⲦⲀⲦⲈⲦⲈⲚ, Pref. p. 66.

ⲈⲦⲀⲨ, Pref. 2. Perf. 3. p. plur. p. 48, 66.

ⲈⲦⲀϥ, Pref. 2. Perf. 3. p. sing. m. p. 48, 65.

ⲈⲦⲈ, when, Prefixed to verbs. p. 65.

ⲈⲦⲈⲦⲈⲚ, Pref. 2. Pres. 2. p. plur. p. 47.

ⲈⲦⲈⲦⲚ̄, Pref. 2. Pres. 2. p. plur. p. 47.

ⲈⲦⲈⲦⲚⲀ, Pref. 2. Fut. 2. p. plur. p. 51.

ⲈⲦⲈⲦⲚⲈ, Pref. 3. Fut. 2. p. plur. p. 51.

ⲈⲦⲈⲦⲚⲚⲀ, Pref. 2. Fut. 2. p. plur. p. 51.

ⲈⲦⲢⲈ, Auxiliary verb. p. 90, 91.

ⲈⲨ, Pref. 2. Pres. 3. p. plur. p. 47.

ⲈⲨⲈ, Pref. 3. Fut. 3. p. plur. p. 51.

ⲈⲨⲚⲀ, Pref. 2. Fut. 3. p. plur. p. 51.

Ⲉⲱ, Sign of the Potential Mood. p. 78.

Ⲉϥ, Pref. 2. Pres. 3. p. sing. m. p. 47.

ⲈϥⲈ, Pref. 3. Fut. 3. p. sing. m. p. 51.

ⲈϥⲚⲀ, Pref. 2. Fut 3. p. sing. m. p. 51.

Ⲉ︦ⲞⲦⲈ, Sign of the Comparative. p. 25.

ⲎⲞⲨⲦ, Participles. p. 65.

ⲎⲨ, Participles. p. 65.

ⲎⲨⲦ, Participles p. 65.

Ⲑ, Defin. Artic. p. 10.

Ⲑⲁ, Posses. Article. p. 13.

ⲐⲢⲈ, Auxiliary Verb. p. 89.

Ⲓ, Suff. 1. pers. sing. and 2. pers. sing. f. p. 36, 45, 97.

Ⲕ, Pref. 1. Pres. 2. p. sing. m. p. 45, 46.

Ⲕ, Suff. 2. p. sing. m. p. 36, 45, 97.

ⲔⲈ, Between the Article and noun. p. 103.

ⲔⲚⲁ, Pref. 1. Fut. 2. p. sing. m. p. 50.

ⲔⲚⲈ, Pref. 1. Fut. 2. p. sing. m. p. 50.

λⲁ, much. p. 106. Bash.

λⲈⲘ, a native. p. 105. Bash.

λⲈⳓ, Forms compound nouns. p. 105. Bash.

Ⲙ̀, Pref. to Gen. Dat. Acc. Abl. p. 21, 22.

Ⲙ̀, Pref. Negat. p. 84.

ⲘⲀ, Pref. Imperat. p. 54.

ⲘⲁλⲈ, Pref. Optative. 2. p. sing. f. and 3. p. sing. and plur. p. 54. Bash.

ⲘⲁλⲈⲔ, Pref. Optat. 2. p. sing. m. p. 54. Bash.

ⲘⲁλⲈⲚ, Pref. Optat. 1. p. plur. p. 54. Bash.

ⲘⲁλⲈⲤ, Pref. Optat. 3. p. sing. f. p. 54. Bash.

ⲘⲁλⲈⲦⲈⲚ, Pref. Optat. 2. p. plur. p. 54. Bash.

ⲘⲁλⲈⳓ, Pref. Optat. 3. p. sing. m. p. 54 Bash.

Ⲙⲁλⲓ, Pref. Optat. 1. p. sing. p. 54. Bash.

ⲘⲁλⲞⲨ, Pref. Optat. 3. p. plur. p. 54. Bash.

ⲘⲀⲣⲈ, Pref. Optative 2. p. sing. f. and 3. p. sing. and plur. p. 54.

ⲘⲀⲣⲈⲔ, Pref. Optat. 2. p. sing. m. p. 54.

ⲘⲀⲣⲈⲚ, Pref. Optat. 1. p. plur. p. 54.

ⲘⲀⲣⲈⲤ, Pref. Optat. 3. p. sing. f. p. 54.

ⲘⲀⲣⲈⲦⲈⲚ, Pref. Optat. 2. p. plur. p. 54.

ⲘⲀⲣⲈⲦⲚ̄, Pref. Optat. 2. p. plur. p. 54.

ⲘⲀⲣⲉϥ, Pref. Optat. 3. p. sing. m. p. 54.

ⲘⲀⲣⲓ, Pref. Optat. 1. p. sing. p. 54.

ⲘⲀⲣⲚ, Pref. Optat. 2. p. plur. p. 54.

ⲘⲀⲣⲟⲩ, Pref. Optat. 3. p. plur. p. 54.

ⲘⲀⲋ, Forms the Ordinal numbers. Copt. p. 43.

Ⲙⲉⲋ, Pref. to nouns, Copt. p. 105.

Ⲙⲉⲧ, Pref. to nouns, Copt. p. 105.

ⲘⲚⲧ, Pref. to nouns, Sah. p. 105.

Ⲙⲉⲋ, Forms the Ordinal numbers Sah. p. 43.

ⲘⲘⲀⲩ, Pref. Negat. p. 96.

ⲘⲡⲀⲧⲉ, Pref. Negat. p. 79, 86.

Ⲙⲡⲉ, Pref. Negat. p. 79. 85.

Ⲙⲡⲉⲗ, Pref. Negat. p. 89. Bash.

Ⲙⲡⲉⲣ, Pref. Negat. p. 89.

Ⲙⲡⲣ, Pref. Negat. p. 89.

Ⲛ, Pref. Negat. p. 79.

Ⲛ, Pref. to Gen., Dat., Acc., Abl. p. 21, 22.

Ⲛ, Pref. 2. Pres. 2. p. plur. p. 47.

Ⲛ, Pref. Infinit. p. 54.

Ⲛ, Suff. 1. p. plur. p. 36, 46, 97.

Ⲛ, Definite Artic. plur. p. 11.

ⲚⲀ, Possess. Article. plur. p. 13.

ⲚⲀ, *About.* p. 44.

ⲚⲀⲓ ⲡⲉ, Pref. Imperf. 1. p. sing. p. 47.

ⲚⲀⲓⲚⲀ, Pref. Imperf. Fut. 1. p. sing. p. 52.

ⲚⲀⲓⲚⲉ, Pref. Imperf. Fut. 1. p. sing. p. 52. Bash.

ⲚⲀⲕ ⲡⲉ, Pref. Imperf. 2. p. sing. m. p. 47. ·

ⲚⲀⲕⲚⲀ, Pref. Imperf. Fut. 2. p. sing. m. p. 52.

ⲚⲀⲕⲚⲉ, Pref. Imperf. Fut. 2. p. sing. m. p. 52. Bash.

ⲚⲀⲚ ⲡⲉ, Pref. Imper. 1. p. plur. p. 47.

ⲚⲀⲚⲚⲀ, Pref. Imper. Fut. 1. p. plur. p. 53.

ⲚⲀⲚⲚⲉ, Pref. Imperf. Fut. 1. p. plur. p. 53. Bash.

ⲚⲀⲣⲉ ⲡⲉ, Pref. Imperf. 2. p. sing. f. and 3. p. sing. and plur. p. 47.

ⲚⲀⲢⲈⲚⲀ, Pref. Imper. Fut. 2. p. sing. f. and 3. p. sing. and pl. p. 52, 53,

ⲚⲀⲢⲈⲚⲈ, Pref. Imperf. Fut. 2. p. sing, f. and 3. p. sing. and pl. p. 52, 53.

ⲚⲀⲢⲈⲦⲈⲚ ⲠⲈ, Pref. Imperf. 2. p. plur. p. 47.

ⲚⲀⲢⲈⲦⲈⲚⲚⲀ, Pref. Imperf. Fut. 2. p. plur. p. 53.

ⲚⲀⲢⲈⲦⲈⲚⲚⲈ, Pref. Imperf. Fut. 2. p. plur. p. 53.

ⲚⲀⲤ ⲠⲈ, Pref. Imperf. 3. p. sing. f. p. 47.

ⲚⲀⲤⲚⲀ, Pref. Imperf. Fut. 3. p. sing. p. 52.

ⲚⲀⲨ ⲠⲈ, Pref. Imperf. 3. p. plur. p. 47.

ⲚⲀⲨⲚⲀ, Pref. Imperf. Fut. 3. p. plur. p. 53.

ⲚⲀϥ ⲠⲈ, Pref. Imperf. 3. p. sing. m. p. 47.

ⲚⲀϥⲚⲀ, Pref. Imperf. Fut. 3. p. sing. m. p. 52.

ⲚⲄ, Pref. Subjunct. 2. p. sing. m. p. 53.

ⲚⲈ, Defin. Article plur. p. 11.

ⲚⲈ, Verb. p. 92.

ⲚⲈ ⲠⲈ, }
ⲚⲈ ⲦⲈ, } Irreg. verb. p. 92.

ⲚⲈ Ⲁ ⲠⲈ, Pref. Pluperf. 3. p. sing. m. and f. p. 48.

ⲚⲈ Ⲁⲓ ⲠⲈ, Pref. Pluperf. 1. p. sing. p. 48.

ⲚⲈ ⲀⲔ ⲠⲈ, Pref. Pluperf. 2. p. sing. m. p. 48.

ⲚⲈ ⲀⲚ ⲠⲈ, Pref. Pluperf. 1. p. plur. p. 49.

ⲚⲈ ⲀⲢⲈ ⲠⲈ, Pref. Pluperf. 2. p. sing. f. and 3. p. sing. m. and f. p. 48.

ⲚⲈ ⲀⲢⲈⲦⲈⲚ ⲠⲈ, Pref. Pluperf. 2. p. plur. p. 49.

ⲚⲈ ⲀⲤ ⲠⲈ, Pref. Pluperf. 3. p. sing. f. p. 48.

ⲚⲈ ⲀⲦⲈⲦⲚ̄ ⲠⲈ, Pref. Pluperf. 2. p. plur. p. 49.

ⲚⲈ ⲀⲨ ⲠⲈ, Pref. Pluperf. 3. p. plur. p. 49.

ⲚⲈ Ⲁϥ ⲠⲈ, Pref. Pluperf. 3. p. sing. m. p. 48.

ⲚⲈ ϢⲀⲓ ⲠⲈ, Pref. Imperf. Indef. 1. p. sing. p. 49.

ⲚⲈ ϢⲀⲔ ⲠⲈ, Pref. Imperf. Indef. 2. p. sing. m. p. 49.

ⲚⲈ ϢⲀⲖⲈ ⲠⲈ, Pref. Imperf. Indef. 2. p. sing. f. and 3. p. sing. and pl. p. 49.

ⲚⲈ ϢⲀⲚ ⲠⲈ, Pref. Imperf. Indef. 1. p. plur. p. 49.

ⲚⲈ ϢⲀⲢⲈ ⲠⲈ, Pref. Imperf. Indef. 2. p. sing. f. and 3. p. sing. and pl. p. 49, 50.

ⲚⲈ ϢⲀⲢⲈⲦⲈⲚ ⲠⲈ, Pref. Imperf. Indef. 2. p. plur. p. 50.

ⲚⲈ ϢⲀⲤ ⲠⲈ, Pref. Imperf. Indef. 3. p. sing. f. p. 49, 50.

16*

ⲠⲀⲬⲒⲚ, Particip. pers. sing. p. 54.

ⲠⲈ, Definit. Article. m. sing. p. 11. vocat. p. 21.

ⲠⲈ, Verb *to be,* p. 91.

ⲠⲈⲔⲬⲒⲚ, Particip. 2. p. sing. p. 54.

ⲠⲈϥ, Signifies days. p. 44.

ⲠⲈϥⲬⲒⲚ, Particip. 3. p. sing. m. p. 54.

ⲠⲒ, Defin. Art. sing. m. p. 10, 11. vocat. p. 21.

ⲣⲈ, *a part,* p. 43.

ⲣⲈⲙ, *a native,* p. 105.

ⲣⲙ̄, *a native,* Sah. p. 105.

ⲥ, Pref. 1. Pres. 3. p. sing. f. p. 46.

ⲥ, Suff. 3. p. sing. f. p. 37, 46, 97.

ⲥⲁ, An artificer, p. 105.

ⲥⲉ, Pref. 1. Pres. 3. p. plur. p. 46.

ⲥⲈⲚⲀ, Pref. 1. Fut. 3. p. plur. p. 50.

ⲥⲈⲚⲈ, Pref. 1. Fut. 3. p. plur. p. 50.

ⲥⲚⲀ, Pref. 1. Fut. 3. p. sing. f. p. 50.

ⲥⲚⲈ, Pref. 1. Fut. 3. p. sing. f. p. 50.

ⲥⲞⲨ, Prefixed to days forms the Ordinal number. p. 43.

ⲧ, Defin. Artic. sing. f. p. 10, 11.

ⲧ, Suff. 1. p. sing. p. 36, 97.

ⲧⲀ, Pref. 4. Fut. 1. p. sing. p. 52,

ⲧⲀ, Possess. Article. f. sing. p. 13.

ⲧⲀⲗⲈⲧⲈⲚ, Pref. 4. Fut. 2. p. plur. p. 52.

ⲧⲀⲣⲈⲔ, Pref. 4. Fut. 2. p. sing. m. p. 52.

ⲧⲀⲣⲈⲥ, Pref. 4. Fut. 3. p. sing. f. p. 52.

ⲧⲀⲣⲈⲧⲚ̄, Pref. 4. Fut. 2. p. plur. p. 52.

ⲧⲀⲣⲈϥ, Pref. 4. Fut. 3. p. sing. m. p. 52.

ⲧⲀⲣⲚ̄, Pref. 4. Fut. 1. p. plur. p. 52.

ⲧⲀⲣⲒ, Pref. 4. Fut. 1. p. sing. p. 52.

ⲧⲀⲣⲞⲨ, Pref. 4. Fut. 3. p. plur. p. 52.

ⲧⲈ, Definit. Article. sing. f. p. 11.

ⲧⲈ, Pref. 1. Pres. 2. p. sing. f. p. 46.

TE, Suff. 2. p. sing. f. p. 97.

TEN, Pref. 1. Pres. 1. p. plur. p. 46.

TEN, Suff. 1. p. plur. p. 97.

TENA, Pref. 1. Fut. 2. p. sing. f. p. 50 and 1. p. plur. p. 56.

TENNA, Pref. 1. Fut. 1. p. plur. p. 50.

TENNE, Pref. 1. Fut. 1. p. plur. p. 56.

TEPA, Pref. 4. Fut. 2. p. sing. f. p. 52.

TETEN, Pref. 1. Pres. 2. p. plur. p. 46.

TETENNA, Pref. 1. Fut. 2. p. plur. p. 50.

TETN̄, Pref. 1. Pres. 2. p. plur. p. 46.

TETNA, Pref. 1. Fut. 2 p. plur. p. 50.

TETN̄NA, Pref. 1. Fut. 2. p. plur. p. 50.

TM̄, Pref. negative. p. 87, 88.

TN̄, Pref. 1. Pres. 1. p. plur. p. 46.

TN̄, Suff. 3. p. plur. p. 36. 2. p. plur. and 1. p. plur. p. 97.

TPE, *a part*, p. 44.

TPE, The Auxiliary Verb. *to be, to do,* p. 89.

Υ, Suff. 3. p. plur. p. 46.

Φ, Defin. Article. sing. m. p. 10.

ΦA, Possess. Article. m. sing. p. 13.

Χ, Pref. 1. Pres. 2. p. sing. m. p. 46.

ΧΝΑ, Pref. 1. Fut. 2. p. sing. m. p. 50.

ω, Sign of the vocat. p. 21.

ωΟΥΤ, Participle. p. 65.

ϣ, Sign of the Potential Mood. p. 78.

ϣΑΙ, Pref. Pres. Indef. 1. p. sing. p. 49.

ϣΑΚ, Pref. Pres. Indef. 2. p. sing. m. p. 49.

ϣΑλΕ, Pref. Pres. Indef. 2. p. sing. and 3. p. sing. and pl. p. 49. Bash.

ϣΑΝ, *If,* with the prefixes. p. 67, 88.

ϣΑΝΤΕ, *Until,* with the prefixes. p. 66.

ϣΑΡΕ, Pref. Pres. Indef. 2. p. sing. f. and 3. p. sing. and plur. p. 49.

ϣΑΡΕΤΕΝ, Pref. Pres. Indef. 2. p. plur. p. 49.

ϣΑC, Pref. Pres. Indef. 3. p. sing. f. p. 49.

ⲰⲀⲦⲈ, *Until,* with the prefixes. p. 66.

ⲰⲀⲦⲈⲦⲈⲚ, Pref. Pres. Indef. 2. p. plur. p. 49.

ⲰⲀⲦⲈⲦⲚ̄, Pref. Pres. Indef. 2. p. plur. p. 49.

ⲰⲀⲨ, Pref. Pres. Indef. 3. p. plur. p. 49.

ⲰⲀϥ, Pref. Pres. Indef. 3. p. sing. m. p. 49.

ⲰⲞⲨ, Pref. implying worthiness. p. 79. 105.

ⲰⲦⲈⳘ, Pref. negative. p. 87, 88.

ϥ, Suff. 3. p. sing. m. p. 37, 46, 97.

ϥ, Pref. 1. Pres. 3. p. sing. m. p. 46.

ϥⲚⲀ, Pref. 1. Fut. 3. p. sing. m. p. 50.

ϥⲚⲈ, Pref. 1. Fut. 3. p. sing. m. p. 50. Bash.

ⳅⲀ, *a person, master,* &c. p. 106.

ⳅⲀⲚ, Indef. Article. plur. p. 12.

ⳅⲈⲚ, Indef. Article. plur. p. 12.

ⳅⲚ̄, Indef. Art. plur. p. 12.

ⲬⲀ, Verb. p. 92.

ⲬⲈ, Conjunction p. 99 and verb. p. 92.

ⲬⲒⲚ, Participle, taking the article and infixes. p. 65.

ⲬⲞⲞ, Verb. p. 92.

ⲬⲠ, Forms the Ordinal numbers for hours. p. 45.

ⲬⲰ, Verb. p. 92.

ϬⲒⲚ, Participle taking the Articles and infixes p. 65.

ϯ, Definit. Article. sing. f. p. 10, 11.

ϯ, Pref. 1. Pres. 1. p. sing. p. 46.

ϯ, Suff. 2. p. sing. f. p. 97.

ϯⲚⲀ, Suff. 1. Fut. 1. p. sing. p. 50.

ϯⲚⲈ, Suff. Pref. 1. Fut. 1. p. sing. p. 50.

www.ingramcontent.com/pod-product-compliance
Lightning Source LLC
Chambersburg PA
CBHW021122020726
47500CB00003B/888